REENVISIONING HISTORIES OF AMERICAN ART

CRITICAL ETHNIC STUDIES
AND VISUAL CULTURE

Laura Kina, series editor

Reenvisioning Histories of American Art

Transforming Museum Practice

Michael W. Hartman
and Jami C. Powell

The Hood Museum of Art, Dartmouth, in association with
the University of Washington Press, Seattle

TERRA
FOUNDATION FOR AMERICAN ART

This publication, as well as the exhibition *This Land: American Engagement with the Natural World*, was generously supported by Claire Foerster and Daniel Bernstein, Dartmouth Class of 1987, and by the Terra Foundation for American Art.

Publication of this book has been aided by a grant from the Wyeth Foundation for American Art Publication Fund of CAA.

Design by Mindy Basinger Hill

Composed in Garamond Premier Pro and Avenir Next

29 28 27 26 25 5 4 3 2 1

Printed and bound in the United States of America

UNIVERSITY OF WASHINGTON PRESS / *uwapress.uw.edu*

LIBRARY OF CONGRESS CATALOGING-IN-PUBLICATION DATA

Names: Hartman, Michael W., editor. | Powell, Jami C., editor.

Title: Reenvisioning histories of American art : transforming museum practice / edited by Michael W. Hartman and Jami C. Powell.

Description: Seattle : University of Washington Press, [2025] | Series: Critical ethnic studies and visual culture | Includes bibliographical references and index.

Identifiers: LCCN 2024023390 | ISBN 9780295753386 (paperback) | ISBN 9780295753393 (ebook)

Subjects: LCSH: Art museums—Social aspects. | Museum techniques—Social aspects. | Art, American. | Social integration—United States.

Classification: LCC N430 .R43 2025 | DDC 708—dc23/eng/20240628

LC record available at https://lccn.loc.gov/2024023390

∞ This paper meets the requirements of ANSI/NISO Z39.48-1992 (Permanence of Paper).

FOR BARBARA MACADAM,

whose generosity and willingness to share space
created the opportunity for this project

CONTENTS

John R. Stomberg

ALWAYS BECOMING

Art and History in This Land

In 2007 the poet and sculptor Nora Naranjo-Morse (K'apovi/Santa Clara Pueblo) installed her site-specific artwork titled *Always Becoming* at the National Museum of the American Indian in Washington, DC. Made of materials such as clay, mud, ceramic shards, branches, and sand, the outdoor work necessarily changes with time. Birds build nests, snow and rain lead to erosion, and there are human interactions to contend with as well. The artist works with the museum to rebuild sections on occasion; the changes are inherent to the work, hence the title.

Naranjo-Morse's evocation of perpetual transformation offers an apt metaphor for thinking about ways to tell more complete histories of the art and culture generated within the lands encapsulated by the present-day United States. Past versions of American art were not wrong but, rather, incomplete. Instead of striving for a fixed and finite story, we need to embrace a multitude of narrative strands simultaneously reaching back thousands of years and spreading out across geographies that extend beyond current political boundaries.

There is some consensus that the onset of human habitation on the North American continent was well under way by 15,000 BCE—and maybe even much, much earlier. As that is the case, it hardly seems reasonable to start the art historical record of this land with the arrival of European explorers in the sixteenth-century CE or to focus on the cultural output of those new arrivals and their successors. And yet that is what the field of American art history has typically done—begun with the onset of colonizers from abroad and focused almost exclusively on their culture in isolation from rich Indigenous traditions.

Reenvisioning Histories of American Art: Transforming Museum Practice is rooted in a question that is simultaneously a challenge: How can we tell a more comprehensive story of the art and culture created within the geographic boundaries of the present-day United States? Further, what happens to the narrative when we center on the people who lived here first? That is, could we tell the story with Native American art at its core and non–Native American art as something that also happens—that is, the reverse of past histories?

This is no mere intellectual exercise but, rather, a much needed, and inherently justifiable, rethinking of the historical narrative. It is also a monumental undertaking. The essays in this volume offer pathways to further dialogue and ideas for sustaining the work initiated by *Reenvisioning Histories of American Art* and other projects like it. The change has begun, and the future is bright for historical narratives like these that generate expansive art histories, inclusive of a richer variety of important, vibrant, and lively artistic practices throughout the United States.

ACKNOWLEDGMENTS

This publication would not be possible without the support of many people whose knowledge, time, and talents contributed to the exhibition *This Land: American Engagement with the Natural World* and the convening held in conjunction with the exhibition in April 2022.

First and foremost, we want to recognize other members of the *This Land* curatorial team: Barbara J. MacAdam, Jonathan Little Cohen Curator of American Art Emerita; Morgan E. Freeman, former Native American Art Fellow; and Thomas H. Price, former Curatorial Assistant for American Art. Their genuine commitment to collaboration, desire to expand and change the field, and good humor resulted in an exhibition that has become a touchstone at the Hood Museum and other institutions for what a thoughtful reinstallation of American art can accomplish. When planning for *This Land*, these co-curators also engaged in conversation with curators at other institutions dedicated to similar work, particularly those at the Peabody Essex Museum: Austen Barron Bailly (now at Crystal Bridges Museum of American Art), Karen Kramer, and Rachel Allen (now a doctoral candidate at the University of Delaware). At Dartmouth, we also want to acknowledge the exhibition's faculty advisors, whose knowledge shaped the curatorial team's conceptual and methodological approach: Maurice S. Crandall, associate professor of history and Native American studies (now at Arizona State University);

Mary Coffey, professor of art history; Jorge E. Cuéllar, assistant professor of Latin American, Latino, and Caribbean studies; Abigail H. Neely, associate professor of geography; Laura A. Ogden, professor of anthropology; and Cristina Seeley, associate professor of studio art. We are also grateful to Hood Museum of Art interns and students in Museum Club, whose keen insights and feedback throughout the process also shaped our interpretive strategies.

Many individuals and foundations support the Hood Museum's ongoing work to critically reinterpret and reinstall American art to be more inclusive, meaningful, and engaging for our students and broader publics. We offer our sincerest thanks to Claire Foerster and Daniel Bernstein, Dartmouth class of 1987, and the Hood Museum of Art Board of Advisors past and present for funding the exhibition; the Luce Foundation's financial support, which funded Thomas H. Price's position at the Hood Museum; and the Ford Foundation and the Walton Family Foundation for funding Morgan E. Freeman's fellowship, as well as the initial funding for Jami C. Powell's curatorial position at the Hood Museum of Art under the Diversifying Art Museum Leadership Initiative. This book and the convening that led to its creation were funded through the Terra Foundation for American Art's "Re-envisioning Permanent Collections" initiative.

Past and present staff of the Hood Museum of Art have supported these projects. In addition to those already mentioned, we would like to thank the following individuals for their overall support of this project: John R. Stomberg, Virginia Rice Kelsey 1961s Director; Juliette Bianco, former deputy director; Stephanie Fournier, former business assistant; Kathryn Gilbert, former assistant to the director; Giselle Hart, business assistant; Jessica Havrda, former associate director of finance and administration; Nils Nadeau, former associate director, external relations and operations; Ramie Speicher, business officer; and Nathalia Whitecar, collection information and digitization assistant. The planning, development, and interpretive strategy of this exhibition owes much to the expertise and generosity of the following individuals: Katherine Hart, senior curator of collections and Barbara C. and Harvey P. Hood 1918 Curator of Academic Programming Emerita; Jessica Hong, former associate curator of global contemporary art; Isadora Italia, former campus engagement manager; Amelia Kahl, Barbara

C. and Harvey P. Hood 1918 Curator of Academic Programming; Vivian Ladd, teaching specialist; Neely McNulty, Hood Foundation Curator of Education; Taylor Rose Payer, former Cultural Heritage and Indigenous Knowledges Fellow; Jamie Rosenfeld, former museum educator; and Meredith Steinfels, assistant director, digital platforms, media, and archives. The work of preparing, installing, and deinstalling an exhibition of this scale would not have been possible without many individuals, including Susan Achenbach, lead preparator; Kristie Couser, associate registrar; Patrick Dunfey, former head of exhibitions design and implementation; Andrew Gabrysiak, former exhibitions designer; Nicole Gilbert, head of exhibitions; Cynthia Gilliland, registrar; Laurie Kobar, museum preparator; Matthew Oates, museum preparator; Molly Papows, former exhibitions manager; John Reynolds, former lead museum preparator; Lauren Silverson, former registrar; and Matthew Zayatz, former museum preparator.

For the convening that inspired this publication, we also offer our thanks to the excellent planning and coordination of Sharon Reed, programs and events manager, and Laura A. Howard, assistant to the director and advancement manager, along with assistance from Nichelle Gaumont, Board of Advisors Mutual Learning Fellow in Registration and Collections, and Jayde Xu, Board of Advisors Mutual Learning Fellow in Education and Public Programming. Presenters at this event who also shaped many of the thoughts that informed this publication include Mary K. Coffey, professor of art history and affiliated faculty in Latin American, Latino, and Caribbean studies; Zachary Miller, former cultural heritage and indigenous knowledges fellow, Teresa Montoya, assistant professor of anthropology, University of Chicago; Scott Manning Stevens (Akwesasne Mohawk), associate professor of English and director of Native American studies, Syracuse University; Kristen Swan, independent copyeditor, and Royce K. Young Wolf, assistant curator of Native American art, Yale University Art Gallery.

In addition to the wonderful staff at the University of Washington Press, we want to acknowledge the Hood Museum of Art's publications team: Alison Palizzolo, head of communications, content, and brand; Anna Kaye M. Schulte, communications coordinator; Anna Patten, communications and digital content assistant; and Alexander Bortolot, deputy director. Lastly, this publication would not have been possible without the intellectual contributions of Ana "Beatriz" Yanes Martinez, 2021–24 Board of Advisors Mutual Learning Fellow in Curatorial and Exhibitions. As a "mutual learning" fellow, we have had the pleasure of working with and learning alongside Beatriz through the convening and publication. Most significantly for this project, Beatriz took on the gargantuan task of securing images and permissions, and we are grateful for their tireless efforts. Evonne Fuselier, 2024–27 Board of Advisors Mutual Learning Fellow in Curatorial and Exhibitions, also helped bring this project to completion during her first few months at the Hood Museum. We appreciate her eager support.

This publication grew out of an exhibition, and it is our hope that the authors and exhibitions featured in this publication build upon past conversations and inspire our colleagues, present and future, who are dedicated to reenvisioning histories of American art.

REENVISIONING HISTORIES OF AMERICAN ART

Michael W. Hartman / Jami C. Powell

INTRODUCTION

Beyond the Land Acknowledgment

In recent years, museums in the United States have faced increasing pressure to reckon with our histories and to consider the relevance of our field amid a global pandemic, ongoing international conflicts, and social movements in response to racism, violence, and the erosion of human rights here and abroad. While it was once acceptable for museums to posture ourselves as separate or even a space of refuge from what was going on outside of our walls, the idea that inherently colonial institutions can separate ourselves from the realities of colonialism and its ongoing legacies is no longer acceptable to our publics, the artists with whom we work, and our colleagues entering the field. As a result, growing institutional self-reflection and transformation have emerged in tandem with a focus on incorporating antiracism and decolonization throughout museum practice. Much of this work has focused on particular areas of art within what is now the United States—Native American art, African American art, Asian American art, and Latine/x art—with innovative scholarship and approaches emanating from people trained not only in art history but also in anthropology, gender and sexuality studies, history, and American or ethnic studies.[1]

In this book, curators and professors working at the intersection of these fields and across disciplinary boundaries write about the actual processes of transforming theory and methodology into museum practice. Exhibition catalogs dedicated to expansive and critical narratives rarely, if ever, reveal how museums function, the questions they ask themselves, and the methods by which they operate. Often celebratory in tone and focused on the outcomes of projects, these publications do not shift the focus to process or emphasize how arts workers collaborate with one another, as well as community stakeholders, to broaden and expand their narratives to be more inclusive of, relevant to, and truthful about issues taken up by artists past and present. Similarly, professors who write on these topics are seldom the practitioners who work day-to-day within museums and other arts and cultural institutions, creating a gap between theory and practice within art historical and museum-focused scholarship.

This edited volume begins to bridge this gap, providing curators from academic and civic museums a space to reflect upon the challenges and possibilities for expanding the canon of American art. Professors likewise argue for the critical importance of museums in educating broader publics and college students by making accessible the multiple histories of American art. While recognizing possibilities and shortcomings of curatorial approaches, contributors to this volume demonstrate how sustained dialogue and engagement with antiracist and decolonial practices have made forward strides in the museum field.

Many of the approaches in this book center on Native American and African American art, and to a lesser degree Asian American art, within the museum. Latine/x art is relatively absent, a topic that will be discussed further in this introduction. Just as a single exhibition can never fully engage with every topic relevant to its thesis due to limitations on gallery space, the length of label texts, or availability of artworks, this volume can highlight only a fraction of the transformative and often tedious work of our colleagues throughout the field. This volume serves as an entry point or opening to what we hope is a sustained dialogue about the future of American art, its display in museums, and how it is taught in university classrooms. This book is not about the art of underrepresented and disenfranchised Americans as something that exists outside the canon of American art but as something essential to it. When appointed as the director of the National Museum of African American History and Culture, poet Kevin Young said, "The museum is such a beacon of thinking about the way that African American culture is at the center of the American experience, and you can't tell the story of America without the story of African Americans."[2] Similarly, this book and the authors who have created it make the case that you cannot tell the story of American art without Native American art, African American art, Asian American art, and Latine/x art.

LAND ACKNOWLEDGMENT: A STARTING POINT

When the Hood Museum of Art reopened after a renovation and expansion in 2019, the following land acknowledgment was written and placed at the museum's entry:

> The Hood Museum of Art at Dartmouth is situated upon the ancestral and unceded lands of the Abenaki people. This acknowledgement reminds us of the significance of place, the continued existence of Indigenous people, and the museum and Dartmouth's commitment to building respectful relationships with those who call these lands home today.

This statement serves as a reminder of the complex histories of colonialism at the Hood Museum and Dartmouth College, but it also includes an ongoing commitment to fostering and maintaining relationships with the original inhabitants and stewards of the land on which these institutions now exist. In the years since this statement was placed at the entrance to the museum, critiques about the role of land acknowledgments and broader conversations about historical accountability served as the impetus to rework this statement with faculty colleagues in the African and African American Studies and Native American and Indigenous Studies departments.[3] As a result of this critical reflection and dialogue, a *land and labor acknowledgment* was created in 2021. It reads:

> The Hood Museum of Art at Dartmouth occupies the lands and waters of the Abenaki peoples and was built *without* permission from the Abenaki nation. This institution also has benefitted from the

> economies of slavery and the labors of African descended captives. This acknowledgement reminds us of the significance of place and the legacies of dispossession and enslavement that sustained and enriched New England. Furthermore, it provides a crucial foundation for building respectful relationships with all those who call these lands home today and into the future.

This statement, which has yet to be officially approved by Dartmouth College, begins to acknowledge the complex entanglements that characterize not only the founding of our particular cultural and academic institutions but also the United States as a nation. Although a statement is only a statement, and must be followed with action steps and accountability, the recognition that the foundations of our institutions are deeply rooted in the dispossession of land from Indigenous nations and the dispossession of labor from enslaved Africans and their descendants marks a significant shift in museum practice within the United States.[4] The land and labor acknowledgment provides an invitation to think beyond decolonization and antiracism as separate methodological practices, situating them as part of larger movements that consider and utilize Indigenization and collective liberation.

One of the debates happening within the museum field and beyond is whether or not land acknowledgments have become an empty gesture entirely.[5] For institutions that have created land acknowledgments and failed to engage in other decolonial or antiracist practices, this is certainly the case. For many, the land acknowledgment has become a box to be checked before beginning programs, a self-gratifying exercise to assuage personal and institutional guilt regarding inherited colonial baggage we have inherited and continue to perpetuate in our roles at museums and other institutions. What makes land and labor acknowledgments meaningful is when they serve as an opening for reparative actions, as an invocation to form and sustain relationships with Indigenous nations whose lands we occupy and with descendant communities whom our institutions have historical and ongoing relationships. These statements can also serve as reminders for museum professionals and academics to truly hold ourselves accountable to the ideals and values we so eagerly affirm in our mission statements and strategic plans—or in more candid terms, when we put our money where our mouths are, we open generative spaces and truly stand to benefit from these investments within our shared communities.

The consideration of site and context is key when forming and delivering these recognitions or acknowledgments. Within an academic setting, it is important for students to hear faculty, administrators, and others in relative positions of power speak about the complexity and messiness within institutions and to validate the feelings of ambivalence and anger they might be experiencing. For our colleagues and peers at universities and museums, these statements can serve as a reminder that we must work toward reconciliation and meaningful engagement, that these statements are words alone if not followed with concrete actions in our daily practice and at larger, structural levels. This dynamic work begins with a statement, but it must be followed with sustained action, investment, and ongoing critical reflection.

This edited volume brings together the work of curators, professors, graduate students, and community members whose exhibitions and practices go beyond land acknowledgments and make sustained and critical contributions within the field of American art. The act of reading a land acknowledgment without following up with action is the equivalent of placing works of art by Black and Indigenous artists in preexisting exhibitions without reframing or recontextualizing the gallery as a whole. While this strategy of insertion places artworks in conversation with other works of American art, it also reinforces the position of European American institutions as the arbiters of value and beauty and erases integral social, cultural, religious, ecological, and epistemological roles these works served before they were brought into museum spaces.[6] Instead of inserting artists into preexisting histories, the contributors to this volume deconstruct long-dominant narratives of American art and expand the framework to offer new methods for curating, exhibiting, and teaching a more truthful and inclusive art history.

BEYOND THE LAND ACKNOWLEDGMENT

The Hood Museum's 2022 exhibition *This Land: American Engagement with the Natural World*, grew from the work around the land acknowledgment

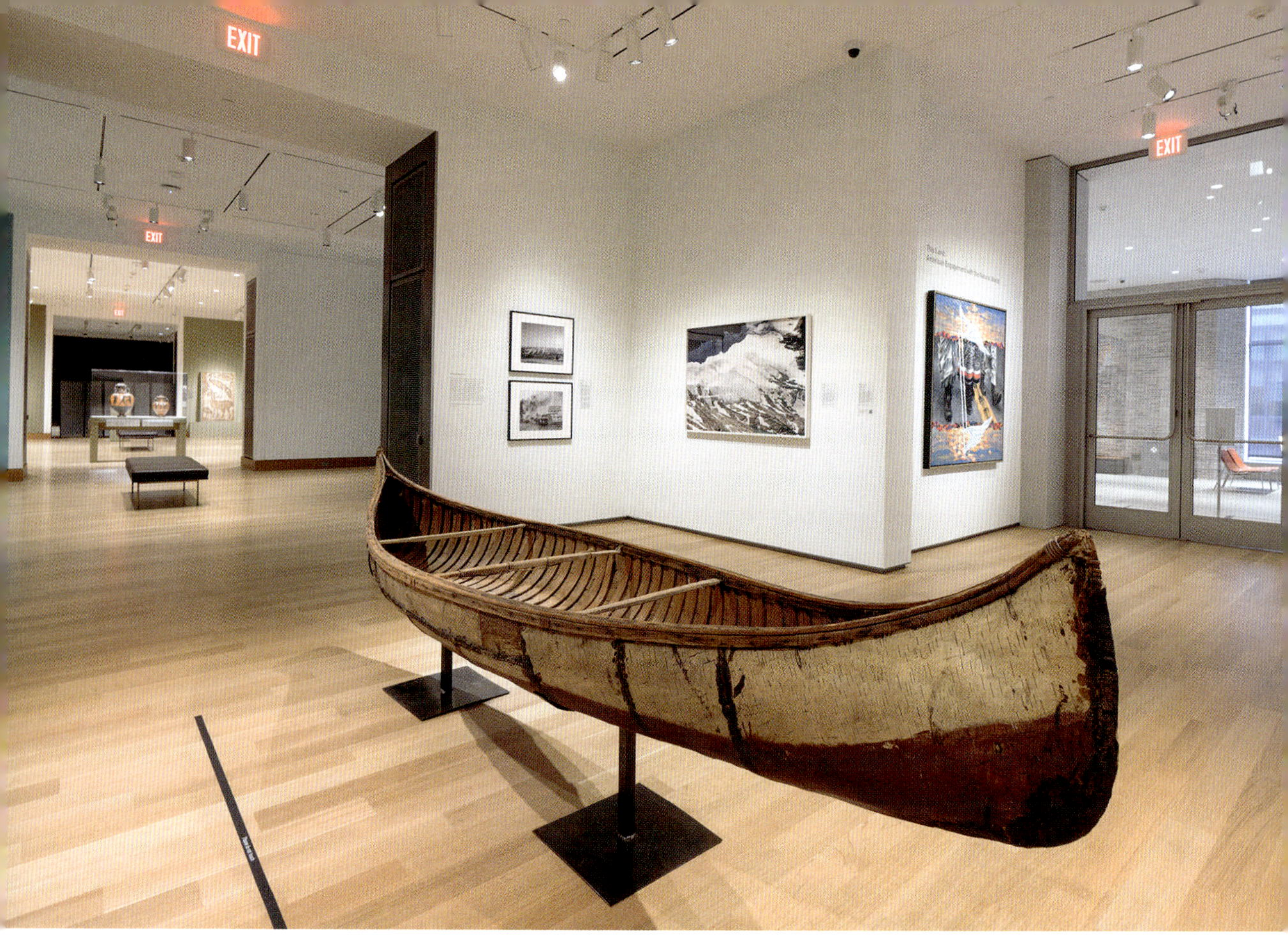

FIGURE I.1 Installation view, entry gallery of *This Land: American Engagement with the Natural World* featuring a birch-bark canoe made by Louis Gill (Abenaki). Image by Rob Strong. © Hood Museum of Art, Dartmouth.

and an ongoing commitment to meaningfully engage with descendant communities and those who call New England—and, more specifically, the Upper Valley region of New Hampshire and Vermont—home today. When visitors first entered *This Land*, they encountered an early twentieth-century birch-bark canoe made by Louis Gill, a citizen of the Abenaki First Nations reserve at Odanak (fig. I.1). Situated at the center of the museum's entry gallery, Gill's canoe grounded the exhibition and museum on Abenaki land while testifying to Gill's immense skill, knowledge, and artistry. The bark of this canoe was carefully soaked, shaped, sewn, and sealed with a mixture of tree resin, charcoal, and deer tallow (fat), making it durable and watertight. The knowledge required to construct such a work and subsequently navigate an intricate highway system comprised of ocean and inland waterways spoke to the importance of place for the maker and users of this canoe. Positioned at the museum's entrance, Gill's canoe also encouraged visitors to consider their personal relationship to places in the world. The introductory panel for *This Land* emphasized these relationships further, ending with a deceptively simple question: "What land holds special meaning for you?"

Using place as an organizing concept, the exhibition's thematic installation of the museum's permanent collection explored the visual, intellectual, spiritual, and social relationships between American artists and the natural world from the early nineteenth century to the present. *This Land* was also the museum's first exhibition to feature Native American art—both historical and contemporary—alongside artworks by African American, Asian American, European American, and Latin American artists. Included in the introductory panel was also the recognition that:

> No single narrative or selection of objects can mine the depth and breadth of such an expansive topic . . . *This Land* raises as many questions as it answers, urging us to consider our own relationships with the natural world and our hopes for its future. *This Land* features works of art that express reverence and concern for the lands now known as the United States. Many perspectives are shared, but not all.

Featuring works both beautiful and challenging, *This Land* compelled viewers to consider new perspectives on historical and contemporary art by diverse artists, Native and non-Native, and to reflect on our own relationship to place and land.

A particularly poignant comparison of a Diné (Navajo) saddle blanket and Georgia O'Keeffe's *Taos Mountain* demonstrated the importance of place for two women living in the same region who portrayed the world within their own artistic traditions and informed by their unique lived experiences (fig. I.2). Woven by a Diné woman, the saddle blanket dates from the so-called Transition Period (1880–1895) that followed the arrival of the railroad to the Navajo Reservation. Increased access to brightly colored commercial yarns and synthetic dyes in the late nineteenth century sparked experimentation

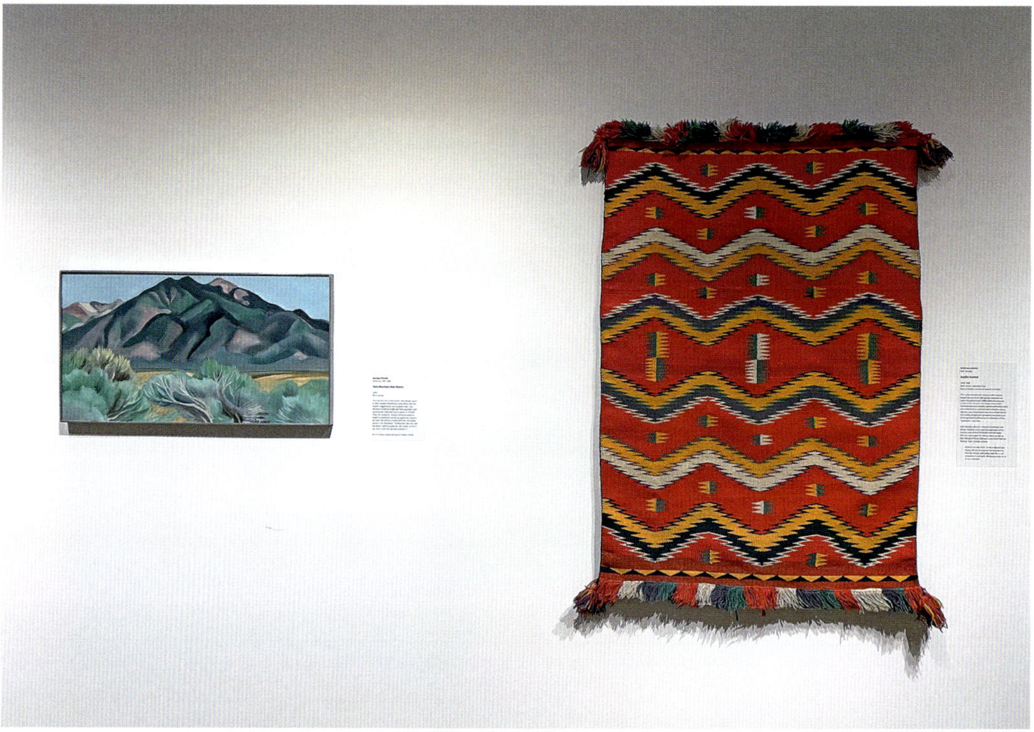

FIGURE I.2 Installation view, "Power of Place," in *This Land: American Engagement with the Natural World*. (Left) Georgia O'Keeffe, *Taos Mountain, New Mexico*, 1930; (right) once-known Diné (Navajo) artist, saddle blanket, 1880–1900. Image by Michael W. Hartman.

among weavers, who incorporated new, more vibrant colors into existing designs and generated new styles, such as the geometric patterns and serrated lines of this "eyedazzler" blanket.[7] Diné weaving expressed the lessons learned from Na'ashjé'ii Asdzáá (Spider Woman), who taught the Diné to weave and introduced the concept of Hózhó. Scholars Lynda Teller Pete and Barbara Teller Ornelas explain: "Hózhó is our way of life, to live in balance and beauty. We do not separate the weaving arts from our culture, spirituality, daily life, or our connection to the earth. Weaving is a way for us to live in balance."[8] Inspired by the local landscape, the Diné woman incorporated bands of yellow, green, and purple, portraying the mountainous landscape in her design. O'Keeffe, who painted the region a few decades later, saw similar colors and forms in the landscape and incorporated them into her oil-on-canvas painting. This region's rugged terrain, crystalline light, and Tewa association with sacred power likely held special appeal for O'Keeffe. She rounded the contours of Taos Mountain and accentuated its height by pushing the summit up against the canvas's top edge. She wrote to a friend after this, her second season in the Southwest, saying, "The Mountain calls one, and the desert—and the sagebrush—the country seems to call one in a way that one has to answer it."[9] When side by side, the shared recognition of the importance of place for these women became ever more apparent through their formal similarities.

Elsewhere in the gallery, the curatorial team incorporated multiple and sometimes divergent viewpoints by juxtaposing historical and contemporary artworks by Native and non-Native artists that spoke to a common theme or idea. Within the exhibition's third section, titled "Sustenance," a grouping of three works by Lloyd Harrison, Tonita Vigil Peña (Quah Ah) (Po-Woh-Ge-Owinge [San Ildefonso Pueblo]), and Nicholas Lampert considered the diversity of American relationships with corn, a food staple that has shaped US cultural and national identity (fig. I.3). Harrison's World War I–era propaganda poster hailed corn as "The Food of the Nation" and extolled the abundance and diversity of corn products—corn meal, grits, hominy, corn muffins, corn pancakes, and even corn syrup—at a time when wheat, meat, and sugar were being rationed. Long before corn was an American food staple, however, it was also a staple for many Native North American nations. Tonita Peña's depiction of a basket dance—one of several annual dances practiced by Puebloan communities to ensure agricultural success—reminds us that crops are not always abundant. Juxtaposed alongside these historical images, Nicholas Lampert's print *Solidarity with Migrant Workers, Not Agribusiness* portrays a migrant family running beneath a weaponized cob of corn. Lampert illustrates the connections between agribusiness and US foreign policy and the impacts these policies have on migrant families. With just these three artworks, Dartmouth students and the broader public engaged with representations of a familiar food staple in a manner that was both present and contemporary but rooted within entangled histories of celebration, dispossession, immigration, and violence.

While this temporary exhibition presented many opportunities, it also posed many challenges. Lampert's print calls for solidarity with migrants,

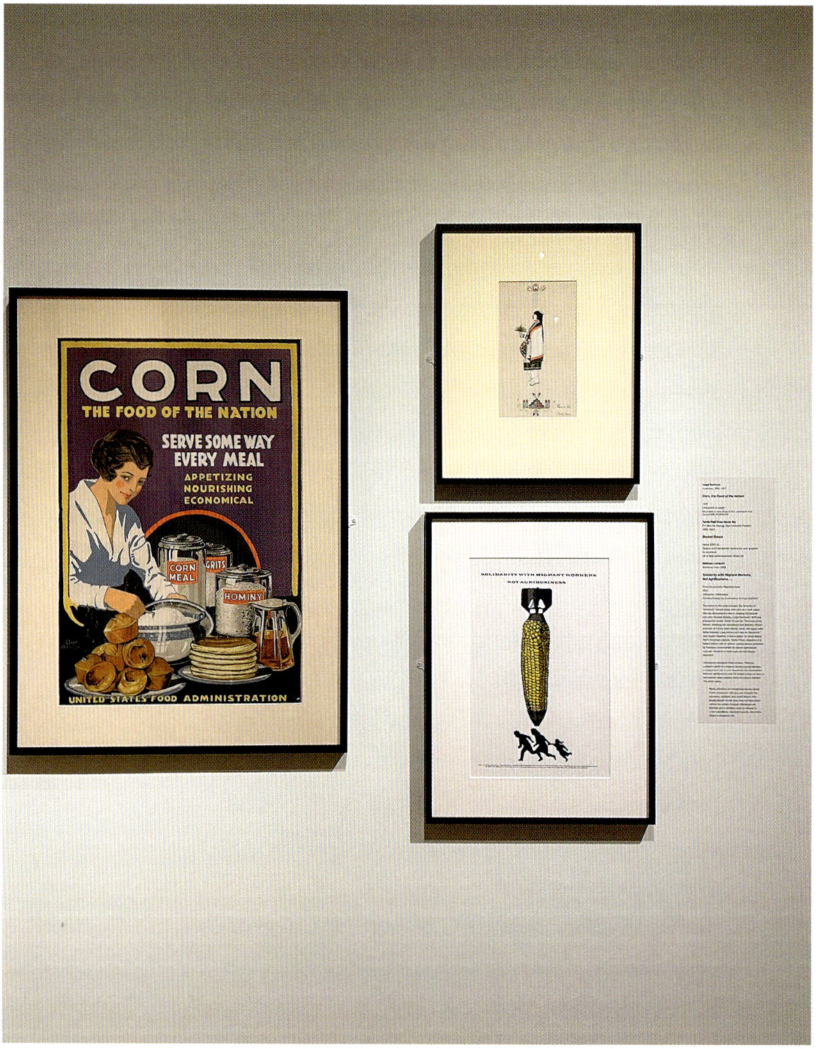

FIGURE I.3 Installation view, "Sustenance," in *This Land: American Engagement with the Natural World*. (Left to right) Lloyd Harrison, *Corn, the Food of the Nation*, 1918; Tonita Peña, *Basket Dance*, 1930–31; Nicholas Lampert, *Solidarity with Migrant Workers, Not Agribusiness . . .* , 2012. Image by Jami C. Powell.

although the inclusion of this work—rather than a print by a Latine/x artist more directly impacted by migration across the US southern border—revealed one of many shortcomings in the Hood Museum's collection. The process of mining the collection to develop *This Land* revealed that we cannot fully tell all stories or represent all perspectives, because we lack the artworks to do so, a sentiment reflected in the exhibition's introductory text. Many themes were disproportionately represented solely in works on paper—a light-sensitive medium that cannot remain on view for long periods of time—which meant the exhibition could be on view for only six months. Refining our collecting priorities and writing a Collections Development Plan has ensured that we will expand our collection in ways that highlight diverse voices in our galleries through artworks across media that better reflect Dartmouth's student body. Since the closing of *This Land*, we have strategically grown the collection to encompass many more works by Latine artists, including Laura Aguilar, Carolina Aranibar-Fernández, Steven Molina Contreras, Guillermo Galindo, Scherezade García, Ester Hernandez, Kiara Aileen Machado (fig. I.4), Poli Marichal, Michael Menchaca, Alexander Maldonado, Álvaro D. Márquez, Javier Piñón, Sonia Romero (fig. I.5), and Karla Rosas. Because this edited volume grew out of the Hood Museum's exhibition, American art by Latine/x artists is not fully addressed in this text. It is our hope that our colleagues at other institutions who are doing this work will continue to help the field redefine and complicate American art histories on display in the museum and taught in the classroom.

Furthermore, the COVID-19 pandemic slowed progress and delayed installation, especially with the retirement of Barbara J. MacAdam early in the pandemic and the hiring of Michael W. Hartman as her replacement in mid-2021. Morgan E. Freeman and Thomas H. Price both left the Hood Museum to attend graduate school. Jami C. Powell shepherded the project to completion despite these challenges to bring the exhibition to fruition and worked closely with the Terra Foundation and their responsive granting program to create the opportunity for this publication. As a co-curated project, the team intentionally developed an exhibition that would contribute to emerging discourses about the boundaries of American art. Reading scholarship, discussing artworks, and coming together across disciplines resulted in

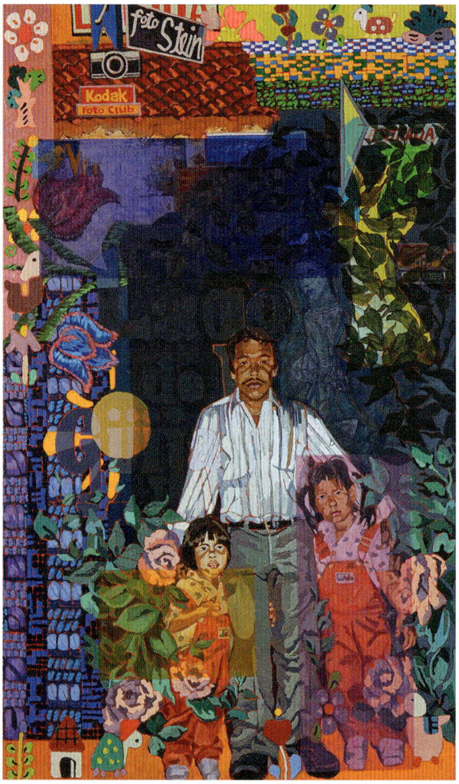

FIGURE I.4 Kiara Aileen Machado (Guatemalan/Salvadoran, born in the United States, 1993), *Tres Fronteras (Three Borders)*, 2019. Oil on canvas, 54 × 36 in. Hood Museum of Art, Dartmouth: Purchased through the Robert J. Strasenburgh II 1942 Fund; 2023.27. Image by Sara Jamback. © Kiara Aileen Machado.

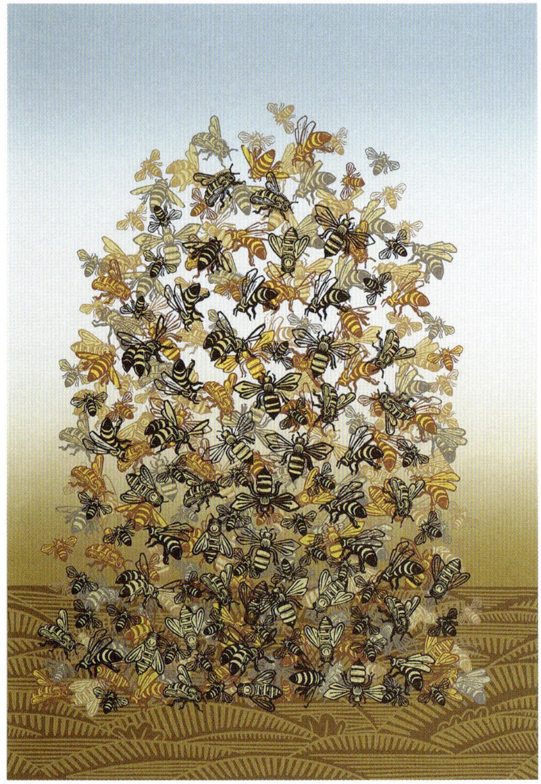

FIGURE I.5 Sonia Romero (American, born 1980), *Bee Pile*, 2010. Screen print, 43 x 31 in. Hood Museum of Art, Dartmouth: Purchased through the Phyllis and Bertram Geller 1937 Memorial Fund; 2023.36.2. Image by Sara Jamback. © Sonia Romero.

an expansive exhibition that attempted to fully incorporate artworks from diverse backgrounds, encouraging visitors to see and learn about multiple viewpoints. But even with years of planning, what was originally intended as the anticipated final checklist changed after the exhibition opened.

During a press walk-through, we realized that some of our object choices and interpretive strategies did not fully contribute to a productive conversation. The label for the Hood Museum's *Cowboy Bargaining for an Indian Girl* by Charles Marion Russell (fig. I.6) rightly drew attention to how such works

> blur the lines between reality and fiction and, in the case of this painting, perpetuate harmful stereotypes about the availability and assumed promiscuity of Indigenous women. Furthermore, these depictions flatten the experiences of Native women, who played important social and economic roles as interlocutors, mediators, and traders through interracial relationships.

FIGURE I.6 Installation view, *This Land: American Engagement with the Natural World*. (Left to right) Saddle blanket made by a once-known Diné (Navajo) artist, 1880–1900; Ansel Adams, *Moon and Half Dome, Yosemite National Park, California*, 1960; Len Jenshel, *Arches National Park, Utah*, 1985; John Steuart Curry, *The Plainsman*, 1945; John McGahey after George Catlin, *Wi-Jun-Jon, An Assiniboine Chief*, 1844; and Charles Marion Russell, *Cowboy Bargaining for an Indian Girl*, 1895. Image by Rob Strong. © Hood Museum of Art, Dartmouth.

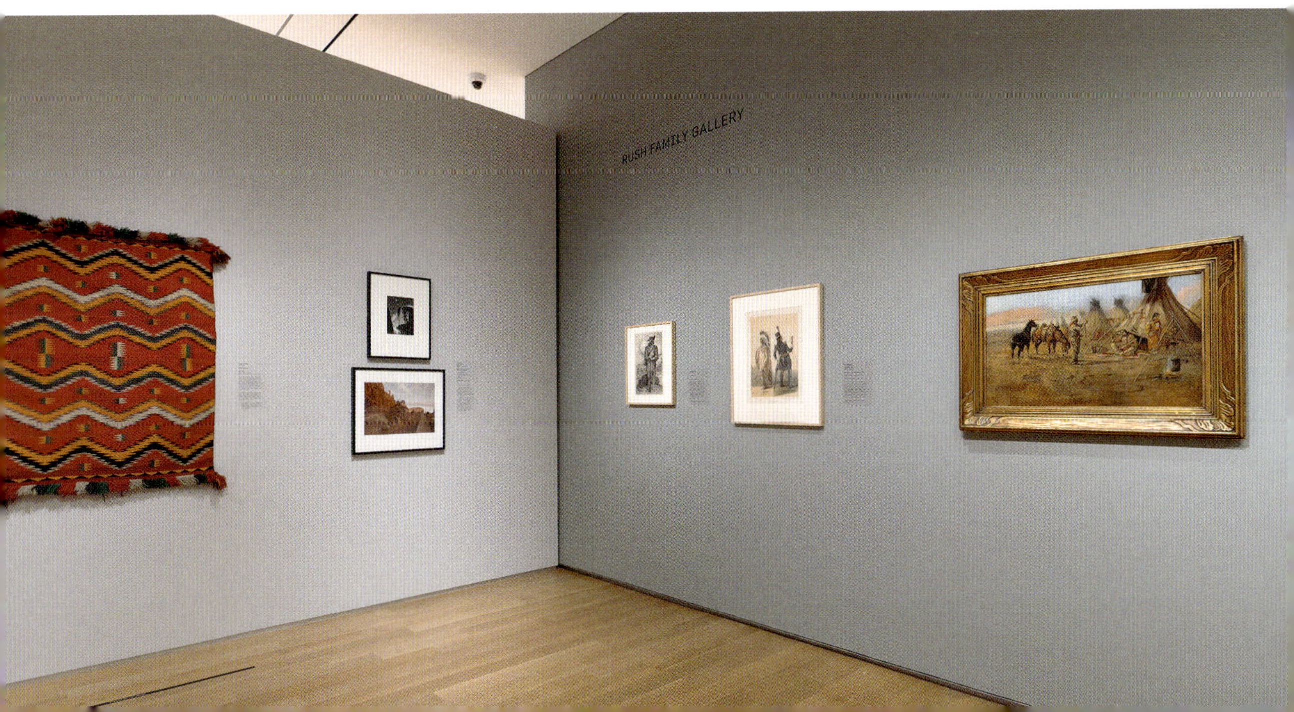

Even so, one early and unpublished review of the exhibition fixated on this painting's "authentic" representation of a "real" event, failing to grasp the complexity. Instead of altering the text further, we removed the work from the gallery. Like the exhibition's evolving changes over time, this book is just a step in a broader process of relearning and reevaluating how we interpret, collect, and exhibit American art in US museums.

EXPANDING AMERICAN ART HISTORIES

This book originated in *This Land*, an exhibition that contributed to the emerging discourse about the boundaries of American art, but grew out of a convening held in April 2022 at the Hood Museum. Titled "Re-envisioning Histories of American Art," this convening featured curators, professors, and graduate students working within and beyond the field of art history to challenge, rethink, and expand traditional definitions of American art. The contributors to this volume pull back the curtain to highlight other curatorial projects and scholarly approaches that similarly seek to refine and expand American art across a range of institutions, including academic, civic, encyclopedic, and national museums. Although an increasing number of museums are seeking to diversify and make their collections, exhibitions, and staffs more inclusive, very little has been published about the actual processes involved in this meaningful work and the ways individuals and teams must navigate institutional constraints and opportunities, particularly when projects disrupt existing practices or expectations.

This book contributes to and expands ongoing conversations regarding the development of more inclusive narratives of American art that employ curatorial and community collaboration and multivocality to share fuller histories of our variegated, and often problematic, histories. The authors in this volume speak about their work highlighting diverse artists and untold stories and about the possibilities and challenges of this meaningful practice. They embrace collaborative approaches to research and curatorial practice and represent varied specialties, academic backgrounds, and career levels. Organized into three sections, this scholarly book generates important new scholarship and compels the field to widen the lens when teaching and curating American art. Above all, the essays in this volume demonstrate that there is no singular or "one size fits all" approach to the work of expanding the canon of American art but, rather, that this long-term work requires a multiplicity of strategies employed across exhibitions, collecting, and teaching.

Part 1: Complicating Histories: Curating across Disciplinary Boundaries

Increasingly, museums are seeking to diversify their collections, exhibitions, and staffs to make them more inclusive, though very little has been published about the actual institutional and curatorial processes involved in these significant undertakings. The first section of this book provides an opportunity to hear from curatorial collaborators about their experiences regarding the challenges and possibilities of this meaningful work. Morgan E. Freeman and Thomas H. Price reflect on their experiences as co-curators for *This Land: American Engagement with the Natural World*. Freeman and Price provide an overview of the exhibition's planning and installation while arguing for the critical importance of curatorial collaboration; the openness to critique; the need to honestly communicate an exhibition's limitations and possibilities to the public; and the time, effort, and institutional support required to curate projects that embrace Native American and American art. To tell a story about American art and the natural world, Freeman and Price demonstrate how limitations can become generative conversations driven by open collaboration and thoughtful dialogue. They ask us, "How do you tell a story about American art and nature?" While their answer, "Tell more than one story," sounds quite simple, the two authors demonstrate the value in having open, honest, and challenging conversations in order to expand the definition of American art on display in museums.

Their essay is followed by one from Janet Dees and Alisa Swindell, who write about their collaborative experience working with each other and the Chicago community to curate *A Site of Struggle: American Art against Anti-Black Violence* at Northwestern's Block Museum of Art. Highlighting the importance of Black feminist curatorial perspectives, Dees and Swindell demonstrate how curated spaces can grapple with difficult topics while becoming spaces of care, both for visitors and museum staff. Their project reveals how reenvisioning histories of American art cannot just elevate underrecognized histories but requires a complete rethinking of how exhibitions are made and viewed by diverse audiences. By "centering care," Dees and Swindell argue that methodologies working across real and perceived differences, institutional hierarchies, and collaborations with community stakeholders are what ultimately help us reenvision "content-specific models" for exhibiting the multiple stories told about American art within museum spaces. They advocate for the importance of institutional support to work with communities in more sustained ways that might lengthen the exhibition planning process but create deeper and more impactful results.

The first section concludes with a conversation moderated by Jami C. Powell and Michael W. Hartman with Austen Barron Bailly and Karen Kramer, scholars who have collaborated on numerous curatorial projects at the Peabody Essex Museum, including the permanent collection reinstallation *On This Ground: Being and Belonging in America*. Bailly and Kramer first speak about their own trajectories into the field of curatorial practice, demonstrating how canonical histories of American art have long excluded Native artists and how institutional support is critical to readdressing and correcting this omission. Using a variety of curatorial projects as examples, they underscore the importance of highlighting Indigenous voices within museums, arguing for how curatorial collaboration across disciplines, with museum staff and fellows, and with people from Indigenous communities can disrupt canonical art historical narratives. At the same time, they demonstrate the importance of maintaining a distinct or sovereign space for exhibiting works by Indigenous artists on their own terms. Kramer speaks of this distinction in metaphor: "Native art practitioners want a piece of the pie that is American art, but we want our own pie too."

Part 2: Reframing Collection Practices and Care

As museums continue to revise and redefine their collecting priorities, essays in the second section of this book critically reconsider how museums can implement collections practices in meaningful ways. Looking at case studies regarding museum collecting and collections care, curators embrace interdisciplinary and intersectional approaches that open new possibilities for contending with past and present with an eye toward the future of museum collections practices. This group of scholar-curators considers the ethical considerations involved in identifying collection needs, boundaries, and possibilities. They center place and locality in their discussions, providing new frameworks for how museums develop institutional priorities.

The fiftieth anniversary of the Smithsonian American Art Museum's Renwick Gallery of American Craft and Decorative Arts anchors Anya Montiel's (Mexican and Tohono O'odham descent) essay, which reckons with the reality that Native arts comprised just 0.5 percent of the collection (twelve artworks) prior to the anniversary acquisitions campaign. Montiel outlines how an acquisitions plan was developed, ensuring that living artists were prioritized to balance historical artworks already in the collections of other Smithsonian institutions. She writes, "Living artists can work with the curatorial, collections, conservation, and exhibit staff about the materials and techniques in their works while advising on how best to store, display, and care for them. Living artists also can assist the education and visitor services staff with interpretive strategies for their works." Through a series of case studies, Montiel argues how "these artworks demonstrate to museum visitors that Native people are contemporary and not of the past" by emphasizing the collaborative nature of working with artists and other curators. Even in what seemed to be an unsurmountable obstacle of working within a collection that neglected Native arts for decades, Montiel's essay and curatorial practice envisions paths forward for other museums that lack Native representation in their collections.

Mindy N. Besaw begins her essay by asking, "Who are the arbiters of taste, and why does inclusion in the canon remain such a powerful benchmark, even while museums across the country are working hard to undermine the canon and instead turn attention to underrecognized artists?" Using the example of well-known artist Frederic Remington, who even within the history of American art is considered secondary due to his focus on the American West, Besaw's essay discusses Crystal Bridges's fall 2024 exhibition *Knowing the West*, the first major traveling exhibition to focus on the coexistence of art created in the nineteenth and early twentieth century by Native American and non–Native American artists. Co-curated and developed with an advisory council of Native and non-Native scholars, *Knowing the West* embraces an interpretive philosophy that acknowledges how audiences approach the American West through many ways of knowing while prioritizing Indigenous perspectives and other untold stories. In doing so, Besaw demonstrates how placing a single work by Remington in a gallery otherwise dedicated to Native artists—the opposite of recent approaches that add Native American art to galleries previously installed with paintings and sculptures—changes the perspective of whose histories are told and how they are communicated. She argues that curatorial reckoning and accountability must balance label texts that are simultaneously invitational, additive, and inclusive, allowing museums to become spaces for dialogue and provide opportunities for conversation and growth, complicating inherited art historical narratives while simultaneously expanding them.

A collaborative essay by curator Layla Bermeo and Wabanaki Educator and Language Keeper Roger Paul (Passamaquoddy/Wolastoqey) concludes this section. When rewriting labels for *Translating American Stories* at the Museum of Fine Arts, Boston, Bermeo designed a multilingual presentation that would reorient the gallery's traditionally heroic tales of the American Revolution, emphasizing community members' interpretations of artworks written in their native language. Presented as a dialogue between Paul and Bermeo, this essay outlines how the process unfolded for a label to accompany Robert Feke's *Portrait of Isaac Winslow*. Both authors speak to the importance of sharing authority and welcoming many voices. Importantly, Paul also reflects on the ambivalence of knowledge partners who carry with them unease for institutions that have long excluded them and exploited their cultures. For Bermeo, "the yearlong process of writing a single, 127-word label" speaks to the importance of time, openness, and reciprocity required to care for collections and to care for collaborators who help make museum collections more broadly accessible. Bermeo emphasizes that instead of translating labels into languages that reflect the museum community's demographics, the museum can collaborate directly with community members to tell their histories in their own languages.

Part 3: Interrupting Colonial Structures

Recent scholarship has challenged the assumed neutrality of the scholarly voice, especially in the construction of the canon of American art. Thinking about our own voices and multifaceted positionalities, the book's final section reconsiders how we define American art. Museum curators and college educators suggest new modes of teaching and presenting American art to speak to the past, the present, and a shared future. Navigating historical and ongoing negotiations of who is "American," scholar-curators challenge the legacies of colonialism, racism, and White supremacy that have historically defined these discussions. Whereas essays in section one and two focus more on the practice and application of these ideas, authors in the final section of the book reincorporate this applied work within broader theoretical frameworks and demonstrate the significant, co-constitutive role of art and museums within academic knowledge production. Embracing interdisciplinary approaches, these authors offer new possibilities for the ethical study and exhibition of artists and media traditionally left out of the art historical canon.

"How effective can institutional critique be when the invitation is fulsome and eagerly extended?" Kirsten Pai Buick offers this question as a critique of museums that invite art historians and contemporary artists to critique or disrupt their historical collections. Buick argues that the purpose of these engagements is to keep "Old Masters" relevant because if the invitation to critique comes from the museum itself, critique is already circumscribed within what the museum deems appropriate and allowable. The terms "invited," "interrupted," and "uninvited" ground Buick's essay, which opens by describing her own experience as a scholar invited to speak about the "Black sublime" in Kehinde Wiley's work on view at the National Gallery in London. The paper Buick proposed critiqued the imperial museum, arguing that "Kehinde Wiley's offering is actually closer to Mary Shelley's depiction of the monster among the picturesque as she relies on the experiences of the 'un-monstrous' and Wiley the 'un-Black' to complete their pictures and to question their own status." Because Buick's proposed lecture did not offer a self-congratulatory narrative, the museum declined it. Buick continues to the theme of interruption, arguing that inviting contemporary Native artists to interrupt galleries displaying nineteenth-century landscapes must be accompanied by institutional prerogative to critique the imperial narratives that these paintings uphold. Buick's essay concludes with an artwork by Isaac Otchere "Azey," which was removed from a gallery at the Detroit Institute of Arts. Uninvited by wealthy racist White donors, the painting celebrated Barack Obama's election to the presidency in 2008. Using art as "absolving agents . . . in our redemptory installations in imperial museums" limits perspectives on view and upholds the same narratives, giving them a different pictorial form. The "invited disruption" results in an interruption that renews "relevance and absolution for the real monsters of empire."

Hazel V. Carby's essay uses *This Land: American Engagement with the Natural World* as a case study to consider the importance of interdisciplinary perspectives within museums for critiquing settler colonial narratives and giving "voice to those who protest and oppose colonial corporate predation." Carby grounds her essay in her belief that art museums hold pedagogic potential but that the "White noise" of institutional DEAI programs fails to inject real institutional change. She argues that DEAI programs are not commitments to end structural racism because they sidestep naming and critiquing the settler colonial narratives they inherit and perpetuate. Within this framework, Carby argues that "museums wishing to fulfill their role as public educators in spaces welcoming to a broad audience and . . . for universities seeking to expand the diversity of their student body," the real work of "unearthing, confronting, and acting to repair the violence and violations of settler colonialism and racial capitalism will require more than platitudes." Carby traces how "White noise" subverts, if not obliterates, creative thought because the impetus to truly change does not exist. Museums have the potential to explicitly recognize dispossession, displacement, and enslavement and accompany this recognition by actions that "remediate and repair."

Using metaphors of braiding, stitching, and sweeping, Alexandra M. Thomas demonstrates the importance of highlighting the experiences of Black women to enrich art histories and incorporate new perspectives. Thomas's 2023 exhibition *Homecoming: Domesticity and Kinship in Global African Art* embraced the concept of "Black feminist domesticity" to argue for the importance of developing new critical methods for presenting African diasporic art histories. Thomas encourages us to consider "what it means to collaborate on a vision for a different world through our work and its intersections with creative practice" while centering on Black feminist perspectives that attempt to "dislodge the hierarchies and borders of the art world." Grounding her practice and exhibition within Black women's domesticity, Thomas begins with the practice of braiding hair, which opens a dialogue about entanglements and connections within communities. She expands to include a discussion and collaboration with Indigenous artists who incorporate braiding into their practice, demonstrating the importance of braiding to Black and Indigenous feminisms and their interconnectedness across tribes, nations, and diasporic experiences. Thomas then grounds stitching as "a Black feminist gesture of care, repair, and creative expression" used in textiles and beadwork. Centered on a discussion of Bhasha Chakrabarti's double-sided quilt *It's a Blue World*, Thomas demonstrates how this artwork mobilized intergenerational and feminist approaches to reveal stitching as both utilitarian and political. Sweeping centers Black women as caregivers in their communities who sweep streets after protests. Thomas reveals how "protesting police brutality, in all forms, and cleaning up afterward are public demonstrations of love and care for community." Black women's domesticity and labor (often unacknowledged or unpaid) become sources of resistance and help build a future "world in which Black women's creative labor, innovative designs, and speculative worlds are celebrated for their abundant offerings."

Yinshi Lerman-Tan speaks to how nontraditional artworks, such as large-scale murals or small sketches with conservation concerns, must be collected and preserved by museums if these institutions are truly dedicated to telling more inclusive art histories. Using a recently acquired eight-by-eight-foot mural by Chinese American artist Tyrus Wong designed for the Los Angeles restaurant Dragon's Den, Lerman-Tan compels readers to see a more complex and diverse history of American art, touching on everything from Walt Disney to Hallmark. His work, like that of other artists of color working in the period, achieved "a radical layering of American icons typically coded as white with an Asian American sensibility and politics." Collecting a large-scale mural once splattered with American Chinese restaurant food—something previously unheard of in most museums—demonstrates The Huntington Museum's critical dedication to preserving this artist's work and experience, as well as a broader American Chinese experience in 1930s California. Over the course of her essay, Lerman-Tan emphasizes the importance of American art history's continued engagement with area studies programs, noting how Asian American art has been crucially informed by scholars in Asian American studies. She argues that institutions must expand "institutional collecting interests and practice to more robustly include and display the varied media produced by artists like Wong." Lerman-Tan uses Tyrus Wong's life and career as "an example of how expanding the disciplinary boundaries of American art informs our interpretation and understanding of historic artists of color."

Rather than a traditional exhibition catalog, this collection of essays provides multiple methods for widening the lens when teaching and curating American art by featuring a selection of authors already engaged in this practice. Instead of focusing on the results of the exhibition, the emphasis on pedagogical and curatorial methodologies generates important new scholarship that will inspire change in our institutions for years to come. Embracing the broad perspective of American art, the authors and editors of this volume attempt to fully include diverse histories and perspectives, providing a timely resource for our colleagues, present and future. The ideas that drove the exhibition *This Land: American Engagement with the Natural World* continue in this volume and are expanded upon, offering art history a series of questions for how the field and museums can continue to expand their narratives by being honest about the past, incorporating voices from artists of differing backgrounds while not limiting these artists to engaging only with inherited narratives and offering reparative actions for a path forward.

NOTES

1. This list is not exhaustive and not intended to be comprehensive. It reflects our own academic training and the limits of our knowledge. We know there are others in the field also doing this work. In addition to the authors included this

volume, we also want to recognize the following scholars: heather ahtone, Aleesa Pitcharmarn Alexander, Anna Arabindan-Kesson, Renée Ater, La Tanya Autry, Mia Bagneris, Martin Berger, Janet Berlo, Stephen Best, Alexis Boylan, Adrienne Childs, Huey Copeland, Philip J. Deloria, Jacqueline Francis, Ximena Gómez, Camera Dia Holloway, Shana Klein, Marci Kwon, Anthony Lee, Amy Lonetree, Kobena Mercer, Alexis Monroe, Kelli Morgan, Rachel Grace Newman, Ruth Phillips, E. Carmen Ramos, Tatiana Reinoza, Kirk Savage, Tanya Sheehan, Shawn Michelle Smith, Krista Thompson, Jennifer Van Horn, ShiPu Wang, Adrianna Zavala, and Claudia Zapata. *Panorama*, the open access journal for the Association of Historians of American Art, has also made significant contributions to this area.

2. Graham Bowley, "Kevin Young, Poet and Author, Is Named to Lead African American Museum," *New York Times*, September 30, 2020, https://www.nytimes.com/2020/09/30/arts/design/kevin-young-to-lead-african-american-museum.html/.

3. Colin Gordon Calloway, John Kimball Jr. 1943 Professor of History and professor of Native American and Indigenous studies; Bruce Duthu, Samson Occom Professor of Native American and Indigenous Studies; Jessica Hong, formerly associate curator of global contemporary art, Hood Museum of Art; Deborah King, associate professor of sociology; and Trica Keaton, professor of African and African American studies.

4. See also Horace D. Ballard, Ximena Gómez, and Jami C. Powell, "Beyond the Land Acknowledgment: Native Voices, Institutions, and Scholars in Conversation," Harvard Art Museums, May 5, 2022, https://youtu.be/XXM2et6TFfg/. For a similar discussion at the MFA Boston, see Marina Tyquiengco, Layla Bermeo, and Tess Lukey, "Beyond Land Acknowledgments," in "Art History and the Local," In the Round, *Panorama: Journal of the Association of Historians of American Art* 8, no. 1 (2022), https://doi.org/10.24926/24716839.13208/.

5. Joseph M. Pierce, "Your Land Acknowledgment Is Not Enough," *Hyperallergic*, October 12, 2022, https://hyperallergic.com/769024/your-land-acknowledgment-is-not-enough/.

6. See Jami C. Powell, review of *Art of Native America: The Charles and Valerie Diker Collection*, Metropolitan Museum of Art, *Panorama: Journal of the Association of Historians of American Art* 5, no. 1 (2019), https://doi.org/10.24926/24716839.1710/.

7. Laurie D. Webster, "Changing Markets for Navajo Weaving," in *Navajo Textiles: The Crane Collection at the Denver Museum of Nature and Science*, ed. Laurie D.

Webster, Louise I. Stiver, D. Y. Begay, and Lynda Tellerpete (Boulder: University Press of Colorado, 2017), 49–77.

8. Barbara Teller Ornelas and Lynda Teller Pete, *How to Weave a Navajo Rug and Other Lessons from Spider Woman* (Loveland, CO: Thurms Books, 2020).

9. Georgia O'Keeffe to Dorothy Brett, early April 1930, transcribed by Sarah Greenough in *Georgia O'Keeffe: Art and Letters*, ed. Jack Coward, Juan Hamilton, and Sarah Greenough (Washington, DC: National Gallery of Art, 1987), 200.

PART I

COMPLICATING HISTORIES

Curating across Disciplinary Boundaries

1

Morgan E. Freeman / Thomas H. Price

COLLABORATIVE METHODOLOGIES FOR AN EXPANDED AMERICAN ART

This Land / American Engagement with the Natural World

How do you tell a story about American art and nature? While simple in structure, this question, which drove our work on the exhibition *This Land: American Engagement with the Natural World*, quickly expanded in myriad directions, raising both complications and possibilities. How do we, as curators or as museums, define the borders of cultural and artistic production, and do we separate them at all? Is our exhibition a story about American art, and how do we define that? Art in the United States? Art in part of North America? How can we embrace a model of "story" telling by providing nuanced perspectives, histories, and accounts while offering a comprehensible exhibition structure and resisting the reductive simplicity of a singular narrative? And, crucially, how do we tell an expansive story with the inevitable limitations of an institutional collection?

In many ways, *This Land* was a new endeavor for the Hood Museum of Art. A thematic collection show about artistic interactions with nature, the exhibition was the first time that the historic American art and Native American art collections were displayed together. The stakes, as such, were notably high. With such an important first, there is an urge to "get it right" and tell as expansive an account as possible, to address every issue and concern that might arise for our viewers. Yet this standard, of course, is impossible to meet. How might limitations, then, be generative?

The exhibition, which was on view at the Hood Museum from January through July 2022, began some four years earlier, in 2018, in the wake of a major renovation and expansion project. After being closed for more than two years, the Hood Museum reopened in January 2019 with an additional seven thousand feet of gallery space and an entirely new teaching facility, the Bernstein Center for Object Study, which includes three object study classrooms and a swing storage space to accommodate art movement from the museum's off-site storage facilities. With the galleries filled by new permanent collection installations, reintroducing the Dartmouth and Upper Valley community to the museum's wide-ranging collections, new work began on future shows.

Having freshly updated the American art galleries, Jonathan Little Cohen Curator Emerita of American Art Barbara J. MacAdam began conceptualizing an exhibition on nineteenth-century naturalism that would bring together mainstays as well as underutilized objects in the collection. When Jami C. Powell joined the museum in early 2018 as the inaugural associate curator of Native American Art, MacAdam soon asked her to collaborate, envisioning a more expansive exhibition together.[1] Later that year, when we started at the museum as the curatorial assistant for American art (Price) and Diversifying Art Museum Leadership Initiative (DAMLI) Native American art fellow (Freeman) and settled into our respective roles under MacAdam and Powell, we were asked to join the project and quickly began working as a curatorial team.[2] Three years of work followed, designing and redesigning the exhibition to fit into noncontinuous galleries. Over time our roles grew from assistants to collaborators, and we participated in the exhibition development as co-curators. This development was a natural progression, with our supervisors taking our ideas seriously, though, unfortunately, it remains unusual for curatorial teams to acknowledge lower-ranking curatorial staff as co-curators. This reflects an obvious intellectual generosity on MacAdam's and Powell's parts as well as a concerted effort to forge an atmosphere of thoughtful dialogue and open collaboration with others.

The resulting exhibition, which eventually stretched across two floors of the museum, explored the visual, intellectual, spiritual, and social relationships between American artists and the natural world. Covering a broad temporal period, from the early nineteenth century to the present, the show was comprised of more than 180 objects, from a Thomas Cole painting to Casadei boots beaded by Jamie Okuma in 2021 (fig. 1.1). And while *This Land* reflected the collection's particular strengths in European American and Native American art, artists from a wide variety of backgrounds were represented. *This Land*, we hoped, would present as many facets of "American" art as possible.

This Land was developed and displayed during an ongoing period when museums are reevaluating their collecting and display practices and combining collections to tell more holistic stories. This work is slow, and the inevitable gaps often reveal the troubling history of museum acquisitions. Other institutions, such as the Peabody Essex Museum, were actively

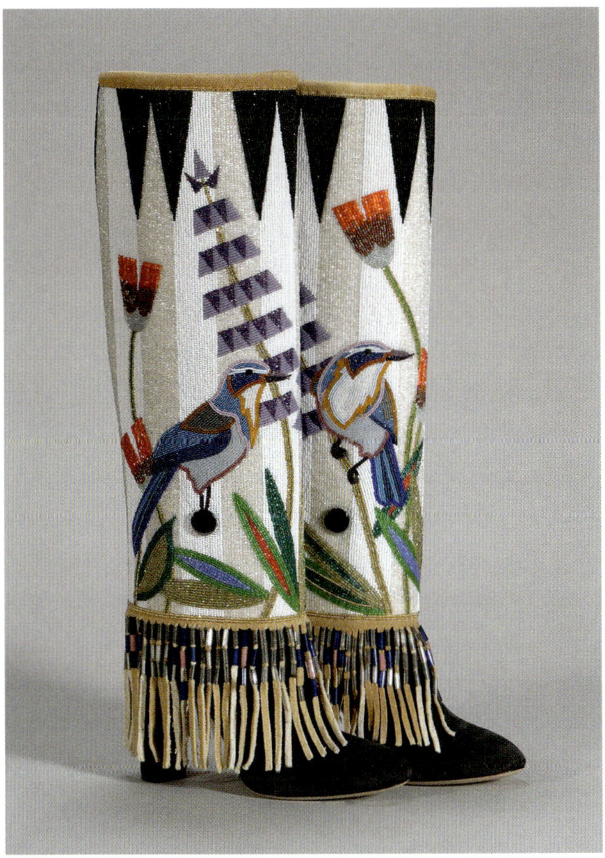

FIGURE 1.1 Jamie Okuma (Luiseño/Shoshone-Bannock/Japanese American), *Peep*, 2021, antique glass beads, brain-tanned deer hide, and vintage basket beads on Casadei boots, 20½ × 8⁷⁄₁₆ × 4¾ in. Hood Museum of Art, Dartmouth: Purchased through the Evelyn A. and William B. Jaffe Fund; 2021.8.1-2. Image by Jeffrey Nintzel. © Jamie Okuma.

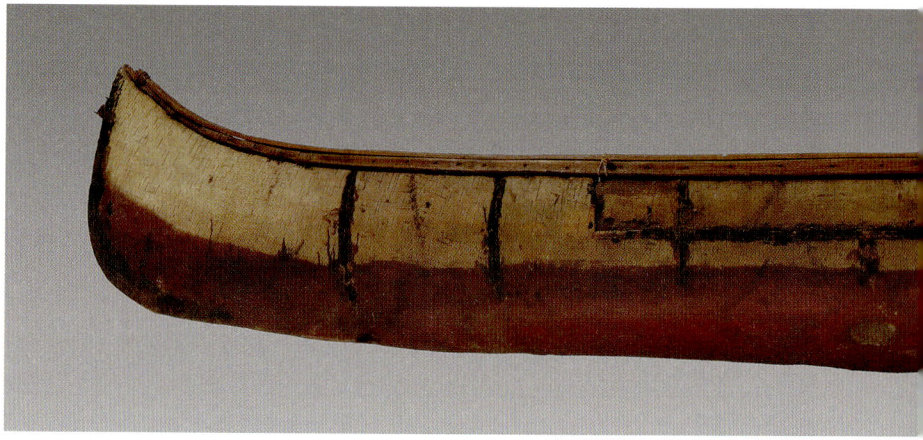

FIGURE 1.2 Louis Gill (Abenaki), birch-bark canoe, early twentieth century, birch bark and wood, 168½ × 32⁵⁄₁₆ × 12⅝ in. Hood Museum of Art, Dartmouth: Gift of Sinclair Week; 162.27.14802. Image by Jeffrey Nintzel. © Hood Museum of Art, Dartmouth.

engaged in reinstalling their permanent galleries, resulting in the long-term exhibition *On This Ground: Being and Belonging in America*, as discussed by Austen Barron Bailly and Karen Kramer in their essay in this volume. Others, such as the Art Gallery of Ontario, had recently completed similar permanent collections reinstallations. A number of major exhibitions, too, were experimenting with new ways of presenting expansive histories of American art and pushing against the accepted "canon." An important contribution here was *Hearts of Our People: Native Women Artists*, curated by Jill Ahlberg Yohe and Teri Greeves and organized by the Minneapolis Institute of Art, which not only reframed Native art through women artists but also relied on collaborations with a large number of Indigenous community members and knowledge keepers to shape the exhibition. *Nature's Nation: American Art and Environment*, organized by Karl Kusserow and Alan C. Braddock for the Princeton University Art Museum, also began its tour in 2018, an influential show that notably argued for the ecological basis of all American art. The exhibition's installation at the Peabody Essex Museum was particularly influential for our curatorial team. A small sixteenth-century bear sculpture, probably Pawtucket, accompanied the museum's land acknowledgment, centering the history of local artistic production and inspiring our own choice to

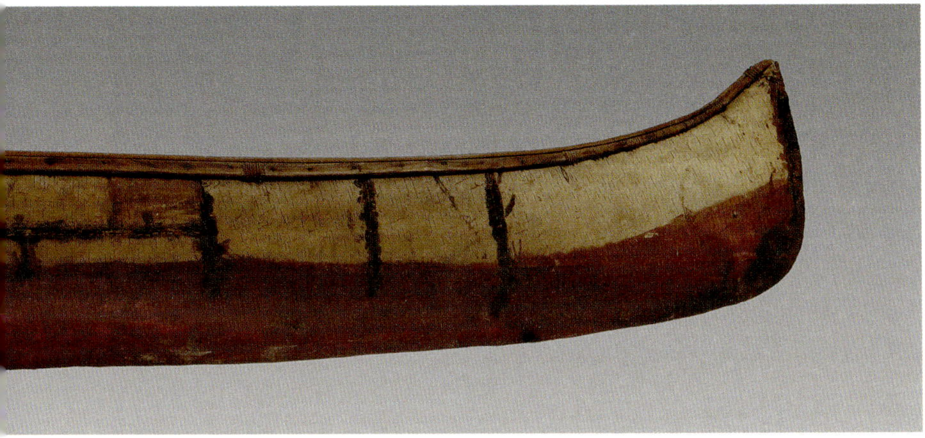

begin with an Abenaki birch-bark canoe made by Louis Gill (fig. 1.2). The presentation of *Nature's Nation* at the Peabody Essex Museum was also reframed with the explicit goal of centering Indigenous art and perspectives. The layout was adjusted, for example, so that it began with a balloon from Postcommodity's *Repellent Fence* and ended with Cannupa Hanska Luger's *Mirror Shield Project*, a revision that helped address the inherently colonial vision laden in much American landscape representation.[3]

TEAM COLLABORATION

Considering the concurrent curatorial work of our peers, and subsequently the work and scholarship that informed their own installations, required a collective engagement with literature interrogating the framework of American art, the Anthropocene and its utility as an analytic, and collections stewardship that account for these matters. Our team of four decided to collaborate on a foundational reading list that reflected this discourse, with the goal of facilitating shared terminology and reference points across our respective areas of focus. Among these resources was a selection of essays from the fall 2018 issue of *Panorama: Journal of the Association of Historians of American Art*. The issue featured guest editor Kathryn Bunn-Marcuse, who asked a selection of leading curators of Native American art—including our team's own Jami C. Powell, contributor Karen Kramer, and heather ahtone—the question "How might technology restore the connections between the tangible and the intangible that text-based art-historical practices and their often singular focus on the visual have damaged or elided?" Across their respective responses was a common urging to account for the affective, as well as meanings that cannot be realized in the deracinated setting of the museum. Bunn-Marcuse poignantly reminds us, "Museums excel at spotlighting the visual aspects of art but struggle to engage the fundamental sensorial and performative aspects of art tied to movement, song, and language."[4] A major contribution to this pitfall, ahtone argues, is the learned tendency to center material as an object's defining property. In other words, such an understanding becomes problematic when *material* is defined by its absence of *life*, a paradigm that maintains a stronghold in Western visual culture.[5]

In their coauthored article, "Beyond the Mirror: Indigenous Ecologies and 'New Materialisms' in Contemporary Art," Native studies scholars Jessica Horton and Janet Berlo contend with this divide that we would go on to encounter throughout the duration of this project. The two critique claims of novelty in the scholarly study of materialisms that seek to be more expansive about that which is living, writing explicitly from Indigenous studies and intellectual traditions within which the human is not prioritized above all else. "Once we take indigenous worldviews into account," they argue, "the 'new materialisms' are no longer new."[6] The four of us strived to account for this in our curatorial practice and narrative, both in the contents of the exhibition and in the claims we made of the exhibition itself. There are times when deemphasizing the monumentality of curatorial or academic intervention can seem antithetical to the work we set out to perform; nevertheless, it remains critical that we engage generous citational practices, naming with humility the intellectual work that has preceded us.

While our goal was to broadly deepen our familiarity with American art, including the art and artists that traditionally fall outside of the "canon," our readings primarily focused on scholarship addressing Native art. This choice points to a greater gap in the quantity of scholarship published in the field or, rather, the lack of publications supporting the circulation of such work. Such an absence is reflected in the curricula and specializations of faculty in art history programs today, as the parameters of academia often relegate Indigenous visual cultures to the fields of archeology and anthropology. Professor of gender studies Nancy Marie Mithlo (Chiricahua Apache) has urgently written that the textual absence of Native studies scholarship is stark and has remained so for decades, even more drastically in the fields of Native art and visual culture.[7] Today a new generation of academics is being trained in the study of Indigenous artistic practices across disciplines (e.g., art history, American studies, visual culture) and expanding the methodologies used to write about this work, though it will take years to see this shift reflected in universities across the United States. The scholars and writers named here whose work we engaged with in collective discussion was paired with more widely read texts in the field of American studies at large, such as William Cronon's frequently cited "The Trouble with Wilderness; or, Getting Back to the Wrong Nature," to parse through commonly held beliefs of the American wilderness over time and if such a consensus can even be reached.[8]

Whereas the coming together of four contributors with differing levels of experience and varying training may have, under other circumstances, easily lent itself to a hierarchical structure, our team worked laterally, relying on opportunities for mutual learning. This precedent, which was set by MacAdam and Powell from the moment we joined the curatorial team, allowed the four of us to present knowledge and arguments freely while deferring to the respective expertise held by one another. In other words, a horizontal structure wherein we all shared the title of "co-curator" did not imply that we were working from shared backgrounds but instead recognized that our individual contributions were made stronger when conceding to what we did not know and listening with excitement to each other as colleagues, across seniority.

As a collective we sought to maintain this work structure outside of the bounds of our curatorial team and agreed that successfully executing such a wide thesis depended on the inclusion of a swath of voices beyond our own. Funds from DAMLI allowed us to invite peers to visit, such as Anya Montiel (Mexican and Tohono O'odham), curator at the Smithsonian's National Museum of the American Indian, who traveled to the Hood Museum to consult on a number of Southwest basketry items that were preliminarily on our object checklist. Montiel's guidance was central to the inclusion of an early twentieth-century Akimel O'odham plaque woven of cattail and willow, a paradigmatic representation of O'odham creator I'itoi, who resides within their homelands. The design, often colloquially referred to as "the man in the maze," portrays a figure in a labyrinth, which iconographically represents the critical turning points within an individual's lifetime or people's history, more broadly. This plaque was made following the wake of the 1853 Gadsden Purchase, from which the United States acquired 29,670 square miles of land from Mexico, which had no regard for and ruptured O'odham ancestral territory. Montiel reminds us that today this matter of place remains a quotidian issue for Tohono O'odham people, who remain separated by an international border, a labyrinth in and of itself.[9]

The questions posed by the inclusion of this work alone generated threads that brought us into conversations with other objects that were eventually displayed around it. What geographical features of this landscape (also known as Arizona, US, and Sonora, Mexico) inform the visual and material culture we see before us? The same could and should be asked of the Diné weaving that hung just beyond the plaque. What happens when borders do not account for kinship and tribal nations? Let us turn left to Lawren Stewart Harris's painting *Lake Superior*, to ask a similar question regarding people toward the North whose communities were disrupted by the Canada–United States border. The insight we received from colleagues like Montiel not only shaped how we began to conceptualize the exhibition's sections but also how we were conceptualizing land itself. Terrain became a limited descriptor of the kinds of stewardship, ways of inhabiting, and ontological principles within which the artists of *This Land* were working.

This sentiment was reaffirmed during our Dartmouth faculty advisory workshops wherein we presented the in-progress work of the exhibition after nearly a year of research to faculty from various disciplinary backgrounds.[10] Within the space of these advisory sessions, we made clear that we were seeking constructive criticism rather than positive feedback. Several faculty members, for example, expressed a strong desire for a clearer critical voice and sense of urgency amid our ongoing climate crisis, leading to several layout changes and informing our choice to open the exhibition with ecocritical art.

These discussions also further encouraged a move away from dichotomous traps such as flora versus fauna, human versus nonhuman, so as to build a greater sense of relationality across the copious and diverse material we were presenting. Our idea to open *This Land* with the birch-bark canoe crafted by Abenaki maker Louis Gill—with aforementioned inspiration from our colleagues at the Peabody Essex Museum—was received with enthusiasm as a work that would first and foremost recognize the unceded lands upon which Dartmouth and the Hood Museum are built and, second, as a signifier that water is not the antithesis of land but instead exists in co-constitutive relation to it. Mobility made possible by the distinctive, intricate waterways of the Northeast have long been a defining characteristic of the region, the navigational knowledge of such routes even serving as a source of reprieve.[11]

It was our aim to be receptive of the same level of critique and collaboration internally, between the *This Land* curatorial team and other staff members across the museum. Most notably, this effort took shape in the form of regular interpretation meetings with members of the museum's education department from early in the exhibition's development and continued to evolve after our departures to pursue our doctoral degrees—Freeman at Yale University and Price at the University of Delaware. Remaining true to our initial ideals around transparency, however, we remained active participants as the project transformed, recording audio labels for a selection of works alongside our former colleagues, new additions to the staff and artists represented in the exhibition. For this we relied greatly on the pedagogical expertise of Neely McNulty, the Hood Foundation curator of education, and a team of interns tasked with coordinating this supplementary digital material.

EXHIBITION WALKTHROUGH

From the earliest planning stages, *This Land* was envisioned as a thematic exhibition, eschewing a traditional chronological layout. With such a broad conceptual scope—exploring the visual, intellectual, spiritual, and social relationships between American artists and the natural world—no singular narrative or selection of objects could appropriately mine its depth and complexity. Instead, *This Land* was broken into seven interrelated sections: "An

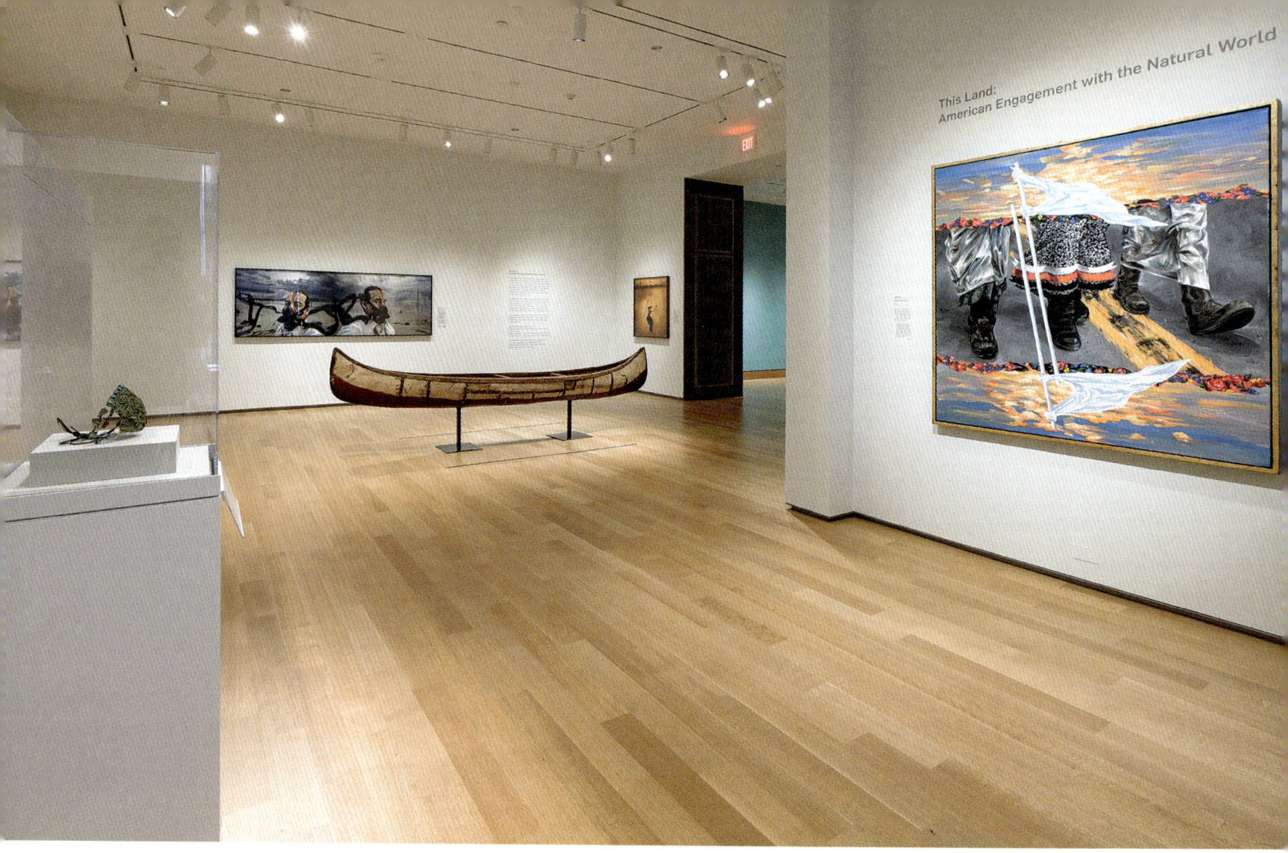

FIGURE 1.3 Installation view, "An Ecocritical Lens," in *This Land: American Engagement with the Natural World*. (Left to right) Shayai Lucero, *Breath of Life*, 2021; Will Wilson, *Auto Immune Response No. 5*, 2005; Louis Gill, birch-bark canoe, early twentieth century; Cara Romero, *Oil Boom*, 2015; and Yatika Starr Fields, *White Buffalo Calf Women March*, 2017. Image by Rob Strong. © Hood Museum of Art, Dartmouth.

Ecocritical Lens"; "Knowing Nature"; "Sustenance"; "Expansion, Encounter, and Exchange"; "Power of Place"; "Force of Nature"; and "Reimagining American Landscapes." This arrangement allowed us to delve into a smaller number of topics in greater depth, often finding commonalities between objects of different temporal, cultural, geographical, or material origin. The resonance of objects across the exhibition allowed visitors multiple entry points into the complex and varied epistemologies between artists and the natural world. The introductory text concluded with a question, rather than a statement, encouraging them to consider "What land holds special meaning for you?"

The exhibition opened in the museum's entry gallery, on the ground floor, with "An Ecocritical Lens" (fig. 1.3). Drawing from the Hood Museum's substantive collection of environmental photography, this section presented the ecological and political stakes of climate change while reflecting the urgency many of us across the United States and the world feel concerning global environmental degradation. Through vivid color and elegant compositions, photographers such as Edward Burtynsky, Diane Burko, and Will Wilson (Diné) temper the catastrophic human impacts of development, pollution, consumption, and resource extraction. Spanning the middle of the gallery, the birch-bark canoe made by Louis Gill (Abenaki) grounds the exhibition in *Ndakkina*, or Abenaki homelands, highlighting the ongoing impacts of colonization and dispossession and exemplifying the inextricable link between water and land. This latter idea was a prominent subtheme of this section, evoked in photographs by Cara Romero (Chemehuevi) exploring the capacity of water to hold memory, and Josué Rivas's images documenting the protests against the Dakota Access Pipeline at Standing Rock in North Dakota in 2016.

This Land continued upstairs on the second floor of the museum with "Knowing Nature" (fig. 1.4). This broad section asked how artists come to understand and represent nature, whether through intergenerational knowledge transfer, close observation, touch, book learning, storytelling, or art making. A grouping of works by John James Audubon, Walton Ford, and a once-known Acoma artist representing birds was foundational to the development of the exhibition (fig. 1.5). Portraying artistic depictions of birds spanning over one hundred years, these three works reflect the multiple and sometimes fraught relationships between human and nonhuman beings. Within Acoma and other Pueblo communities, birds—in this case the parrot or macaw—have long served as connections between people and the gods who live in the upper or sky world. Birds, which can carry messages or prayers for rain, are often depicted on *ollas,* or water jars, marking a connection between the object's form and its function. The 1810 Audubon pastel of a juvenile red-tailed hawk includes detailed notations of the bird's dimensions, weight, and taxonomic classification, suggesting an element of possession and claiming that goes beyond aesthetic appreciation. Known for his meticulously executed images of animals in a style resembling Audubon's naturalistic scenes with a critical twist, Ford's print features the Carolina parakeet, which was declared extinct in 1939 as a result of agricultural deforestation and farmers killing large numbers of the birds, which were considered pests. Unlike Audubon's pastel,

Ford's rendering is more than observational, giving voice to the now-extinct parakeet. Using a familiar motif, in this case a bird, this grouping and others invited visitors to consider the multiple and intersecting knowledge systems and entanglements across different time periods and cultures, as well as interactions between humans and nonhumans. They invited viewers to reconsider what these objects suggested about the artists' knowledge and understanding of the environments in which they were created.

An adjacent, smaller gallery continued with "Sustenance," which explored the complexities of food acquisition in relation to necessity, abundance, nourishment, and labor (fig. 1.6). Consumption, among the most foundational elements in any society, has played a central role in shaping American cultural relationships to the land. The hierarchy of enslaved people, indentured servants, sharecroppers, and free peoples in the United States dominated the structure of food production through the early twentieth century. At the

FIGURE 1.4 Installation view, "Knowing Nature," in *This Land: American Engagement with the Natural World*. Image by Rob Strong. © Hood Museum of Art, Dartmouth.

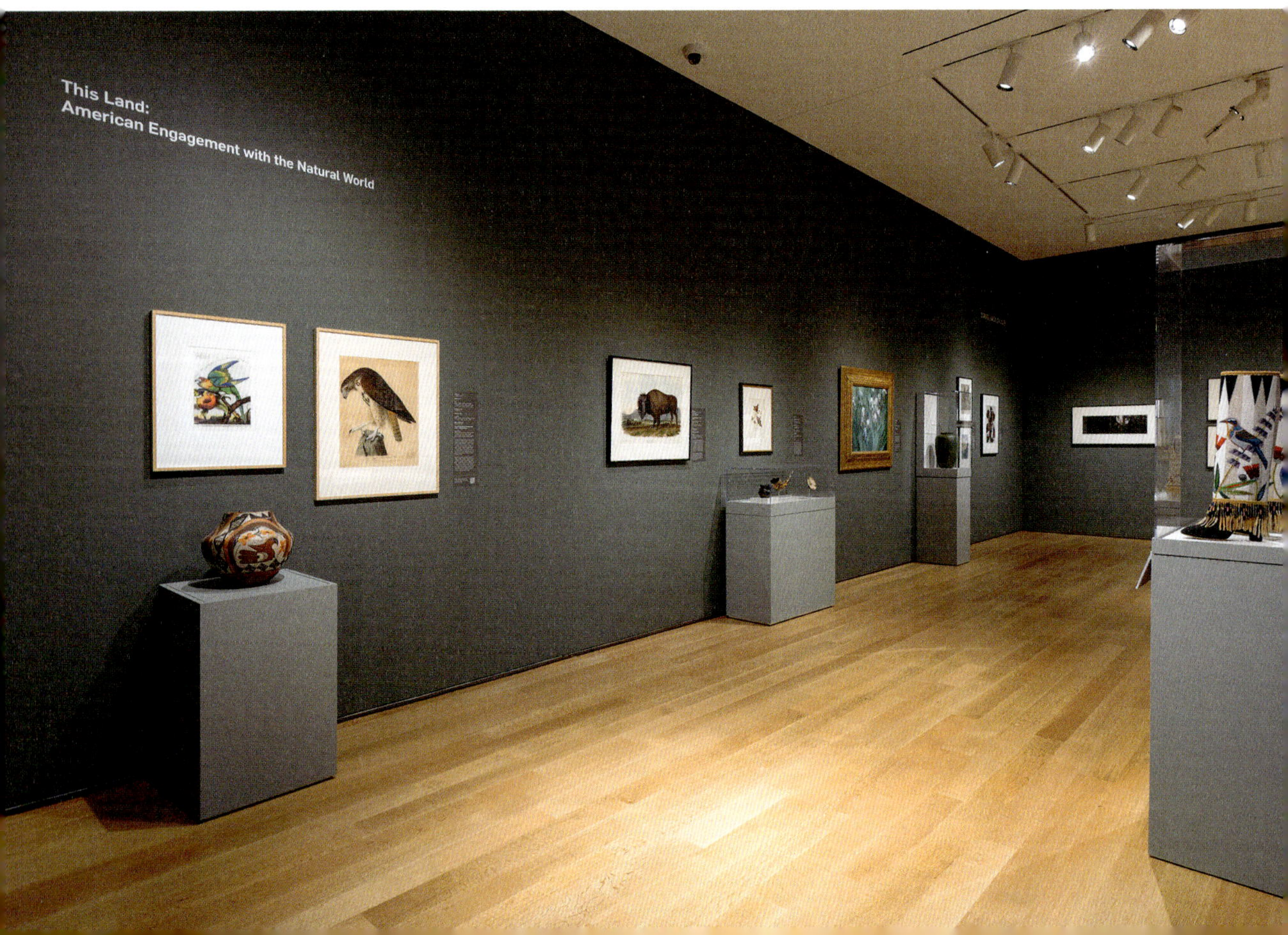

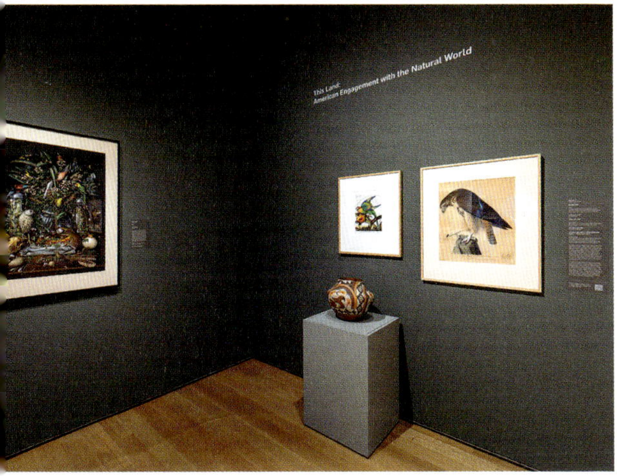

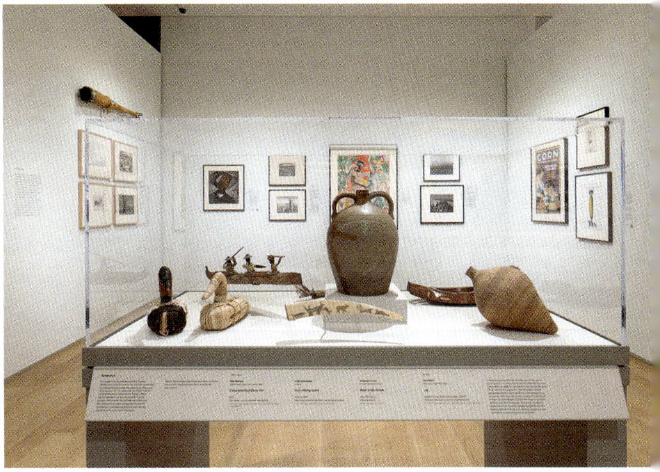

FIGURE 1.5 *left* Installation view, "Knowing Nature," in *This Land: American Engagement with the Natural World.* (Left to right) Isabella Kirkland, *Gone*, 2004; Walton Ford, *Condemned*, 2006; *Olla* (water jar) made by a once-known Acoma artist, about 1900; and John James Audubon, *American Buzzard or White Breasted Hawk . . . Falco Leverianus*, 1810–12. Image by Rob Strong. © Hood Museum of Art, Dartmouth.

FIGURE 1.6 *right* Installation view, "Sustenance," in *This Land: American Engagement with the Natural World.* Image by Rob Strong. © Hood Museum of Art, Dartmouth.

same time, scenes of rural agricultural labor have come to be a hallmark of American identity, reinforcing nationalist ideals of landownership and self-sufficiency. Russell Lee's Works Progress Administration photographs of rural farmers paired importantly with Elizabeth Catlett's iconic *Sharecropper*, reflecting both visible and invisible agricultural labor. In addition to survival, the works in this section of the exhibition considered the specialized ecological knowledge that communities hold and how those knowledges sustain our lives. A Sugpiaq three-hatch kayak model, for example, not only portrays men on a hunting expedition but also meticulously details kayak construction techniques, demonstrating a relationship to materials and animals for future generations.

The other side of the gallery moved to "Expansion, Encounter, and Exchange" (fig. 1.7). First defined in the 1840s, manifest destiny asserted that the United States was predestined to expand its territory across the North American continent.[12] Visual expressions of this imagined inevitability often erased the violence of westward expansion, focusing instead on the aesthetic beauty of the Western landscape. The idea of the "West" became a new

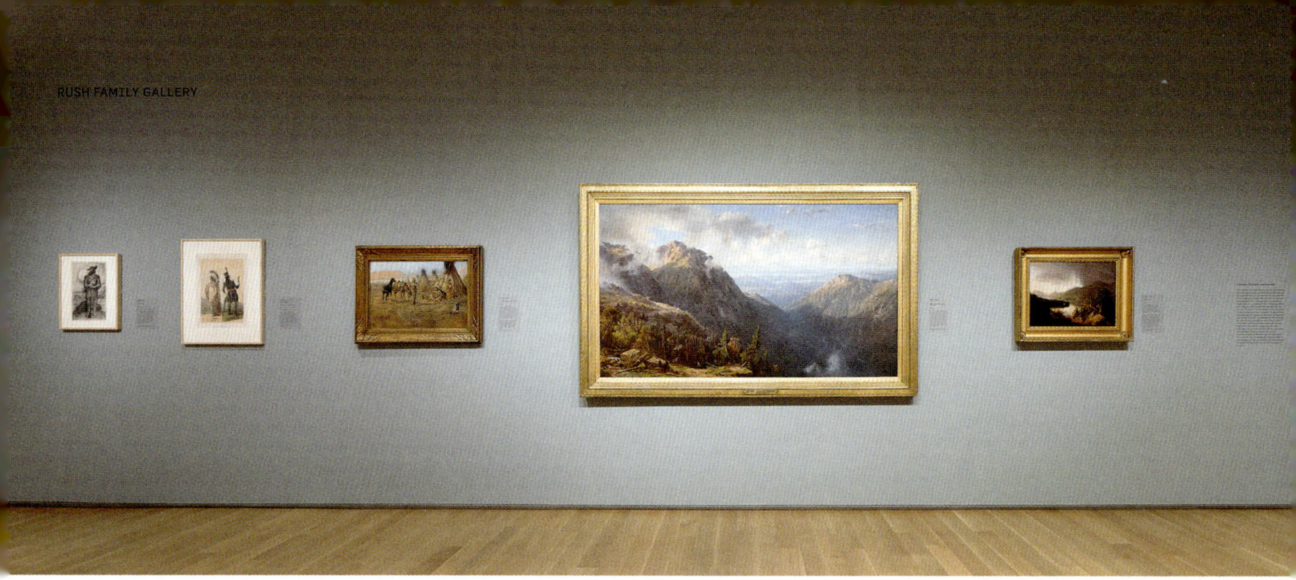

FIGURE 1.7 Installation view, "Expansion, Encounter, and Exchange," in *This Land: American Engagement with the Natural World*. (Left to right) John Steuart Curry, *The Plainsman*, 1945; John McGahey after George Catlin, *Wi-Jun-Jon, An Assiniboine Chief*, 1844; and Charles Marion Russell, *Cowboy Bargaining for an Indian Girl*, 1895; Régis François Gignoux, *New Hampshire (White Mountain Landscape)*, about 1864; and Thomas Cole, *View on Lake George*, 1826. Image by Rob Strong. © Hood Museum of Art, Dartmouth.

foundation for an American ideology of "progress" as government-sponsored surveys mapped the landscape, preparing the way for settlers, miners, and transcontinental railroads. Informed by the work of artists like Albert Bierstadt and Eadweard Muybridge, colonialist policy continued throughout the early twentieth century as Native American nations were forced from their homelands and largely stripped of their sovereignty. Newly formed national parks strengthened the tie between American identity and the land, becoming symbols of national unity. At the same time, art served as an impetus for more complex exchanges between Native and non-Native peoples in the West, with artists such as Elizabeth and Louise Hickox (Karuk/Wiyot) continuing traditions of basket weaving while also participating in the commercial art market.

Without ignoring the complexities of land and history, the next section of the exhibition, "Power of Place," encouraged visitors to consider our individual and communal relationships with the landscape (fig. 1.8). The Western United States continued to be a prominent theme, providing a transition from the previous section while emphasizing its importance to national identity. More intimate relationships took form along an adjacent wall as prints by New York–based Dominican artists collective Dominican York

Proyecto Grafica evocatively articulated the complexities of "home." Works by Truman Lowe (Ho-Chunk) and Lawren Stewart Harris framed the Great Lakes region from opposite shores, critiquing and complicating the colonial border between the United States and Canada. In examining associations with lived-in space, both near and distant, "Power of Place" examined how connections with the land have changed over time through experiences such as displacement and diaspora while also inviting visitors to reflect on their own homes and relations to land. How can a place, we asked, inform our understanding of ourselves?

"Force of Nature" displayed a range of works that considered the destruction and weaponization of nature and our aesthetic responses to these events (fig. 1.9). Natural forces, which can be beneficial in moderation and destructive in extremes, feed human desire to control and manipulate our environment. Many of the works in this theme depicted the devastating power of natural phenomena, including floods, forest fires, droughts, volcanic eruptions, and landslides. Severa Tafoya's (Santa Clara Pueblo [Kha P'o Owingeh]) vessel

FIGURE 1.8 Installation view, "Power of Place," in *This Land: American Engagement with the Natural World*. Image by Rob Strong. © Hood Museum of Art, Dartmouth.

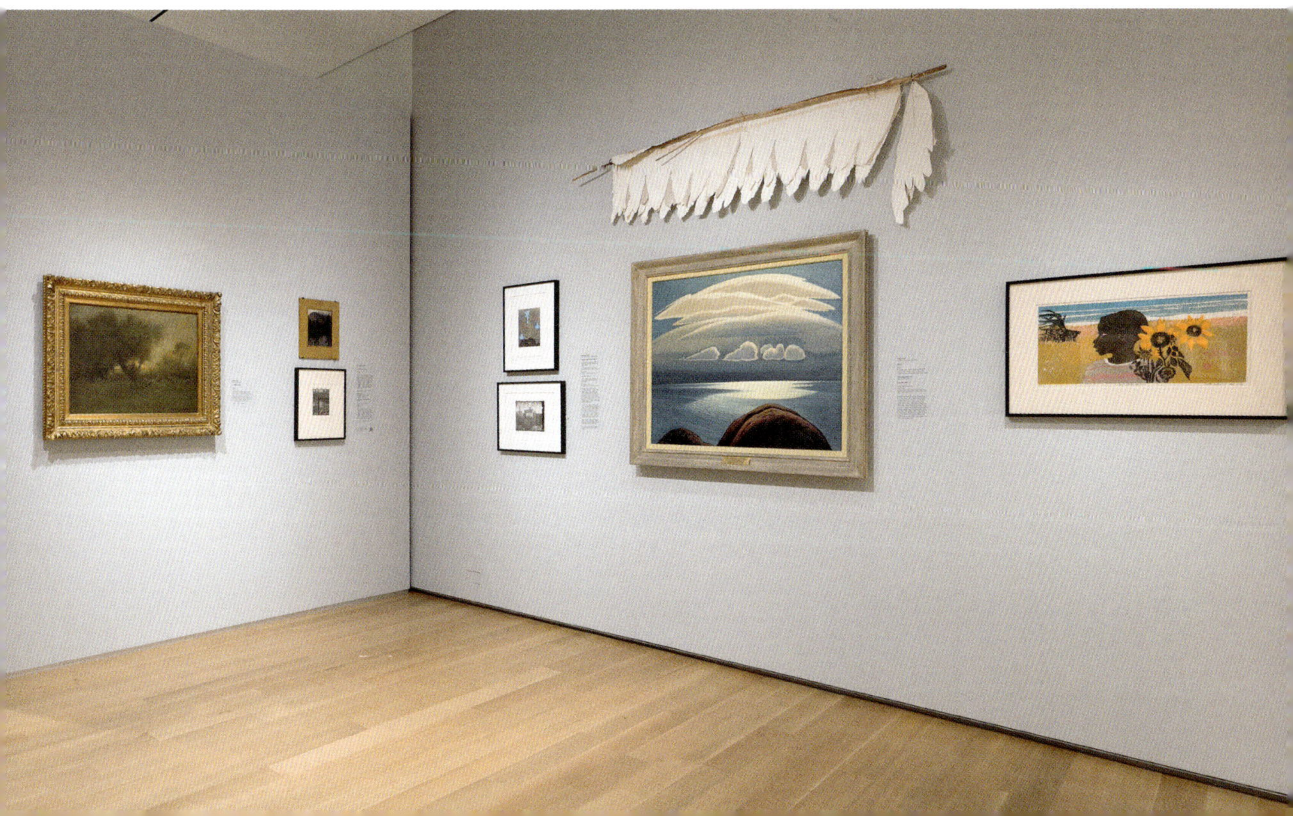

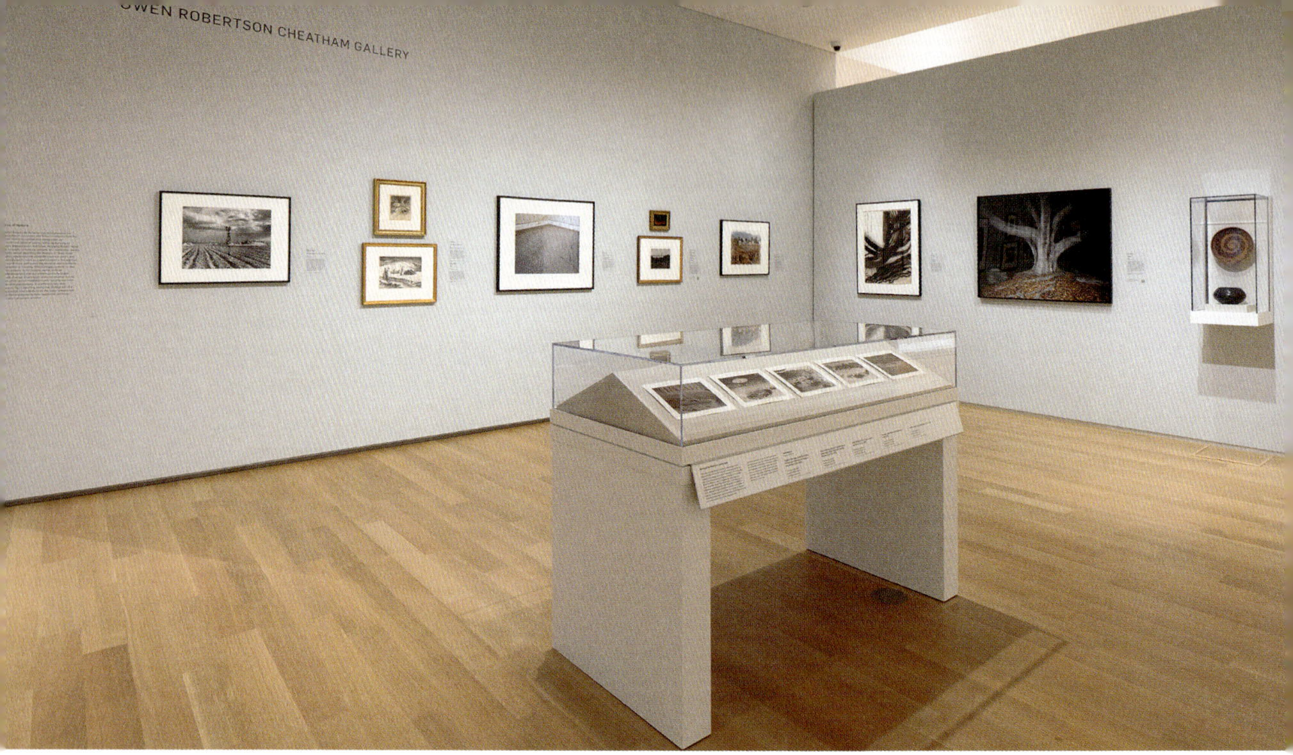
OWEN ROBERTSON CHEATHAM GALLERY

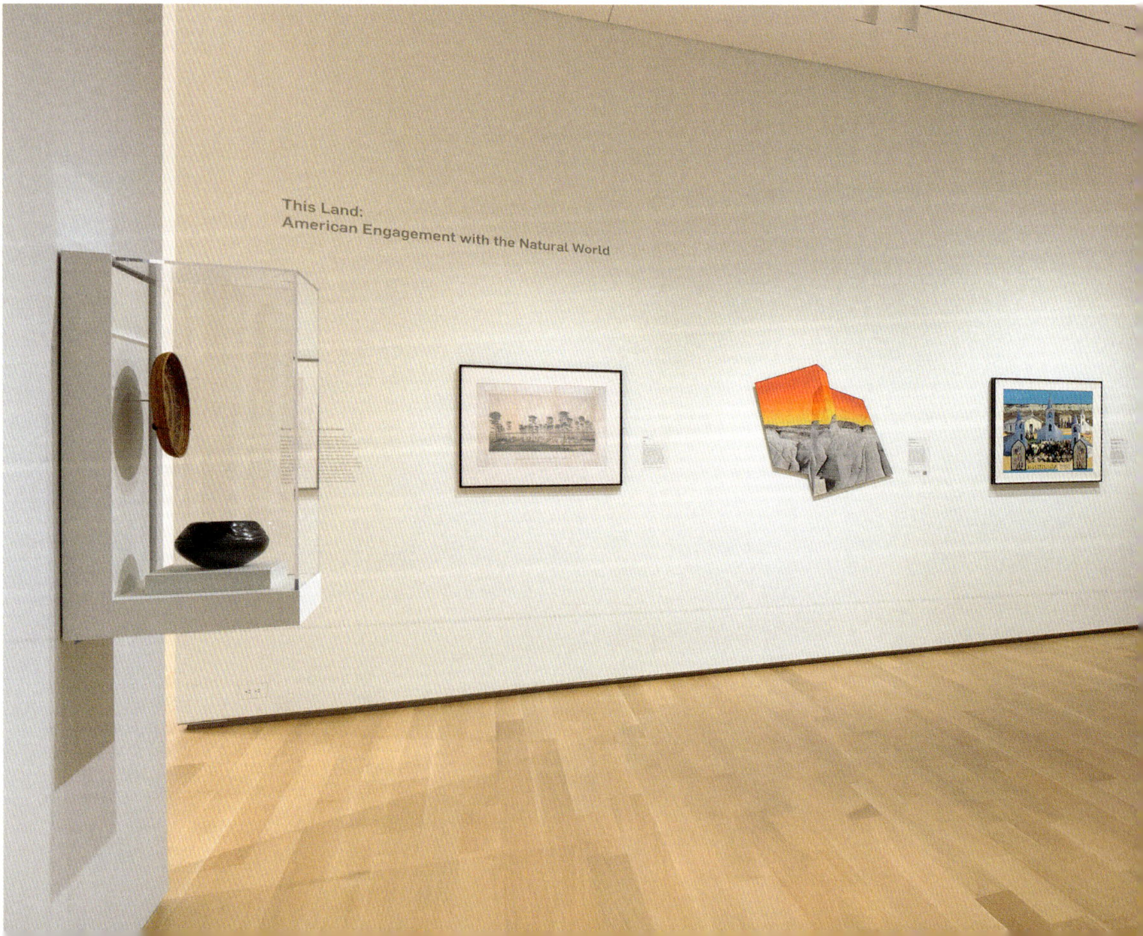
This Land:
American Engagement with the Natural World

depicting Avanyu, or Tewa water serpent, expresses the unstable nature of water, while Brenda Garand's work on paper created in the wake of Hurricane Irene in 2011 addressed the physical and emotional impacts of flooding. These images remind us that human actions in the natural world, such as overdevelopment and our contributions to global climate change, can exacerbate extreme weather events, which often ravage neighborhoods housing the most financially disenfranchised populations. Recounting more direct intervention, Ken Gonzales-Day's haunting nocturnal photograph *Nightfall I* clearly evokes the weaponization of nature. A monumental tree rises alone in the center, its branches reaching out into the darkness, standing in for the many weaponized trees that are known to have supported lynchings, most often of people of color.[13]

This Land concluded with "Reimagining American

FIGURE 1.9 *opposite* Installation view, "Force of Nature," in *This Land: American Engagement with the Natural World*. Image by Rob Strong. © Hood Museum of Art, Dartmouth.

FIGURE 1.10 *below* Installation view, "Reimagining American Landscapes," in *This Land: American Engagement with the Natural World*. Image by Rob Strong. © Hood Museum of Art, Dartmouth.

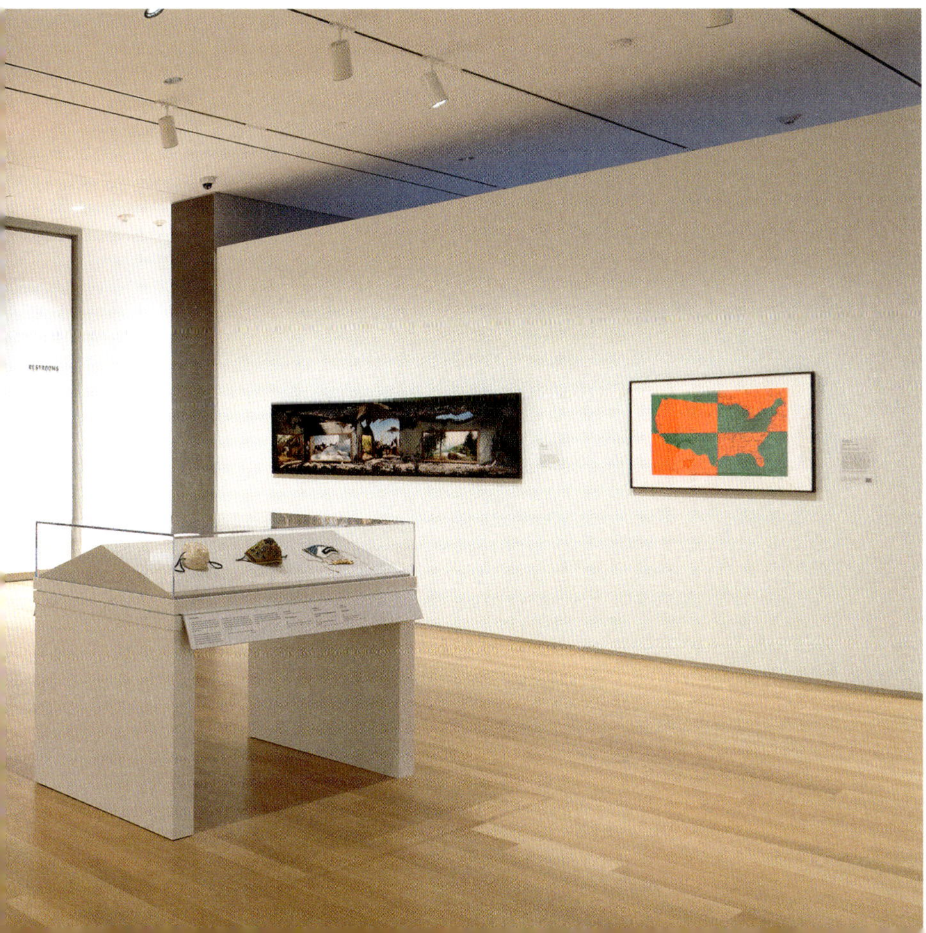

Landscapes," which displayed works by artists who critically appropriate the landscape tradition (fig. 1.10). The work of nineteenth-century landscape painters, such as Thomas Cole, serve as ubiquitous and romanticized representations of the United States. These works were largely made by and for wealthy White Americans. Today many artists are challenging these conventions and the disenfranchisement and erasure they can engender. Faith Ringgold's offset lithograph *United States of Attica*, for example, urges a reexamination of historical narratives of violence in our nation. Elsewhere, Fred Wilson's *1863* places glassine over a reproduction of John Henry Bufford's Civil War–era print depicting a camp of Massachusetts soldiers, obscuring the White regiment and highlighting the labor of a Black washerwoman, visible through a singular perforation. The works in this section contribute critical visions of America that help us imagine possible futures and reckon with the complexity of the past.

OUTCOMES

Despite recognizing the expectation to write with a single curatorial voice, as a team we were quite wary of using the neutral tone common to museum labels. While we had something to say, and years of research to support our thoughts, ours are not the only voices of authority. Inviting others in became an important way for us to move away from an overly didactic tone. "*This Land* features works of art that express reverence and concern for the lands now known as the United States," we stated at the end of the introductory text. "What land holds special meaning for you?" Questions were one way that we brought visitors into dialogue with us, making a point, at least in text, to acknowledge that their thoughts and opinions are valuable.

Perhaps even more important, writing with one voice did not mean we needed to maintain a singular point of view. The great benefit of having a team is having unique perspectives and outlooks, and losing that in the resulting exhibition would have wasted years of careful work. The show's thematic groupings, we hoped, would help us display similar kinds of objects that represented multiple viewpoints. "Subsistence," after some consideration, became "Sustenance," a title we thought better reflected the spiritual nourishment that often accompanies food production and consumption while simultaneously recognizing the deep relationships between many American communities and the food that sustains us. George Tice and Russell Lee photographs depicting antiquated farming methods hung next to a Romare Bearden screenprint, *In the Garden*, which conjures a Black woman in a striped dress as the biblical Eve paying homage to her herbal knowledge and spiritual insight.

Including works by a range of artists does more than add diversity to an exhibition, though. At its best—and what we strived for—*This Land* was a show that allowed for multiple frameworks, or epistemologies, to coincide within the same galleries. For us, this often meant dwelling in irreconcilability. A Diné saddle blanket hung in the center of one wall, its eyedazzler pattern commanding attention from across the room and anchoring part of the section "Power of Place" (fig. I.2). The textile relates a story of colonization, the bright colors reflecting the new availability of synthetic or aniline dyes and commercially produced yarn to Indigenous makers, and expresses the teachings of Na'ashjé'ii Asdzáá (Spider Woman), who showed the Diné how to weave. Beside it, to the left, hung Georgia O'Keeffe's *Taos Mountain, New Mexico*, the result of one of her first trips to the Southwest. The lands of New Mexico would come to hold great personal meaning for O'Keeffe, but recent scholarship has also tied her aesthetic sensibility to concurrent colonialism in the region.[14] To the right were photographs by Ansel Adams, evoking the perception of the untouched beauty of America's national parks, and Len Jenshel, underscoring the intentionality of that construction (fig. I.6). These works highlight the deep personal and collective affinities with particular places held by many Americans. Yet they stand in profound contradistinction to one another; the creation of national parks, for example, which have come so much to define an image of the United States and its lands, reflects a direct erasure of Indigenous presence and history in those same spaces.[15] A singular interpretation of land and its inhabitants cannot be made when one does not truly exist.

This interpolation of epistemologies took different form elsewhere. Audio labels accompanied a number of works scattered throughout the exhibition, offering historical analyses or personal perspectives from curators, other staff members, outside scholars, and Dartmouth students. A poem by Mali Obomsawin, a recent Dartmouth alum and Odanak First Nation (Abenaki) bassist, singer, composer, and songwriter, narrates the production and use of the birch-bark canoe at the beginning of the exhibition (fig. 1.02). "N'manhikewáteman," she begins. "I peel the bark for a canoe."[16] The work is transportive, providing an affective understanding of the vessel and its importance for everyday life. Yet the words certainly hold more meaning for some than for others—for those, say, who do not need the translations that follow each Abenaki phrase, or for others familiar with the process of building a canoe. Audio labels like this offer storytelling where pedagogical label text sometimes fails. More deeply, though, they insert a voice that is not equally legible to all museumgoers. This is not a failure. Finding common ground is important, but it can sometimes erase the specificities that give meaning to certain works. Striving to do both, to educate while also preserving the complexity of a work's creation and cultural origin, better serves the general public and the communities that objects come from or directly speak to.

By the time *This Land* went on view in January 2022, we arrived at a place that felt like a beginning rather than an end to the project. Throughout its conceptualization and production, *This Land* was an experiment, an introduction to new ways of thinking about and curating exhibitions at the Hood Museum and beyond rather than a final statement. With objects on the walls and visitors in the galleries, new work could begin.

From the outset, it was obvious that there were significant gaps in the collection and stories that we did not have the ability to tell. A number of strategic purchases, such as Ken Gonzales-Day's *Nightfall I*, were made between 2018 and 2020 to expand the scope of the exhibition, an unusual move for a collection show but one that we felt bolstered the museum's holdings in important places while also supporting its teaching mission. This work was continued by Hartman when he joined the museum in 2021, acquiring an additional four objects that were rotated into the show, preserving some works from overexposure and making some necessary adjustments to the exhibition's narrative. A particularly notable acquisition was Toshio

Aoki's watercolor *Untitled (Allegorical Scene)*, from about 1890–1900 (fig. 1.11). The exhibition, and the museum's collections more broadly, feature very few works by Asian American artists, especially any works prior to the twentieth century, so this addition provided an almost entirely new point of view.

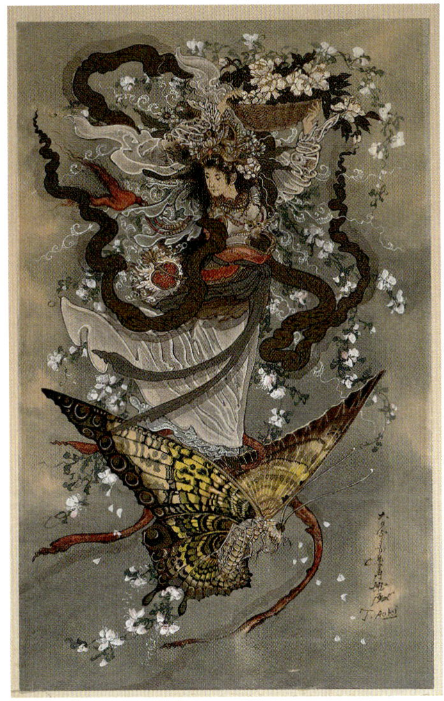

FIGURE 1.11 Toshio Aoki (Japanese, active in United States, 1854–1912), *Untitled (Allegorical Scene)*, 1890–1900. Watercolor and gouache on paper, 22½ × 14¼ in. Hood Museum of Art, Dartmouth: Purchased through the Evelyn A. and William B. Jaffe 2015 Fund; 2021.58. Image by Jeffrey Nintzel.

Beyond acquisitions, though, the thinking that drove *This Land* has rippled outward, setting a precedent for framing the collection in new ways. In 2023 Hartman curated *Historical Imaginary*, a permanent collection show that paired an unfinished study for Emanuel Leutze's *Washington Crossing the Delaware* (Metropolitan Museum of Art) with other historical and contemporary American art. Inspired by the way *This Land* invited visitors to explore how works from the past speak clearly to our present moment, *Historical Imaginary* reversed that logic, asking how artworks have shaped and continue to shape our perception of the past.

Now, three years since the exhibition was on view and some seven since ideas first began to take shape, *This Land* continues to resonate, inspiring new growth. While examining images of the past, Hartman's vision for *Historical Imaginary* included the desire to "build upon our shared, complex, and sometimes violent history to imagine and create a more equitable future."[17] In a period when the United States is increasingly pluralistic, politically discordant, and openly intolerant, holding hope for a better future seems at once naïve and remarkably brave. Envisioning "America"—both its future and its past—in new ways holds particular importance for such hope. Exploring how we view the lands of the United States, and how we might shape a future, relies on new and more open forms of storytelling. How do you tell a story about American art and nature? Tell more than one story.

NOTES

1. Jami C. Powell is now the associate director of curatorial affairs and curator of Indigenous art at the Hood Museum.

2. We both left our roles at the Hood Museum in summer 2020 to start PhD programs, Morgan Freeman at Yale University and Thomas H. Price at the University of Delaware. Barbara J. MacAdam retired from her position at the Hood Museum in August 2020. Michael Hartman, Jonathan Little Cohen Associate Curator of American Art, joined the museum the following year in September 2021 and became an important member of the curatorial team.

3. The Peabody Essex Museum's reconsiderations of *Nature's Nation: American Art and Environment* (2019) went beyond an altered layout with revised gallery text. As Bailly and Kramer discuss in their essay in this volume, the curatorial team worked with the museum's Indigenous fellows and, particularly with the insight of Rachel Allen (Northwest Museum of Arts and Culture and PhD candidate, University of Delaware) provided suggestions and substantive alterations to the *Nature's Nation* exhibition catalog. Their work and the reading guide Allen produced were crucial for our development of *This Land*.

4. Kathryn Bunn-Marcuse, "Textualizing Intangible Heritage: Querying the Methods of Art History," introduction to Bully Pulpit, *Panorama: Journal of the Association of Historians of American Art* 4, no. 2 (2018), https://doi.org/10.24926/24716839.1659/.

5. heather ahtone, Bully Pulpit, *Panorama: Journal of the Association of Historians of American Art* 4, no. 2 (2018), https://doi.org/10.24926/24716839.1662/.

6. Jessica L. Horton and Janet Catherine Berlo, "Beyond the Mirror: Indigenous Ecologies and 'New Materialisms' in Contemporary Art," *Third Text* 27, no. 1 (2013): 18.

7. Nancy Marie Mithlo, *Knowing Native Arts* (Lincoln: University of Nebraska Press, 2020).

8. William Cronon, "The Trouble with Wilderness; or, Getting Back to the Wrong Nature," in *Uncommon Ground: Rethinking the Human Place in Nature*, ed. William Cronon (New York: W. W. Norton, 1996), 69–90.

9. Anya Montiel, "The Tohono O'odham and the Border Wall," *American Indian Magazine*, https://www.americanindianmagazine.org/story/tohono-oodham-and-border-wall/.

10. Christina Seely (associate professor of studio art), Laura Ogden (professor of anthropology), Abby Neely (associate professor of anthropology), Mary Coffey

(professor of art history), Jorge E. Cuéllar (assistant professor, Latin American, Latino, and Caribbean studies).

11. Lisa Brooks, "'Every Swamp Is a Castle': Navigating Native Spaces in the Connecticut River Valley, Winter 1675–1677 and 2005–2015," *Northeast Naturalist* 24, no. 7 (2017): H45–H80.

12. The desire for continental expansion goes hand in hand with broader US imperialism. A recent exhibition at the National Portrait Gallery, *1898: U. S. Imperial Visions and Revisions*, co-curated by Taína Caragol and Kate Clarke-Lemay with assistance from Carolina Maestre, was the first Smithsonian museum exhibition to examine the history and legacy of the War of 1898 (also known as the Spanish-American War), the Congressional Joint Resolution to annex Hawai'i, and the Philippine-American War.

13. Whereas most historical accounts of lynching in the United States center on Black American victims—the targets of such racially motivated, extrajudicial murders in the South—the work of Gonzales-Day focuses on the lesser-known vigilante murders of Latine/x peoples, Native Americans, and Asian Americans in the state of California.

14. Patricia Marroquin Norby, "Visual Violence in the Land of Enchantment," PhD diss., University of Minnesota, 2013, 85–131; Sascha T. Scott, "Georgia O'Keeffe's Hawai'i? Decolonizing the History of American Modernism," *American Art* 34, no. 2 (2020): 27.

15. Angela L. Miller, "The Fate of Wilderness in American Landscape Art: The Dilemmas of 'Nature's Nation,'" in *A Keener Perception: Ecocritical Studies in American Art History*, ed. Alan C. Braddock and Christoph Irmscher, 101–106. For a broad study of this topic, see Mark David Spence, *Dispossessing the Wilderness: Indian Removal and the Making of the National Parks* (New York: Oxford University Press, 1999).

16. Mali Obamsawin, "Louis Gill: Birch Bark Canoe," audio recording, 1:04, 2022, https://soundcloud.com/user-893524321/louis-gill-birch-bark-canoe/.

17. Michael W. Hartman, email correspondence with authors, June 20, 2023.

2

Janet Dees / Alisa Swindell

A SITE OF STRUGGLE, A METHODOLOGY OF ACCORD

A Site of Struggle: American Art against Anti-Black Violence was an exhibition that originated at the Block Museum of Art at Northwestern University in Evanston, Illinois, and traveled to the Montgomery Museum of Fine Arts in Alabama in 2022. It was curated by Janet Dees, with the assistance of Alisa Swindell, the authors of this essay. Developed and implemented by several colleagues at the Block Museum, this project was also shaped by the input and participation of artists; a community advisory group; faculty, staff, and students at Northwestern University; and a range of scholars and museum professionals from other institutions who think critically about race and visual practices.[1]

A Site of Struggle investigated how artists have engaged with the reality of anti-Black violence and its accompanying challenges of representation and explored the varied strategies that American artists have used to this end. The publication that accompanied the exhibition includes a range of essays by an interdisciplinary group of scholars that explicate the exhibition themes, engage specific artworks, and expand the conversation beyond the time frame addressed by the exhibition.[2] The purpose of the current essay is to articulate the values that guided the project, explore the exhibition's methodological development and presentation, and reflect upon the exhibition's reception. Centering on care, the methodology employed by *A Site of Struggle* is part of a recent movement in the field that is also reflected in several of the other essays in this volume. As Black, Indigenous, and other people of color practitioners have begun to occupy curatorial and other knowledge-generating roles within the museum, their agency to inform content and process has opened possibilities for more diverse perspectives, ways of working, and understandings of the roles of museums. Transforming decades-old ways of working is not always an easy process, and those leading these transitions sometimes face pushback from within and outside the institutions, but their work is necessary to support expanded definitions of American art. As a case study, *A Site of Struggle* demonstrates how reenvisioning histories of American art requires not only the elevation of new or previously underrecognized histories and practices but also the reimagining of the processes of exhibition making and exhibition viewing.

A CARE-FILLED APPROACH: BLACK FEMINIST CURATORIAL PRACTICE

In a retrospective discussion of the exhibition, art historian Huey Copeland lauded *A Site of Struggle* as a paradigm of Black feminist curatorial practice and went on to say, "The show is not only modeling curatorial best practices; it's modeling spectatorial best practices as well."[3] Grounding in Black feminist values was not made explicit in public material about the exhibition but was implicit in our working methods. In her discussion of the work of Black curators Andrea Fatona and Gaëtane Verna, art historian Joana Joachim productively articulates how aspects of intersectional Black feminist values and commitments manifest themselves in curatorial practice.[4] These manifestations include "opening discussion between communities about topics that are difficult to unpack, yet necessary for our collective well-being"; championing the work of underrecognized artists; productive self-interrogation to alert oneself to one's biases and oversights; and valuing "embodied knowledge and everyday individual experience" as "crucial places of knowing that allow for important insights and transformative justice work."[5] These values resonate with *A Site of Struggle*'s commitment to engaging with a necessary but difficult topic through care and collaboration.

One less-public example of how these values manifested in this project was the working relationship between Janet Dees and Alisa Swindell, which eschewed traditional curatorial hierarchies for a more collaborative approach. Coming into the developing project as a research assistant, Swindell was first tasked with reading the notes from earlier convenings with curators who had curated exhibitions on similar themes and scholars working in related areas. This allowed Swindell access to those conversations and provided an understanding of how important it was to the exhibition that voices and knowledge other than those of Dees were not only welcome but crucial. The importance of meaningful collaboration and coproduction of knowledge would serve as a guide throughout the project and made space for Swindell to make significant contributions throughout the exhibition. Swindell supplements her Western art historical education with an interdisciplinary approach to her scholarship. She incorporates what she learns in her activism and community work and what she learns from others doing that work, especially people from communities in which she does not participate. Her belief in the importance of Black liberation is grounded in Black feminism and queer activism, often informed by a more radical stance.[6] Dees would self-describe as a Black feminist who is heavily influenced by contemplative traditions that connect individual psychological and spiritual liberation to collective social and political liberation.[7] Dees recognized, when hiring Swindell, that she brought an honest interest in the topic, knowledge around the sociohistorical and art historical issues that the exhibition addresses, and a perspective that differed from hers but that was ultimately grounded in compatible values.

Here, the model of collaborative curation also becomes a model of mentorship grounded in Black feminist values. Swindell, knowing that what she brought to the exhibit was respected, had the freedom to champion artworks that she thought were essential to the exhibition's thesis and to contribute fully to conversations where decisions were made about the rules of engagement, programming, and partnerships. Over the course of developing the exhibition, Dees and Swindell cultivated a working relationship that engendered a generative push-pull as well as a system of mutual support. These two aspects of the team dynamic kept them from becoming overwhelmed by the nature of the subject and helped them to be mindful of who would be impacted by the show and how the very curation of the exhibition could help to support its audiences. On occasion, Swindell wanted to push the conversation forward in a blunt manner. In those moments Dees's more spiritual approach led her to suggest that they take a moment and show those implicated some grace. On the other side, Dees occasionally wanted to make people comfortable by more diplomatically stating a message that needed to be made with truth to power. And Swindell would press for doing just that despite the discomfort it might engender.

Similarly, the exhibition *A Site of Struggle* did not attempt to close debate but, rather, to wrestle with the nuances, complexities, and contradictions inherent in engaging with the history of how anti-Black violence has been taken up in American art. Accord in the development process and presentation was not achieved by dismissing dissent, or eliding difficulty, but by working with differing approaches and allowing different perspectives to exist alongside one another in productive dialogue. The methodology mirrored the exhibition in reenvisioning the history of American art and the work of exhibition making in a way that is more inclusive.

A COLLABORATIVE AND CONSULTATIVE PROCESS

A Site of Struggle was the result of six years of research and planning, yet for some it may seem as if it was a response to the most current events. The exhibition opened in 2022, in the wake of the summer of 2020, when the murder of George Floyd at the hands of a Minneapolis police officer sparked a national reckoning with the persistence of racialized violence. For many of this current generation, the death of Trayvon Martin at the hands of George Zimmerman in 2013 was another such inflection point, just as the murder by lynching of Emmett Till in Mississippi in 1955 was for an earlier generation. The consistent recurrence of these atrocities has been matched by consistent critical engagement by artists and the development of visual strategies to grapple with the realities of racial violence. This is a history that is critical to understanding *American* history writ large as well as the particularities of the African American experience.

Chronologically, *A Site of Struggle* was framed by the rise of antilynching activism in the late nineteenth century and the founding of Black Lives Matter in 2013. Thematically, it emphasized different artistic approaches to the subject, including exploration of the psychological impacts of racism and racial violence, abstraction and conceptualism as modes of avoiding literal representations of violence, and the use of graphic imagery as a strategy of protest and consciousness-raising. The exhibition was organized in three thematic sections that reflected these three lines of inquiry: "Written on the Body," "Abstraction and Affect," and "A Red Record." The exhibition was grounded in two crucial questions: How has art been used to protest, process, mourn, and memorialize anti-Black violence within the United States? And how can art history help inform our understanding of the deep roots of racial violence? While not a comprehensive treatment of the subject, but through selective attention, this exhibition suggested the depth and breadth of art that engages with and is impacted by the continuing legacy of racial violence. In doing so, *A Site of Struggle* highlighted artists whose work helps us engage with what is difficult to look at but necessary to see in the ongoing struggle for the preservation and flourishing of Black life.

To this end, *A Site of Struggle* presented a pre- (art) history of our present moment. With one exception, it included works created between 1895 and 2013 and works created after 2013 that refer back to pre-2013 moments in history.[8] The exhibition emphasized African Americans as shapers of visual culture. The majority of works were by Black artists, but it also featured art by non-Black artists who supported Black activist causes (fig. 2.1).[9] For example, the oldest object in the exhibition was an original copy of the antilynching pamphlet *A Red Record: Tabulated Statistics and Alleged Cause of Lynching in the United States*. Written in 1895 by Chicago-based journalist and activist Ida B. Wells, it presented the results of three years of her research. Her findings refuted the common claim that Black men were targeted for lynching in retaliation for crimes. Wells exposed lynching as a means of using terror to exert social control over African Americans. Wells is widely considered one of the first activists to appropriate and reproduce lynching photographs in order to make the case for its abolition.

The newest artwork by Molly Jae Vaughan was completed in 2021, just

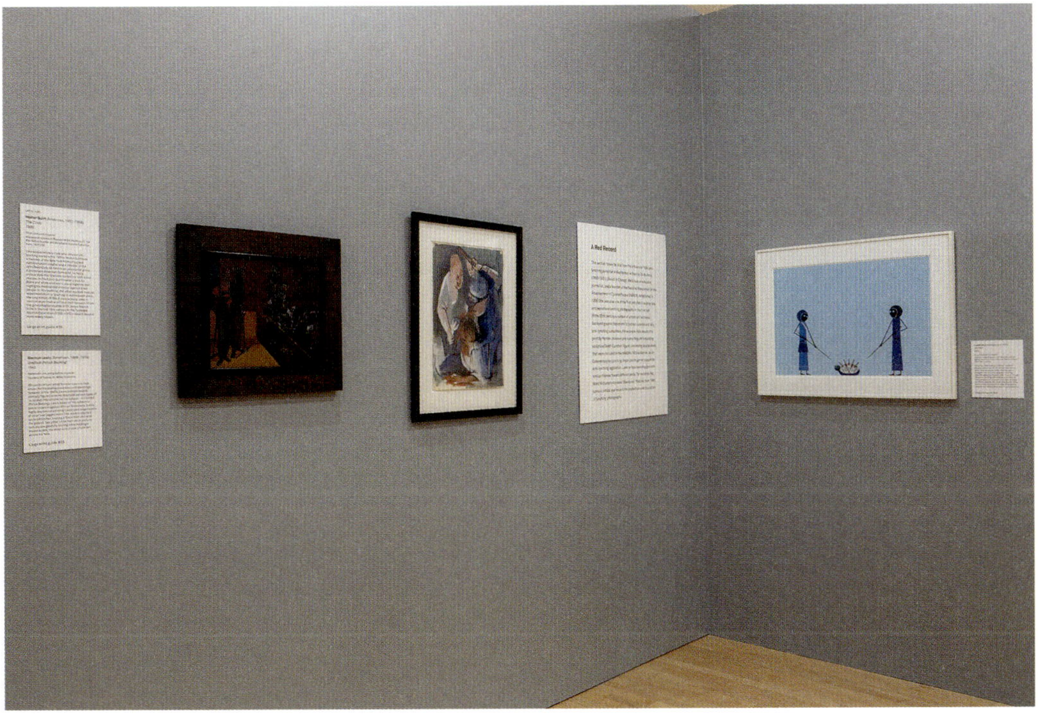

FIGURE 2.1 Installation view, *A Site of Struggle: American Art against Anti-Black Violence*. (Left to right) Walter Quirt, *The Clinic*, 1935; Norman Lewis, *Untitled (Police Beating)*, 1943; Laylah Ali, *Untitled*, 2004. Image by Clare Britt. © Block Museum of Art, Northwestern University.

months before the exhibition opened. *Lateisha "Teish" Green, 400 Block of Seymour Street, Syracuse*, is the most recent work in the *Project 42* series, which Vaughan began in 2012 to help raise awareness about transgender and gender-nonconforming individuals within the United States who were victims of violence, a majority of whom were Black trans women (fig. 2.2). Each garment in the series memorializes the life of a specific individual and is meant to function both as a static work of art and to be activated by performance. This work honors Lateisha "Teish" Green, who was murdered in Syracuse, New York, in 2008. The pattern on the fabric from which the garment and wall covering are made is abstracted from Google Earth imagery of the site where Green was killed. *Project 42* is ongoing as Vaughan works toward the goal of uplifting forty-two lives.

Recognizing the challenging nature of the exhibition's content, the range of responses it would elicit, and the impact it would carry for visitors whose identities and lived experiences intersect with the histories presented, creating structures of care for visitor experience were paramount. From the outset, Dees envisioned a synergistic model soliciting the input of many voices that would include early collaboration with colleagues from different departments within the museum; conversations with different sectors of the campus and larger community; and input from a range of scholars working at the intersection of art history, history, and Black studies along with museum professionals who had experience working on analogous projects. Importantly, the project had early full support from the highest level of the museum's administration and resonated with the museum's stated mission and vision at the time, which was to be a "dynamic, imaginative, and

FIGURE 2.2 Installation view, *A Site of Struggle: American Art against Anti-Black Violence*. (Left to right) Molly Jae Vaughan, *Lateisha "Teish" Green, 400 Block of Seymour Street, Syracuse* from *Project 42*, 2021; Bob Crawford, *Untitled*, 1966; Darryl Cowherd, *Gage Park Protest*, 1967/68; and Paul Rucker, *June 7, 1998, Jasper, Texas*, from the series *Soundless*, 2015. Image by Clare Britt. © Block Museum of Art, Northwestern University.

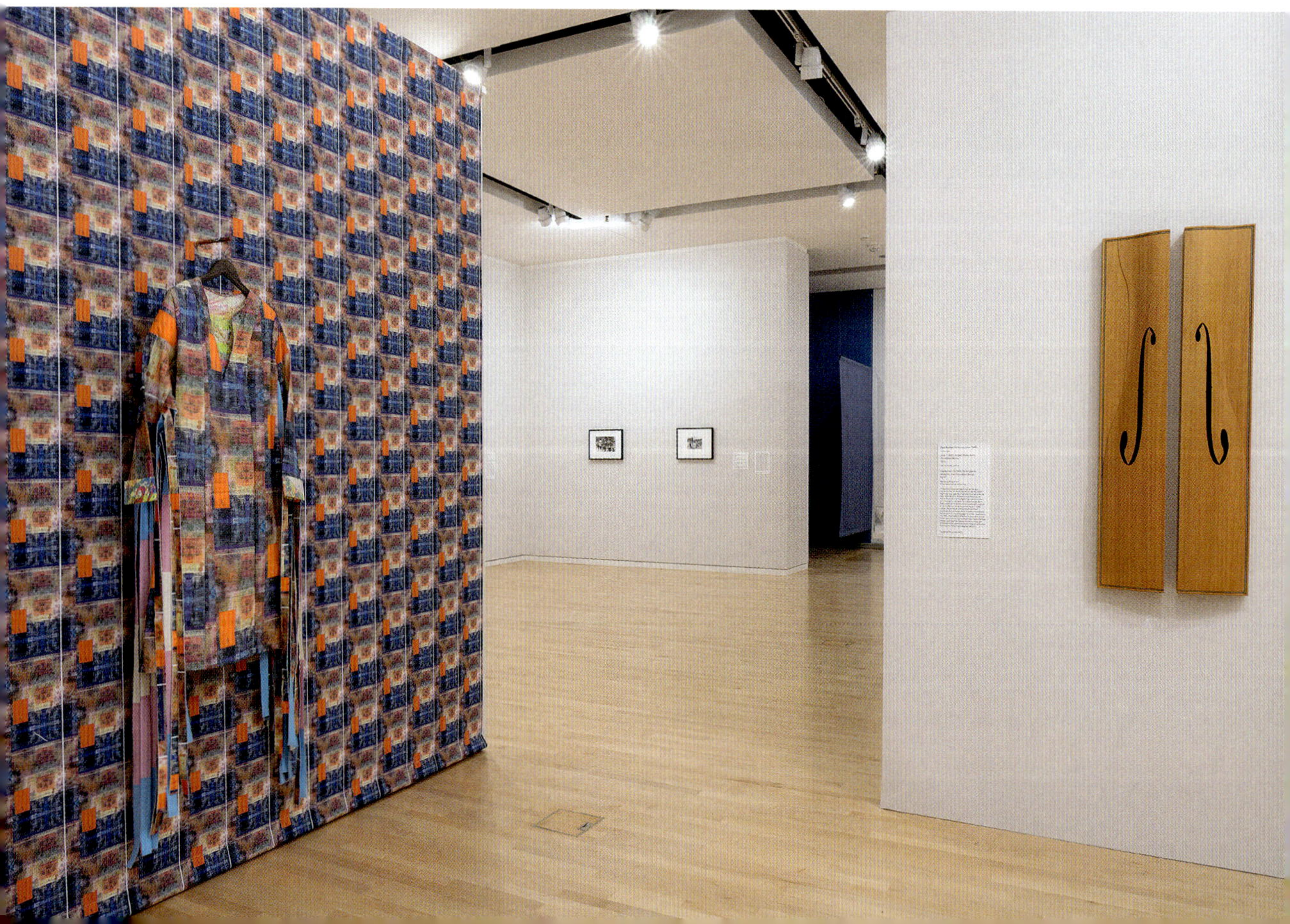

innovative teaching, learning, and research resource that is a springboard for thought-provoking discussions relevant to the [Northwestern University] curriculum and to our lives today."[10]

Early feedback about the exhibition's premise, content, organization, and presentation strategies was solicited from a group of advisors through two convenings held in October 2018 and April 2019. Participants included scholars working in the fields of African American studies, art history, communications studies, history, performance studies, and political science as well as museum educators and curators who had previously been engaged in presenting challenging exhibitions to diverse audiences.[11] Additional conversations with members of our constituent communities—including Northwestern faculty, staff, and students; previous and potential collaborators from Evanston-based organizations; artists; and other colleagues in the above-mentioned fields—focused on providing a preview of the exhibition material, discussing how the exhibition could be a resource for their own work, and soliciting input for structures of care and engagement. This process began in 2019, two and a half years before the exhibition, opening with a forum cosponsored by Northwestern's Black Arts Consortium. This forum brought together undergraduate and graduate students, faculty, and staff with an investment in African American arts and culture. The engagement continued with many one-on-one and small group conversations with colleagues, students, faculty, university administration, and the development of an Evanston community advisory group. The curatorial team, associate director of campus and community education and engagement, and the museum's director variously initiated and participated in these conversations. These dialogues were supplemented by additional research conducted by the Block Museum's engagement staff into different disciplinary models for community care and encouraging conscious visitorship.[12]

There was a lot of thematic consistency in the feedback, including the importance of the exhibition and its relevance in the contemporary environment and to the work of our collaborators. A few students raised concerns about whether the exhibition would reproduce the same type of traumatic visibility provided by the streaming and media coverage of the then-recent murders of Ahmaud Arbery (February 2020), Breonna Taylor (March 2020), and George Floyd (May 2020), among others. Almost all of the participants expressed the necessity of having measures in place to support visitor experience, especially considering the dynamics of viewing in a predominantly White institution with multiracial visitorship.

This highly consultative and collaborative process led to many decisions that impacted the exhibition checklist, exhibition design, programming, strategies for group visits, the development of supplementary materials and experiences, and mechanisms for visitor feedback. We sought to devise a series of solutions that would have the greatest impact while also being achievable. In conversations with partners, it was important to set expectations about capacity while following through on either the specifics or the spirit of many of the most impactful recommendations.

A DYNAMIC CONVERSATION: CHECKLIST DEVELOPMENT

Dees began with a core list of objects that was shaped by dynamic conversations with her and Swindell and through the dialogues noted above. In some cases, scholar-advisors suggested specific artists or artworks to be considered for inclusion in the exhibition. For the most part, their feedback consisted of thematic and organizational recommendations as well as affirmation of preexisting directions. The decision to organize the exhibition thematically rather than chronologically, the careful attention paid to gender dynamics, an emphasis on abstraction, and the inclusion of works that speak to "non-spectacular" kinds of violence were impacted by the critical input of these advisors. Additional guidance included the urge to think capaciously about who would be emotionally affected by the exhibition and to critically articulate the difference, as well as the relationship between the culture of White supremacy and Black experiences of anti-Black violence.[13] The advisors reaffirmed the decisions to develop a concise checklist and offer physical spaces for rest to mediate the potential overwhelming effect of the exhibition. These considerations were then articulated through specific selections of objects and artworks by the curatorial team.

For example, although the original checklist was focused on police violence and a history of lynching—areas of anti-Black violence in the United

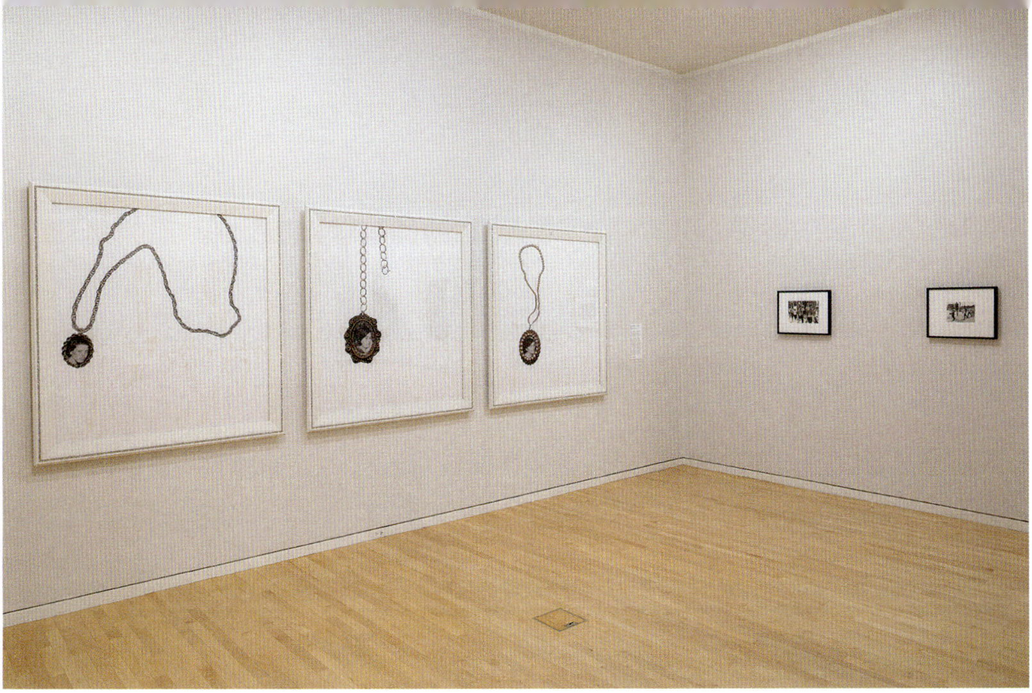

FIGURE 2.3 Installation view, *A Site of Struggle: American Art against Anti-Black Violence*. (Left to right) Kerry James Marshall, *Heirlooms and Accessories*, 2002; Bob Crawford, *Untitled*, 1966; Darryl Cowherd, *Gage Park Protest*, 1967/68. Image by Clare Britt. © Block Museum of Art, Northwestern University.

States that have driven both current and historical conversations around activism for Black lives—Swindell suggested the scope be broadened to include psychological violence and violence aimed at trans and gender-nonconforming (GNC) Black people. The trans community has done a great deal of work to make people outside of their experience aware of their challenges and the threats to their community, but that political capital has been obtained fairly recently. Due to issues surrounding being trans and GNC people having been part of the conversation around Black civil rights and anti-Black oppression for approximately only the last ten years, the same amount of art has not been produced that falls within the time frame of the exhibition as is available on other topics. The curatorial team decided that the violence being perpetrated against this segment of our community was important to include in the exhibition, integrating it into the bigger conversation on fighting anti-Black violence. This commitment was reflected in the inclusion of works by David Antonio Cruz and Molly Jae Vaughan.[14]

Dees underscored the importance of including works that focused on the perpetrators of and spectators to anti-Black violence, drawing attention

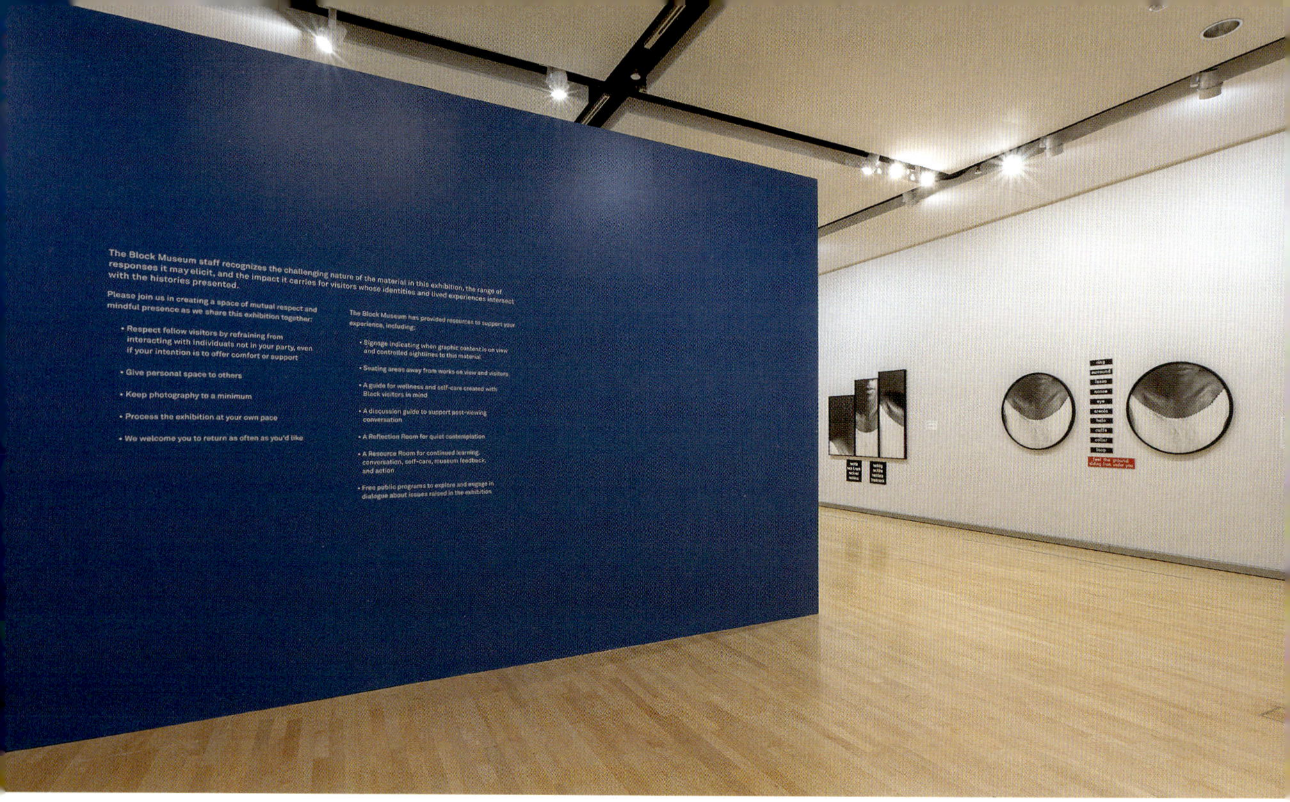

FIGURE 2.4 Installation view, *A Site of Struggle: American Art against Anti-Black Violence* with orientation text. (Left to right) Lorna Simpson, *Untitled (Two Necklines)*, 1989; *Necklines*, 1989. Image by Clare Britt. © Block Museum of Art, Northwestern University.

away from Black people as victims of violence and interrogating racial violence as part of White socialization. This was reflected in the inclusion of works like Kerry James Marshall's iconic *Heirlooms and Accessories* (2002) (fig. 2.3), suggested by one of the project advisors. In this work, Marshall appropriates a well-known 1930 photograph of a lynching in Marion, Indiana, isolating three female members of the crowd of lynching spectators who turned to face the camera as the original photo was taken. Marshall encircled their faces in cameos dangling from chains. The title of the work plays on the double reading of "accessories"—as jewelry, the cameos are accessories, but the women, and all members of the assembled group of lynching spectators, are also accessories to murder. The cameos, as well as the legacy of violence, can be understood as "heirlooms" that are being passed down to and through these women. Other works picking up on this theme included Reginald Marsh's 1934 drawing *This Is Her First Lynching* (as reproduced in the NAACP's *Crisis* magazine), photos by Darryl Cowherd and

Bob Crawford of 1960s anti-integration marches in Chicago, and selections from Ken Gonzales-Day's *Erased Lynching* series (2000–2013).

The checklist was kept intentionally concise—suggestive rather than comprehensive—to mitigate the complete overwhelm that could result from a more exhaustive treatment of the subject. The guiding principle for the exhibition was to do justice to the artists and their works while creating a space and a structure of care that would center Black experience and support diverse visitorship.

A SUPPORTIVE SPACE: EXHIBITION DESIGN AND SUPPLEMENTARY MATERIALS

The importance of employing strategies to promote respectful visitorship was something stressed in feedback with advisors, faculty, and students and by the curatorial team and other members of the museum staff. In the presentation at the Block Museum, the first thing that visitors encountered was an orientation text that asked them to join in creating an atmosphere of respectful viewership and mindful presence and listed resources available to support the visitor experience (fig. 2.4). The text occupied a full wall, signaling its importance to the viewing experience:[15]

> The Block Museum staff recognizes the challenging nature of the material in this exhibition, the range of responses it may elicit, and the impact it carries for visitors whose identities and lived experiences intersect with the histories presented.
>
> Please join us in creating a space of mutual respect and mindful presence as we share this exhibition together:
>
> - Respect fellow visitors by refraining from interacting with individuals not in your party, even if your intention is to offer comfort or support.
> - Give personal space to others.
> - Keep photography to a minimum.
> - Process the exhibition at your own pace.
> - We welcome you to return as often as you'd like.

The Block Museum has provided resources to support your experience, including:

- Signage indicating when graphic content is on view and controlled sightlines to this material.
- Seating areas away from works on view and visitors.
- A guide for wellness and self-care created with Black visitors in mind.
- A discussion guide to support post-viewing conversation.
- A Reflection Room for quiet contemplation.
- Resource Room for continued learning, conversation, self-care, museum feedback, and action.
- Free public programs to explore and engage in dialogue about issues raised in the exhibition.

As a means to control sight lines to the most visually graphic material, a gallery within a gallery was constructed and entrances to the interior gallery were marked with a content warning. This allowed visitors to choose whether they wanted to engage with this material and allowed them to view the other works in the galleries without the most difficult work in their continual sight lines (fig. 2.5).[16] It was also important for providing moments of respite for the visitor services staff, who then did not need to engage with these works unless there were visitors in that particular gallery space. The spacious exhibition design also incorporated dedicated areas for visitors to sit and take visual breaks as needed. Two additional spaces supported the presentation of the exhibition: a dedicated reflection room for quiet contemplation and a resource room where visitors could comfortably sit and peruse a library of books and supplementary materials, write comment cards, and watch a video of interviews conducted with scholars who worked on the project. A guided meditation was also developed specifically for the exhibition by joshua bee alafia. Based in Chicago at the time, alafia is a Black meditation teacher with a strong commitment to social justice. After previewing the exhibition content, alafia devised the meditation to guide visitors through processing strong emotions that may have resulted from engaging with the

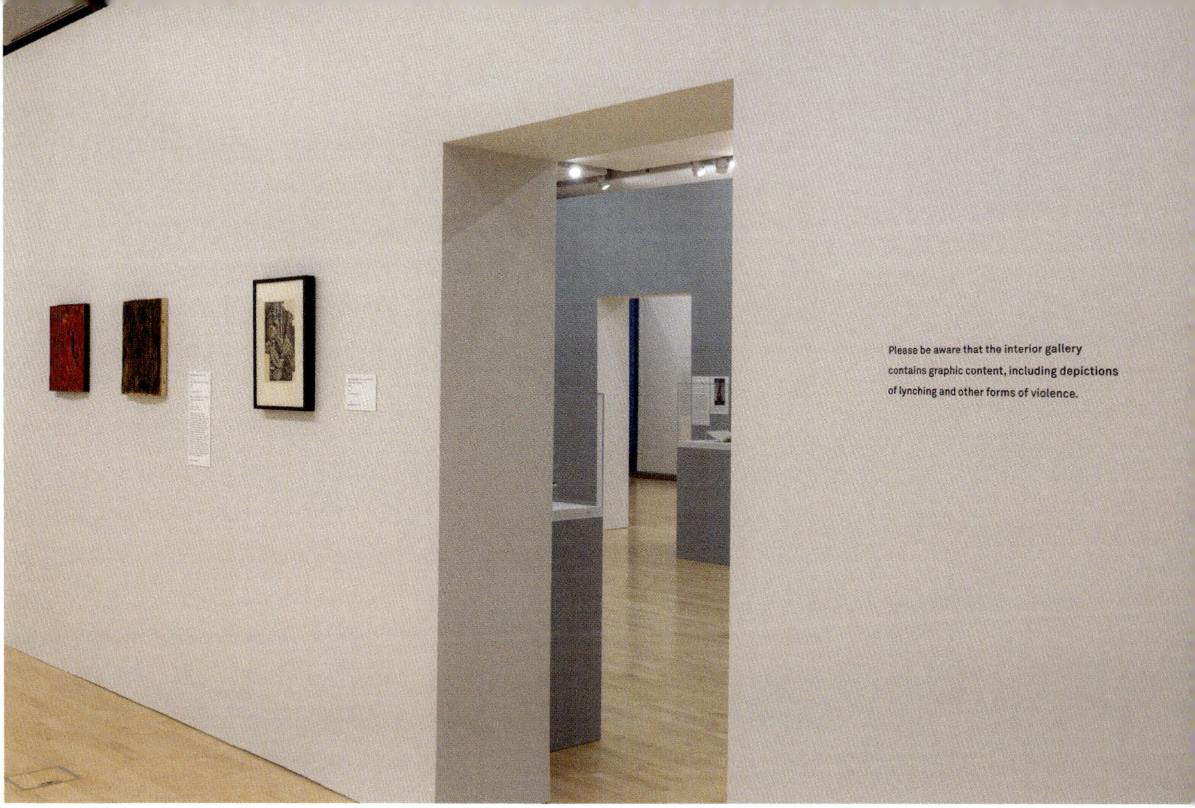

FIGURE 2.5 Installation view, *A Site of Struggle: American Art against Anti-Black Violence*, showing content notice and interior gallery space constructed for graphic material. Image by Clare Britt. © Block Museum of Art, Northwestern University.

exhibition. It was accessible through a QR code or dial-in number for use in the reflection room and even beyond the museum's walls.[17]

The development of supplementary material went beyond what the museum usually does for its exhibitions, including two pamphlets created to support visitor experience. During the development process, visitor services staff indicated that having more comprehensive interpretive materials for visitors would assist their work. The Visitor's Guide contained general information about the exhibition and several additional elements, including a resource list of community and campus organizations working for racial justice and supporting mental health and a set of reflection questions developed in consultation with our community advisory group to aid independent engagement with the exhibition. A Care Guide, developed with the well-being of Black visitors in mind, was created by a graduate fellow.[18] We originally proposed that the fellow devise a more traditional education guide; however, in the collaborative spirit of the project, the guide was shaped by dialogue with the fellow to explicitly address Black audiences as a way of offering additional respite. The Care Guide consisted of visual and poetic meditations of themes implicit to the exhibition, including "Communal Gathering, Mourning, and Joy"; "Motherhood"; "Self-Fashioning and Agency"; and "Black Womanhood."[19]

AN EXTENDED ENGAGEMENT

In partnership with the museum's engagement department and our community advisory group, we created a mission statement and plan for developing exhibition-related programming. The plan addressed five core objectives: deepen historical knowledge, create avenues for conversation, bridge Northwestern campus and the broader community, share calls for action, and provide care and support. Over sixteen programs and film screenings with more than forty Northwestern faculty and staff, outside scholars and museum professionals, Evanston community advisors, as well as exhibition and Block collection artists were presented during the exhibition.[20]

The community advisory group played a crucial role in the ideation and implementation of programs. For example, advisory group member, artist, and psychologist Dr. Melissa Blount advocated for the importance of programming that directly addressed trauma and healing. This resulted in a program with therapist, somatics teacher, facilitator, and political organizer Prentis Hemphill.[21] Hemphill, who was formerly the healing justice director at the Black Lives Matter Global Network, crafted a program that was part lecture and part instruction in embodied healing practices. The program concluded with a discussion and Q&A facilitated by Dr. Blount.

Another program, developed in collaboration with community advisory board member and local NAACP chapter president, Rev. Dr. Michael Nabors, investigated the NAACP's historical role in enlisting art to support its activism and featured Nabors in conversation with noted art historian Dr. Margaret Vendryes. After a presentation in which she discussed the NAACP's 1935 antilynching exhibition *An Art Commentary on Lynching*, Vendryes questioned

Nabors about how and whether the NAACP worked with artists today. This inquiry led Nabors and fellow community advisory board member, artist Fran Joy, to team up to produce an NAACP-supported exhibition of local Black artists. It was held in 2023 and promises to be a recurring event that will continue dialogue and engagement beyond the life of the exhibition.[22]

AN ONGOING DISCUSSION

To be respectful of all visitors, we opted not to hold guided tours of the exhibition. In-gallery programs and group visits were structured so that visitors would be given an introduction by a member of the museum's curatorial or engagement staff or guest speaker(s) drawn from faculty and community advisors. They would then view the exhibition on their own and reconvene for a facilitated conversation in a separate space. This approach honored individual viewing preferences and paces, offered opportunity for processing the exhibition in community, and allowed for real-time feedback about the exhibition's impact. Dees facilitated many of the group visits, which allowed her to hear directly from a diverse group of visitors. This type of ongoing exchange with audiences is atypical for curators.

An additional mechanism for receiving feedback from visitors was the use of comment cards. To encourage use of the cards, we created a writing station near a seating area so that visitors would have places to comfortably sit, reflect, and participate. The communications department collaborated with the curatorial team to ensure that the comment cards were reviewed weekly and that visitors requesting a response were answered. Certain cards, which commenters gave permission to be shared, were scanned and made publicly available on the Block Museum's website. While reflecting a small percentage of the overall visitors, the commentary from the cards was consistent with anecdotal accounts gleaned from group visits.[23] Respondents were overwhelmingly positive, finding the exhibition to be "emotionally impactful and resonant" and "respectful of both the content itself and the visitors' need to emotionally process their experience." For example, one middle-age African American woman wrote:

> Thank you for a thoughtful exhibition. This topic is exceptionally challenging especially as Black people continue to be subject to anti-Black violence in the U. S. and beyond. *A Site of Struggle* feels respectful; it avoids the sensationalism that permeates social media networks. This exhibition feels mediative.[24]

Another visitor who did not provide demographic information shared:

> I have visited museums and exhibitions before that showcase pieces of heavy subject elicit meaningful conversations. I have never been to an exhibition that has so ingrained processing of the subject matter into the experience itself. This made the experience all the more impactful.[25]

As these two examples communicate, the process and consideration that went into the exhibition's development and implementation were noticed and acknowledged by visitors and supportive to their experience of the exhibition.

CONCLUSION

As a case study of Black feminist curatorial practice, *A Site of Struggle* foregrounded relationality, intersectionality, and contextual concerns. This methodology represents a commitment to these values and is not necessarily predicated on ascription to a particular cultural identity. Broad consideration of who would engage with and be impacted by the exhibition shaped processes and decisions involving checklist development, exhibition design, engagement strategies and public programs, and the production of collateral materials. It employed a methodology that required conversations across real and perceived differences; collaboration across imposed hierarchies; and cocreation across institutional departments, and between the museum and individuals and organizational stakeholders. As we seek to reenvision the stories that are told about American art in the context of the museum, we must also reenvision our methods, advocating for content-specific models and conditions that support the sustainability of this deeper and often slower way of working.

NOTES

1. Dees initiated research for the project at the Block in 2018, though the idea had been with her since 2015. Swindell joined the project as a curatorial research associate in May 2019, a position she held throughout the development process of the exhibition, and until leaving to become the associate curator of photography at the Hood Museum of Art, Dartmouth College, in January 2022. Emily Martin served as a curatorial associate for the exhibition from February to December 2022. We would like to thank Emily for her research assistance with this essay. At the Block we would particularly like to acknowledge Lisa Corrin, director, and Kathleen Bickford Berzock, associate director of curatorial affairs, for their early and consistent support of the project; Erin Northington, America Salomon, and Bethany Hill for their research, discussions related to visitor support, and their development of engagement programs and collateral materials; Lindsay Bosch and Emmanuel Ramos-Barajas for their support with communications, documentation, and production of collateral material; Joe Scott and Dan Silverstein for the research and implementation of the exhibition design; and Aaron Chatman and Jeff Smith for coordinating conversations with the visitor services team. Early feedback and advice on the exhibition premise, content, organization, and presentation strategies was anchored on two convenings held in October 2018 and April 2019. We would like to thank the following individuals for their participation in these convenings and for ongoing conversations: Sampada Aranke, LaTanya Autry, Courtney R. Baker, Elisabeth Callihan, Bridget Cooks, Leslie M. Harris, Ross Jordan, Noemi Michel, Valerie Cassel Oliver, Kymberly Pinder, Maurita Poole, Risa Puleo, Veronica Roberts, Shawn Michelle Smith, Nicole Soukup, Lorelei Stewart, LaCharles Ward, Fred Wilson, and Mlondi Zondi. Input from Northwestern University faculty, staff, undergraduate, and graduate students was gathered during an October 2019 lecture and open forum sponsored by the university's Black Arts Initiative and helped with further refinement of the exhibition's approach and plans for interpretation. The community advisory committee consisted of local residents working in the arts, education, social justice, and where these intersect. Thanks are due to Dr. Melissa Blount, Fran Joy, Rebeca Mendoza, Rev. Dr. Michael Nabors, Nathan Norman, Robin Rue Simmons, and Corey Winchester for their participation; and to Dino Robinson, Tiffany McDowell, and LeAnn Jenkins, for their facilitation of this group.

2. Janet Dees, ed., *A Site of Struggle: American Art against Anti-Black Violence* (Evanston, IL: Block Museum of Art, Northwestern University/Princeton: Princeton University Press, 2022). Portions of this essay were adapted from Dees's essay "A Site of Struggle" in that volume. Other publication contributors include Sampada Aranke, Courtney R. Baker, Huey Copeland, Leslie M. Harris, and LaCharles Ward.

3. Huey Copeland, "Critical Care: Huey Copeland Talks with Janet Dees about *A Site of Struggle*," *ARTFORUM* 61, no. 1 (2022): 281.

4. Joana Joachim, "'Embodiment and Subjectivity': Intersectional Black Feminist Curatorial Practices in Canada," *RACAR* 43 (2018): 34–47.

5. Joachim, "Embodiment and Subjectivity," 44–45 and 36–37.

6. Swindell's position is informed by being in community with those advocating for LGBTQ rights and well-being, both through formal organizing and navigation of their personal lives, as well as the work of scholars/activists/public intellectuals James Baldwin, Cathy J. Cohen, Patricia Hill Collins, Saidiya Hartman, and Hortense Spillers.

7. Dees is particularly interested in how this is manifested in the work of Black Buddhist teachers and activists. See, for example, Rima Vesely-Flad, *Black Buddhists and the Black Radical Tradition: The Practice of Stillness in the Movement for Liberation* (New York: New York University Press, 2022); Pamela Ayo Yetunde and Cheryl A. Giles eds., *Black & Buddhist: What Buddhism Can Teach Us about Race, Resilience, Transformation, and Freedom* (Boulder, CO: Shambala, 2020); Rhonda V. Magee, *The Inner Work of Racial Justice: Healing Ourselves and Transforming Our Communities through Mindfulness* (New York: Tarcher Perigee, 2019); and rev. angel kyodo williams, Lama Rod Owens, and Jasmine Syedullah, *Radical Dharma: Talking Race, Love, and Liberation* (Berkeley: North Atlantic Books, 2016).

8. The exception was David Antonio Cruz's painting *anotherroadblockinourway, butifwegowegotogether, the detroit kids* (2020), the subjects of which are three friends, Timothy Blancher, Alunte Davis, and Paris Cameron, who were murdered in 2019, the victims of transphobic and homophobic violence. Later in this chapter we discuss why it was important to make this exception.

9. Artists and activists included in the exhibition are Laylah Ali (b. 1986); George Wesley Bellows (1882–1925); George Biddle (1885–1973); Elizabeth Catlett (1915–2012); Darryl Cowherd (b. 1940); Bob Crawford (1938–2015); Ernest Crichlow (1914–2005); David Antonio Cruz (b. 1974); Emory Douglas (b. 1943); Melvin Edwards (b. 1937); Theaster Gates (b. 1973); Wilmer Jennings (1910–1990); Norman Lewis (1909–1979); Kerry James Marshall (b. 1955); Isamu Noguchi (1904–1988); Howardena Pindell (b. 1943); Carl and Karen Pope (b. 1961); Walter

Quirt (1902–1968); Paul Rucker (b. 1968); Lorna Simpson (b. 1960); Dox Thrash (1893–1965); Molly Jae Vaughan (b. 1977); Lynd Ward (1905–1985); Carrie Mae Weems (b. 1953); Ida B, Wells (1862–1931); Walter White (1893–1955); Pat Ward Williams (b. 1948); and Hale Woodruff (1900–1980).

10. "Block Museum of Art Vision Statement," accessed February 13, 2024, https://www.blockmuseum.northwestern.edu/about-the-block/. The mission statement has since been changed from how it appears in the text.

11. See note 1 for full list of advisors.

12. America Salomon and Erin Northington led research into language involving content warnings and creating space for processing—both within and outside of the realm of visual arts museum. Some references include Jeremy O. Harris's *Slave Play* (2018); the Kigali Genocide Memorial; and the exhibition *Prisoner of Love* curated by Naomi Beckwith (Museum of Contemporary Art Chicago, 2019). Additional references include *Necessary Force: Art in the Police State*, curated by Kymberly Pinder and Karen Fiss (University of New Mexico Art Museum, 2015); *Art and Healing in the Moment*, curated by Valerie Castile with Nicole Soukup (Minneapolis Institute of Arts, 2018); *Vincent Valdez: The City*, curated by Veronica Roberts (Blanton Museum of Art, University of Texas, Austin, 2018); and the online teach-in Art of Collective Care and Responsibility (2020) organized by the Black Liberation Center (founded by LaTanya Autry).

13. To encourage frank and open conversation, the convenings with advisors were held with the understanding of confidentiality. To honor this, feedback is shared in the aggregate here rather than quoting specific individuals. See note 1 for listing of convening participants.

14. For information on Cruz's work, see note 8.

15. At the Montgomery Museum of Fine Arts, this text was given a similar prominent place.

16. This approach was adapted by the Montgomery Museum of Fine Arts in a way compatible with their gallery layout.

17. The mediation was developed by formerly Chicago-based teacher joshua bee alafia. An interview with alafia and a link to the meditation are still available via the Block Museum's website, "May We All Be Free: A Conversation with joshua bee alaafia," March 4, 2022. https://nublockmuseum.blog/2022/03/04/may-we-all-be-free-a-conversation-with-joshua-bee-alafia-on-bringing-meditation-to-the-museum-space/.

18. Bethany Hill was the 2020–2021 art history graduate fellow at the Block Museum and developed the Care Guide.

19. The Visitor's Guide and Care Guide, along with other supplemental material for *A Site of Struggle,* are available on the Block Museum's website at https://www.blockmuseum.northwestern.edu/exhibitions/2022/a-site-of-struggle.html/.

20. Additional programs were developed by the MMFA with their particular audiences in mind.

21. For the work of Prentis Hemphill, see their website at https://prentishemphill.com/, accessed February 29, 2024.

22. See "Art, Activism, and Contemporary Resonances of the 1935 NAACP exhibition *An Art Commentary on Lynching*," *Block Museum of Art* (online), March 9, 2022. A video of the program is accessible at https://nublockmuseum.blog/2022/03/25/art-activism-and-contemporary-resonances-of-the-1935-naacp-exhibition-an-art-commentary-on-lynching-video%EF%BF%BC/. See also "The NAACP Celebrates Black Artists," *Evanston Art Center,* on view May–June 2023, accessed February 29, 2024, https://www.evanstonartcenter.org/exhibitions/naacp-art-exhibition/. Dr. Vendryes (1955–2022) died unexpectedly a few weeks after the Block's program, and the NAACP exhibition was dedicated to her memory. A full discussion of the programming is outside the scope of the current essay. A comprehensive list of programs is available through the *A Site of Struggle* exhibition page on the Block Museum's website. Several of the programs have video documentation accessible online.

23. About 13,000 people visited the exhibition at the Block Museum and there were about 8,500 visitors at the Montgomery Museum of Fine Arts. The number of cards filled our was 389 , and 362 of those provided narrative content. In addition 89.2 percent had a positive tone; 9.7 percent a neutral tone; and 1.1 percent (4 respondents) a negative tone. In terms of race, 18.5 percent of respondents self-identified as Black or African American. This is slightly higher than the percentage of Evanston residents who are Black/African Americans (16.5 percent). Lee Groves Consulting, "*A Site of Struggle* Comment Card Analysis," August 30, 2022.

24. Groves Consulting, "*A Site of Struggle* Comment Card Analysis."

25. Groves, Consulting, "*A Site of Struggle* Comment Card Analysis."

3

Austen Barron Bailly / Karen Kramer,
with Michael W. Hartman / Jami C. Powell

GENERATIVE COLLABORATION

Toward a More Expansive American Art

In August 2023 Austen Barron Bailly, Karen Kramer, Michael W. Hartman, and Jami C. Powell gathered over Zoom to discuss the possibilities for expanding curatorial practice within the field of American art. The conversation presents the challenges and possibilities facing curatorial projects aimed at making American art more inclusive, accessible, and relevant amid larger institutional efforts to reckon with histories and practices rooted in colonialism, exclusion, and dispossession.

JAMI C. POWELL I want to start by setting up the context for our conversation today, which is an informal dialogue that dives into curatorial topics not often covered in publications. During the convening held in conjunction with *This Land: American Engagement with the Natural World*, where we first discussed the ideas for this book, all of us expressed the desire to create a book that would have been useful to us when we were in graduate school or emerging scholars and curators in the field. This round-table format allows us to pull back the curtain and give folks, particularly emerging museum professionals, the opportunity to understand that even established professionals and senior curators have lots of questions and feelings of ambiguity about the work that we do, not to mention the fears we have about whether our work is harmful rather than restorative or reparative.

MICHAEL W. HARTMAN I am trained as an art historian, and Jami is trained as an anthropologist. We often discuss how the work we do is, or is not, informed by our academic backgrounds. Thinking about the perspectives and experiences that inform our curatorial practice, could each of you speak about how you entered the field?

KAREN KRAMER I feel that there are two parallel experiences that have shaped my curatorial practice in my current role.

The first is my academic background. I have undergraduate and master's degrees in anthropology, which is a bit of a dirty word, particularly for the Native stakeholders to whom I am accountable. But having a background in anthropology and working at the Peabody Essex Museum, a museum of world art and culture, has served me well in terms of being aware of the complexities and tenuous relationships between Native communities and museums. My academic training has prepared me to be more sensitive to how and why museums have collected, housed, and displayed Indigenous cultural belongings and to stay grounded in context—why and for what and whom makers created the belongings we now house. More recently, I've been pursuing a doctoral degree in American studies. This interdisciplinary approach is helping me better investigate and navigate the intersections between Native and American politics, history, and art. There is no American art—or America—without Native art, culture, history, and peoples.

The second is working at the same museum for nearly thirty years. When I started at the Peabody Essex in the mid-1990s, I was a curatorial assistant and collections manager. In those roles I gained the professional experience that I really needed to succeed in my current position. My academic background is part of what has shaped me, but being in the job and working with Native community members has also informed and reshaped my experience over time.

AUSTEN BARRON BAILLY I agree with you, Karen. I chose art history as an undergraduate and studied art history all the way through—undergrad, master's, and PhD. I always had this attraction to how museums can provide access to great art, great artists, and great things you've never seen before and maybe never thought about. But I had questions about why certain collections or objects were on view. Why these stories? Questions like these motivated me to go for an MA. I was compelled to leave my job at an art gallery specializing in Impressionist and Old Master artists to pursue the degree because of my exposure to museums while living in New York in the '90s—and my sense that a BA wasn't enough to enter the field. I would describe my academic training as classical because it's rooted in European art. I studied French art before landing my first museum internship researching foreign works of art for a show called *Art in the Empire City* (Metropolitan Museum of Art, 2000). I became captivated by the openness of the American art field, and how this show was paintings and sculpture, it was fashion, it was decorative art and photography.[1] All of these different objects presented multiple ways to tell a story about how something came to be, and I think that really influenced my academic and professional path.

My switch to the American field stemmed from that exhibition project, so I always encourage people to be open to experiences that might shift where you think your primary area of focus is or where you think it is going to be. When I relocated to California, far, far, far from the East Coast, I encountered so many more art histories than I had been taught or seen, including Native American art, and I loved that expansiveness. It's important to acknowledge that there was no Native art taught in my programs. My first introductions to Native American art and opportunities to learn about the field were at LACMA [Los Angeles County Museum of Art].

Working at the Peabody Essex Museum was truly transformative, with such deep collections and specialist expertise, which we will speak to more fully in a moment. But my message is: marry your academic training and interests with curiosity and remain open.

JAMI C. POWELL I think that's a generative and generous way of looking at the field of American art. As an undergrad, I knew I wanted to work in museums, and I knew that I wanted to work with art. But to get a degree in art history—and I think this has changed a bit since I was in school—you had to learn the Western canon. You did not have to learn about art made by Black and Brown folks. For that reason, I was drawn to anthropology because I thought, "Well, even though this comes with its own set of baggage," to which Karen already alluded, I saw a commitment in the field of anthropology to engaging with marginalized communities, a commitment that was lacking in art history. Placing artworks into the existing canon without collaborating with communities is inherently limited, so while I refer to myself as a "recovering anthropologist," I am grateful for my training in community-based participatory research.

I appreciate what Austen said a moment ago about American art having this openness, because I actually think that openness is how we've reached our current moment where people, museums, and foundations are asking questions such as, What is American? Who gets to be part of that? Foundations and funding bodies are now engaging in conversations and driving initiatives that expand the field further, which aligns with what you've both spoken about in terms of your educational and professional experiences over time.

In your presentation at the convening held in conjunction with *This Land*, you shared that you were unfamiliar with major figures in each of your subspecialties.[2] Karen didn't know Thomas Hart Benton and Austen didn't know T. C. Cannon. Michael and I have talked about how much we appreciated your vulnerability in publicly acknowledging the gaps in your knowledge but also how you used that as an opportunity to open a conversation about the importance of collaboration, emphasizing why it's so important for those of us working in institutions to work together and not curate solo projects all the time. Can you recount those stories?

AUSTEN BARRON BAILLY When I joined the Peabody Essex Museum (PEM) in 2013, I was already working on a major exhibition of the American artist Thomas Hart Benton (1889–1975)—*American Epics: Thomas Hart Benton and Hollywood* (2015).[3] We added the show to the calendar, and Karen shared that Benton was totally new to her and not someone she would have studied. In the same way, a giant for Karen was T. C. Cannon (1946–1978, Kiowa/Caddo), and he was completely unknown to me. I had never heard of him, and Karen was curating a traveling exhibition of Cannon's work. These two great artists were living in our parallel but completely separate art historical worlds. In the Benton exhibition, there were many images of Native figures that I thought I had critically engaged through context, through addressing the histories that Benton was representing or trying to represent and through dealing with his methods of stereotype and figuration. But I never fully grasped how those images might land in the galleries. That misperception led to a reckoning of sorts.

KAREN KRAMER Of course, T. C. Cannon has been historically overshadowed by Fritz Scholder (1937–2005, La Jolla Band of Luiseño Indians), his instructor at the Institute of American Indian Arts in Santa Fe, but Cannon is a beloved figure in my field—a painter, poet, and aspiring musician who came of age in the turbulent 1960s and '70s, who died tragically at thirty-one in 1978. He was a super-inventive artist whose mashups of Native and non-Native elements and vivid colors and patterns pulled Native figures out of the staid, romanticized world of black-and-white Indian portraiture. I feel like I've always known T. C. Cannon, even if he wasn't recognized more broadly. But Thomas Hart Benton? I am embarrassed to say that at the time, I had no idea who he was despite his renown in the American canon. I think it speaks to a great divide between Native and American art and how siloed our fields have historically been—a chasm that is slowly starting to narrow.

I remember walking through your magnificent Benton exhibition, and during my first pass-through, there was this room of fifteen panels that you had reunited for the first time called the *American Historical Epic* (1919–1928). There were a few larger-than-life images of glossy, naked, sexy-warrior Mohawk men, and I just thought, "What are these Native people doing in here?" and "How could we not have talked about this when our offices are two doors away from one another?"

When we went through the exhibition with the Native fellows that summer, and they had gone through the exhibition for whatever reason backwards, so that room filled with these murals was their last experience, I think they were also shocked to see the glistening Native bodies portrayed and displayed in this way. But PEM also made an interpretive decision to remove an additional panel about these Native people that discussed their portrayal, what was happening, and the idea of stereotyping. The experience really opened a dialogue between all of us. We went through the exhibition together (including with Austen) and talked about Benton's perspective, our fellows' experiences, and what it means to look at these Brown bodies on view without much interpretation, especially given the heavy histories of museums and Native representation. In addition to Benton's fifteen murals, the show also included a portrait of Metacom (also called Metacomet and Pometacom, as well as his English name King Philip) and an image depicting the Battle of Greasy Grass, also known as Custer's Last Stand. One of our fellows had been to the Little Bighorn Battlefield—his ancestors had fought in the battle—and he shared what it was like to visit it, and what emotions and memories seeing this picture stirred for him. Including Native interpretation could have shaded in some texture and nuance as a contemporary rejoinder to Benton's American epics.

Austen, you were gracious and open to these conversations, and I've always appreciated that about you. That is truly when I felt like we could work together to learn from each other more. I certainly have a lot to learn in the field of American art and also my own field. I'm constantly learning, but that was the first time, for me, that I realized how much work we need to do together to move the dial—and the field—forward.

AUSTEN BARRON BAILLY Yes, I agree, and I think from my perspective, it was just a complete lack of awareness that imagery expressive of histories like westward expansion could be presented without some sort of greater qualification. It wasn't enough to describe how Benton was trying to critique the legacies of westward expansion. Even if Benton was addressing colonization, he was using methods that are visually at odds with a recognition of individual Native peoples and cultures, experiences, and histories. As a famous American artist working in the mid-twentieth century, Benton's default audience was a White majority audience, and the way in which the show was organized reflected that perspective. The dialogue with the Native fellows was a total wake-up call for me to relearn and understand the impact of what gets shared in these museum settings as well as the lasting ripple effects of display decisions.

MICHAEL W. HARTMAN I think there's a perception from some visitors, and even some curators and scholars in the field, that objects are a "product of their time." When I hear people use that excuse, they fail to hold objects accountable to their true histories and legacies of colonialism. Some curators also use this as an excuse to not do the difficult interpretive work, or to not speak with contemporary stakeholders about historical works of art and what they mean today for their communities.

I know that the work and conversations you had about the Thomas Hart Benton exhibition informed PEM's presentation of *Nature's Nation: Art and Environment* (2019).[4] Could you speak more about the importance of incorporating multiple voices into the planning and interpretive process at the beginning of exhibition development?

AUSTEN BARRON BAILLY *Nature's Nation* was a similar kind of origin story, coming from within a pretty narrowly defined field of American art that was, and is, trying to open up. It included not just non-Native artists' images of Native American people and culture but objects made by Native artists. I knew right away that we couldn't consider taking the show unless I discussed it closely with Karen to understand if this project was even moving the field in the right directions.

KAREN KRAMER We met with the curators of the *Nature's Nation*, Alan Braddock and Karl Kusserow, and ultimately agreed to take on the project, with the understanding that the Peabody Essex Museum would augment the checklist by adding about a dozen Native artworks from our own collection. Doing so would tell a more expansive or inclusive story of American art and the environment over four hundred years, which we felt strongly could not be accomplished without additional representation of Native art. In addition to adding Native art to the checklist, we rearranged the order of the exhibition themes and altered the floor plan so that we could really lift up the Native art, which we also did through interpretation.

In addition, Austen and I worked closely with Rachel Allen (Nez Perce), who had been a Native fellow at PEM and had transitioned into a full-time assistant curator over the course of the project. It took all three of us to consider more deeply the objects, the messaging, and the flow when presenting this really wonderful exhibition at PEM, which also informed its later installation at Crystal Bridges.

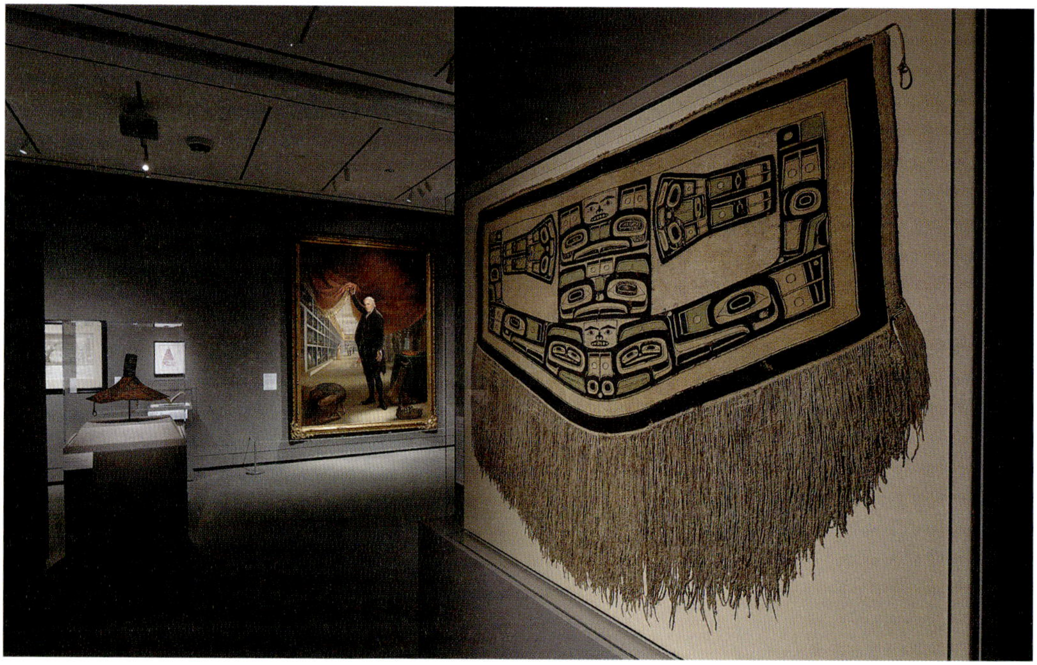

FIGURE 3.1 Installation view, *Nature's Nation: American Art and Environment*, featuring *Tlingit naaxein* (*Chilkat* robe) made by a once-known artist (seen at right in installation), 2019. Image by Kathy Tarantola. © Peabody Essex Museum.

AUSTEN BARRON BAILLY When we committed to the exhibition, we also committed to having an open and honest dialogue with the organizing curators and the coordinating curator for the other venue, which was Crystal Bridges (Mindy Besaw). To plan for the exhibition, we convened in Salem, Massachusetts, to talk candidly through the questions and concerns we had about adapting the exhibition with the curators who conceived the show, did the bulk of the research, and came up with the checklist so that we could make the case for the ways in which we saw the show needing to change for the Peabody Essex Museum and explore how that might influence the project and the national tour.

Some of the proposed changes were significant enough and influential enough to alter their publication. Rachel Allen's analysis of the PDF manuscript version of the catalog was so cogent that Karen and I said to Rachel, "We must share this. We have a moral and ethical responsibility to share this with the organizing curators. Taking into account your expertise and

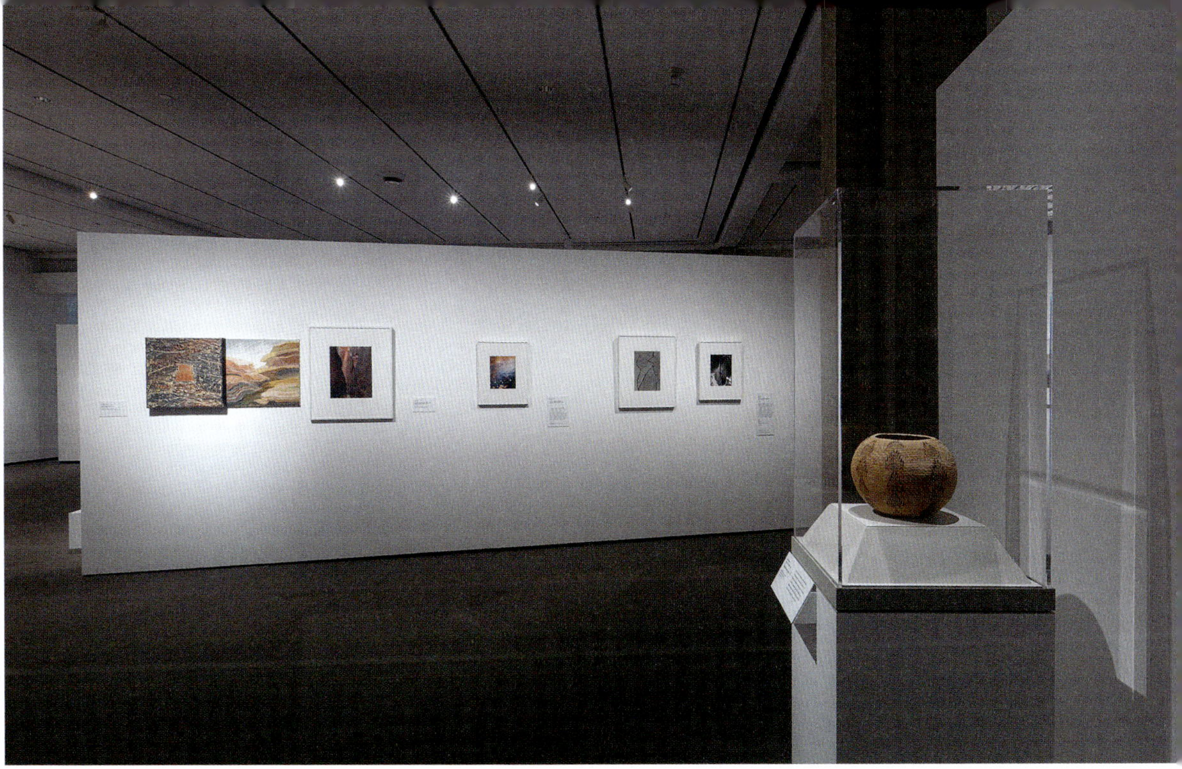

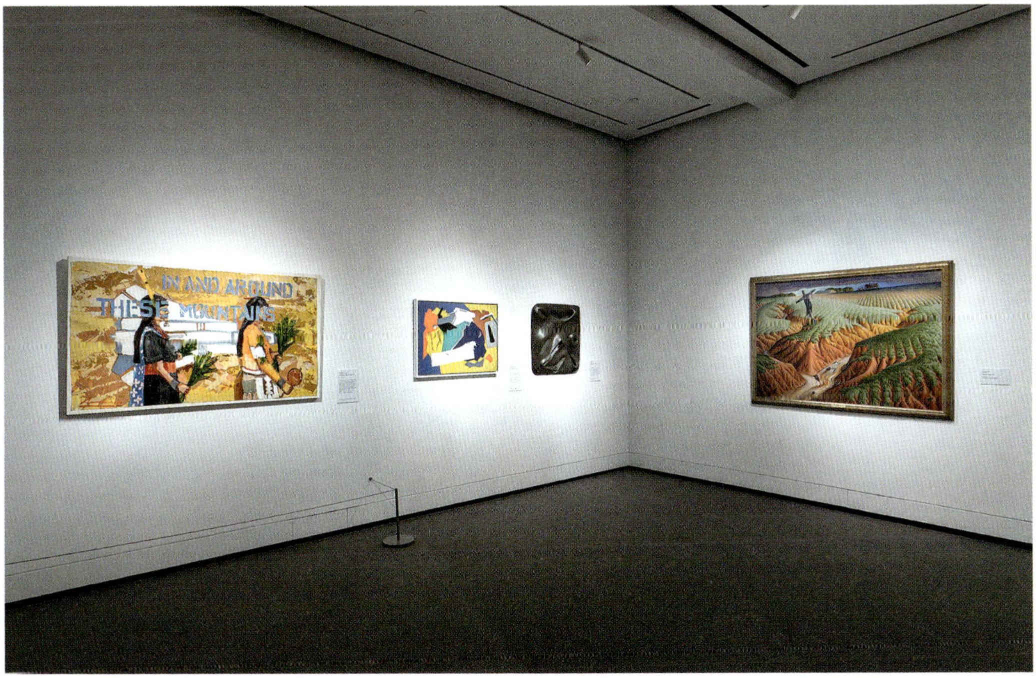

FIGURES 3.2 AND 3.3 Installation view, *Nature's Nation: American Art and Environment*, 2019. Top image by Ken Sawyer, © Peabody Essex Museum. Bottom image by Kathy Tarantola, © Peabody Essex Museum.

perspective, they can't print this catalog without significant changes." Because Indigenous knowledge without citation is often not taken seriously, Rachel's analysis included academic sources from Indigenous scholars, underscoring the importance of engaging decolonizing methodologies that reframe terminology, voice, representation, and agency. Karen also suggested an expert, Miranda Belarde-Lewis (Tlingit-Zuni), to write on the early nineteenth-century *naaxein* (*Chilkat* robe) from PEM's collection, which was added to the exhibition (figs. 3.1–3.3). The organizing curators' openness to Karen's and Rachel's suggestions, along with my advocacy, pushed the project further than it had originally been able to go.

KAREN KRAMER At the Princeton originating installation of *Nature's Nation*, before you even entered the building you encountered Postcommodity's *Repellent Fence/Valla Repelente* (2015), which alerted visitors to the relationship between Native peoples, land, and place. It reminded you of where you're standing and what you're looking at. Similarly, at the Peabody Essex Museum, we wanted to ground *Nature's Nation* in Indigenous expression and honor Native belonging in our space.

In addition to having Postcommodity's artwork as the first experience in the gallery, immediately following we installed an Indigenous-made, beautiful, stylized basalt bear that dates to the 1500s. It was likely created by a Pawtucket artist and was found about a mile from the Peabody Essex Museum in the late 1800s. In conjunction with the bear, we had a land acknowledgment on the wall, which was among the first written land acknowledgments publicly shared by PEM. For us, these artworks and this land acknowledgment were experiments in reminding our visitors that we're always on Native land while upholding a commitment to Native communities in a public setting. Having that encounter at the beginning of the exhibition set our visitors on a path for a deeper engagement with Native and American art for the rest of the exhibition experience.

JAMI C. POWELL Karen, you used the words "expansive" *and* "inclusive" to talk about the work with *Nature's Nation,* which reminds me of a great metaphor you've used before when talking about these issues and is something that I have started to use as well: "Native art practitioners want a piece of the pie that is American art, but we want our own pie too." That visual metaphor perfectly demonstrates how we want the field to expand but also be inclusive.

With the pie metaphor, we also begin to acknowledge the fear within museums and society more broadly that there's only so much pie and that pieces get smaller as we become more inclusive. There's this false assumption that including others means that there are necessarily fewer opportunities for people who have always been included in dialogues and been part of the canon, but it's not a zero-sum game. Can't we make more pies? What about making bigger pies?

KAREN KRAMER When we were planning for *On This Ground: Being and Belonging in America* (2022–ongoing), a permanent collection installation at PEM that integrates our Native art collection with our American art collection, we convened a number of Native and non-Native advisors in 2018, including scholars, educators, curators, artists, elders, and community members. When we all came together, the majority of our discussions centered on the risks and rewards for pulling Native American art together with American art. The overarching feeling or sentiment was that you can't have American art, you can't have American history, and you can't have America without Native Americans. For that reason, Native art needs to be in conversation with American art, but Native art can't only be in service of it. Native art, to quote a phrase that our Native advisors were using, needs "sovereign space" as well. I think that's speaking to this whole metaphor of the pie. We want Native art to be a part of the pie, but we also need to have our own pie and our own slices.

We also found with *Nature's Nation* that contemporary Native art can't always be used to respond to or in service of American art. Native art needs to also be understood on its own terms, and Native art needs to be celebrated in its original context. Native art can do both of these things, but approaching it sensitively and delicately is an imperative of museum professionals.

Speaking to what Michael was asking earlier, the practice of bringing in voices becomes really important when lifting up some of these really complicated histories between Native peoples and these particular objects and contexts. Bringing in voices can sometimes enable a certain freedom that museum curators don't always have because of an institutional imperative or an institutional voice that has become a standard in the field. Bringing in voices enriches the dialogue, and they also unlock a really important perspective that, regardless of your cultural background, adds a really rich layer to the experience and interpretation.

AUSTEN BARRON BAILLY I would add that having seen *On This Ground* come to life and flourish in its full realization, one of the things that is most striking is the balance of the number of objects from different communities. This is so critical to showing the breadth of the American artistic practice writ large across time. So few museums have been able to combine Native and non-Native collections. But what PEM's been able to achieve through that combination is an expansive, inclusive, and holistic way of introducing audiences to a plethora of incredible stories, creativity, and histories that open up so many different perspectives and points of view. These can be grappled with or celebrated, or even frustrating or eye-opening, depending on what a guest is bringing into that space.

Further to Karen's point about having "two pies," a powerful rebalancing takes place when you walk through *On This Ground*'s blended presentations of Native and non-Native art and into a space where you see only Native art and artists, where you might normally have seen only US art and artists. This refocusing is something that I think many museums, if they have the collections and they carefully research the Native collections, could also do. Or if they don't have the collections, they may have the opportunity to build or borrow and, as you say, Karen, to present Native art with other kinds of art and on its own terms.

MICHAEL W. HARTMAN PEM's *On This Ground* features several clever object pairings that encourage dialogue and conversations between the objects, as well as between visitors. Multiple community voices are amplified and present in the galleries, which moves us from a conversation about curatorial collaboration to a discussion about bringing in community voices, as well as the idea of curatorial allyship. Could you both speak more to what generative collaboration actually looks like in a gallery and how it develops? Do you have any specific advice for institutions that want to do this sort of work with their permanent collections?

KAREN KRAMER I want to start with your last question, because it's important to say that the work that Austen and I have done together with the team, and I'm particularly thinking about *On This Ground*, would not have been possible without the support, directive, and freedom granted from museum leadership: our former director, Dan Monroe, and current director, Lynda Hartigan. This institutional prerogative spills into the work that we do with our board of trustees and has shaped our relationships with our project advisors but that also spills into the curatorial work that I do daily. The prioritization of Native voices and Native art being a full part of these conversations, as well as supporting the people who are doing the actual work—the curators, the interpreters, the collections staff, and all the PEM staff—really shapes how we relate to and see Native art in its broadest context. Without that support, it would be challenging, if not impossible, to do this kind of a project. We committed to an equal amount of space for Native art as we did for American art—literally a fifty-fifty split. We committed to calling the gallery "Native American and American"—prioritizing always putting "Native American" ahead of "American." Words matter. These decisions matter.

But you wanted us to talk about curatorial partnerships and allyships, and we can shift to that unless, Austen, if you wanted to add anything?

AUSTEN BARRON BAILLY I would just add that you made an incredibly important point, and I am so glad you brought this up. So far, much of this conversation has reflected on the work Karen and I did at the Peabody Essex Museum before I became chief curator at Crystal Bridges in 2019. One of the reasons I was open to that move was because Crystal Bridges had similar directives in place with our living founder, with our board, with our director, and with the curatorial team. My willingness to move into a leadership role built off what I had learned through collaborations with Karen, the Native fellows, and through the projects that we did at Peabody Essex Museum. These experiences gave me the confidence to continue to advocate for the kinds of acquisitions, for the kinds of curatorial hires, for the kinds of orientations or reorientations of projects that can expand the field further.

We have a lot more work to do at Crystal Bridges. Our collections cannot touch PEM's collections of Native art by any stretch of the imagination. But we have the aspiration and that sense of bringing together an institution with communities, voices, perspectives and to keep learning and growing. These values are in Crystal Bridges' DNA, which gives me hope.

JAMI C. POWELL Hearing your discussion of how leadership informs and supports this work gets us into conversations about how other institutions can move forward. Could each of you give an example of a pairing in the gallery that speaks about this shift from curatorial collaboration to embracing community voices? Or perhaps speak about one portion of an installation that you think exemplifies the strengths of this approach?

AUSTEN BARRON BAILLY In 2018 the curator of American art at Crystal Bridges, Mindy Besaw, worked with a team to reconceptualize the opening experience to the museum. Instead of moving from a textbook chronological unfolding of American art history as traditionally and exclusively defined, the introductory space includes a sweeping wall with Nari Ward's *We the People* (2015) shoelace work (fig. 3.4). The opposite wall features a broad array of portraits by different artists of different backgrounds, painted in different styles and from different time periods. A visitor can still move from a portrait of *Mrs. Jacob Franks (Abigaill Levy)*, a colonial Jewish woman, attributed to Gerardus Duyckinck I (c. 1735), to Susie J. Lee's video portrait of a fracker, *Johnny* (2013), hanging next to a portrait of *George Washington* by Charles Wilson Peale (ca. 1780–82), to Alfred Maurer's full-length portrait of an early twentieth-century woman called *Jeanne* (ca. 1904), to a Mexican American modernist portrait titled *Florida Mexicana* by Alfredo Ramos Martínez (ca. 1936), to Anishinaabe painter Frank Big Bear's *The Poetry of Joseph E Big Bear* (2010) in all its exuberant glory.

When you come into this gallery, there is this sense that you are seeing a

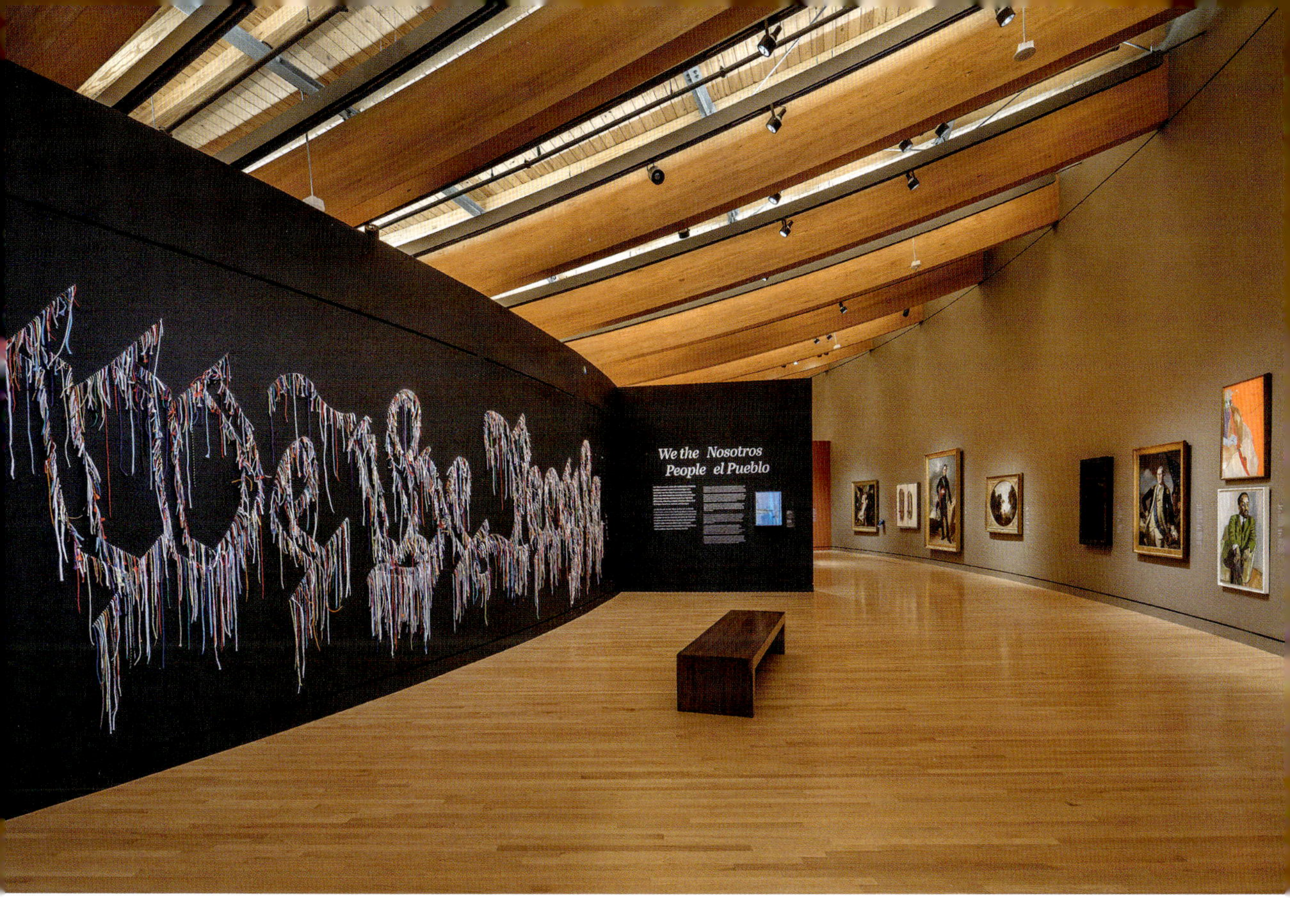

FIGURE 3.4 Installation view, permanent collection entry gallery, featuring Nari Ward, *We the People (black version)*, 2015 (left). © Crystal Bridges Museum of American Art.

glimpse of all that you might imagine about American art as a start to your museum experience. This intermixing sets a tone, but in terms of the combinations of Native and non-Native art we can achieve similar combinations only in modern and contemporary sections of the museum because we don't have as much Native art in the collection. We intend to grow the Native art collection, with a curator of Native American art, and we will be reinstalling the whole museum. As we plan for our reinstallation, we are looking specifically at *On This Ground* as a model.

KAREN KRAMER I love that experience at Crystal Bridges. It was such a powerful moment for me when I walked through that gallery space and I saw a Fritz Scholder next to Alice Neel and Andy Warhol portraits, all displayed directly across from Nari Ward's *We the People* shoelace installation. That experience will stay with me forever. It is a super-inspirational installation.

Within *On This Ground*, we have a small moment where the two collections come together called "Myths and Motives," which is a small constellation of objects that look at westward expansion and how the United States government relied on racialized depictions of Native Americans, African Americans, and Asian Americans to justify ongoing dispossession, displacement, and enslavement. In this space there is an amazing object that Austen brought into PEM's collection, a sculpture by Hank Willis Thomas, *Rich Black Specimen #460* (2017), that is an amazingly vibrant, razor-thin, Technicolor sculpture inspired by nineteenth-century runaway slave newspaper advertisements. Thomas's enlarged male figure appears to be running so fast, he can't be caught by the law, or even by today's contemporary printing press, hence the primary color glitches on his skin. Nearby is David Bradley's (White Earth Ojibwe) painting *American Dream II* (2001), which depicts the Santa Fe Super Chief train barreling down the tracks, advertising death and destruction on occupied Indigenous lands. The train's chimney spits out skulls with a Native man on horseback riding alongside the train trying to outrun it and, by extension, to outrun development and technology. In both Thomas's and Bradley's works, the figures' movements really complicate narratives and understandings. The sum becomes more than each of its parts, because together the artists' vibrant colors, storytelling capabilities, and visual motion tell a powerful story that becomes more exciting through their pairing with one another. These histories are not separate, and not only happened in relation to each other but still inform the present.

JAMI C. POWELL What you said about the sum being greater than the parts reminds me of a pairing that we had in *This Land,* where we hung our Georgia O'Keeffe *Taos Mountain, New Mexico* (1930) landscape painting next to a Diné (Navajo) *Saddle Blanket* (1880–1900). The two women who made these works were living and working in the same region, but even if you just looked at them and did not read the labels, you could see the complementary colors and forms shared between the works. Even though they were created in different media and the artists were from distinct backgrounds, you could see how both women portrayed similar mountain landscapes in New Mexico. As we all know, viewers don't often or always read labels. When a clever pairing of artworks can make the comparisons so clear and do this work of drawing visual connections, it's really impactful. Can you speak more about how we, as curators, can employ strategies to meet audiences where they are and allow artworks to speak for themselves?

AUSTEN BARRON BAILLY Karen and *On This Ground* co-curator Sarah Chasse paired a work by Kay WalkingStick (Cherokee Nation), *Hovenweep #331* (1987), with a painting by John Sloan, *Arroyo Santa Fe* (1919), and commissioned me to write a label about those two pictures in conversation with one another (fig. 3.5). I hesitated because I'm not a voice from the Native community. What I wrote was informed by trying to think about the landscape not as a Native person but from WalkingStick's Native and

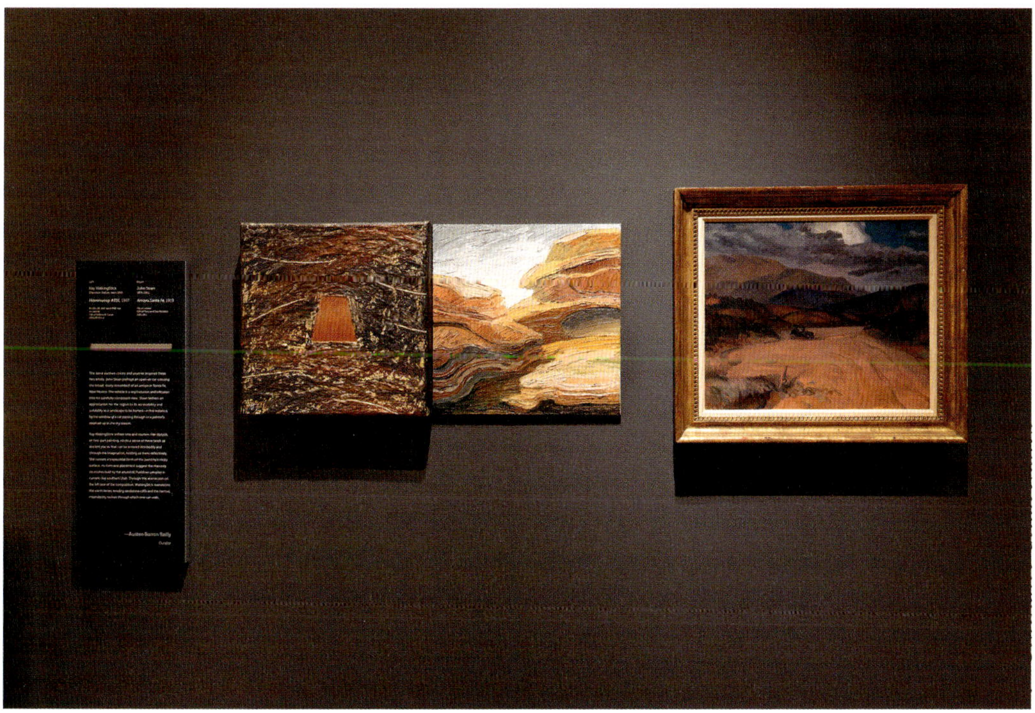

FIGURE 3.5 Installation view, *On This Ground*. (Left to right) Kay WalkingStick, *Hovenweep #331*, 1987; John Sloan, *Arroyo, Santa Fe*, 1919. Image by Kathy Tarantola. © Peabody Essex Museum.

artistic perspective. I considered what it meant to think about these landscapes as Native lands, which just ten years earlier would never have crossed my mind. I would have just written about John Sloan going out to the West and looking at a lovely landscape, but now I was trying to flip the script by asking, "What's actually going on here? How do I think about Sloan's work in relation to WalkingStick's as a Native artist painting the same kinds of places and the same kinds of lands, even though they appear so different from one another?" Karen took my work, edited it, and pushed it further, to get to the essence of what she thought that painting meant for the installation.

KAREN KRAMER I love that example, in part because I think it ties closely into the Hood's *This Land* exhibition, which had that amazing Truman Lowe (Ho-Chunk) feather sculpture paired with a painting by Canadian artist Lawren Harris (fig. 3.6). That pairing is seared into my mind and is, along with Austen's really wonderful example, a pairing that meets audiences where they are in terms of expectations of what American art is and what Native art can do to further expand these ideas. These examples show the promise of moving audiences to understand more deeply what Native art can be and what it can do. They move people away from an idea of Native art being "trapped in time," or Native art as anthropology or anthropological specimen, or as Native art as craft. That really shows through Kay WalkingStick's incredible painting prowess in her depiction of ancient Puebloan ruins in *Hovenweep #331*. She, like John Sloan, was thinking about land and place and a certain timelessness; she captured lightning in a bottle with that one particular painting, which depicts a thousands-year-old masonry structure in what is now called Hovenweep National Monument. WalkingStick's diptych that combines the metaphysical through visual abstraction with the representational, paired with Lonnie Vigil's micaceous pot nearby, just creates this spark, glimmer, and shine that connects the works through materiality, time, people, and space.

AUSTEN BARRON BAILLY I love that phrase—lightning in a bottle—because this pairing is not meant to strike out the John Sloan. WalkingStick's landscape, through the abstraction, through the materials, and through the

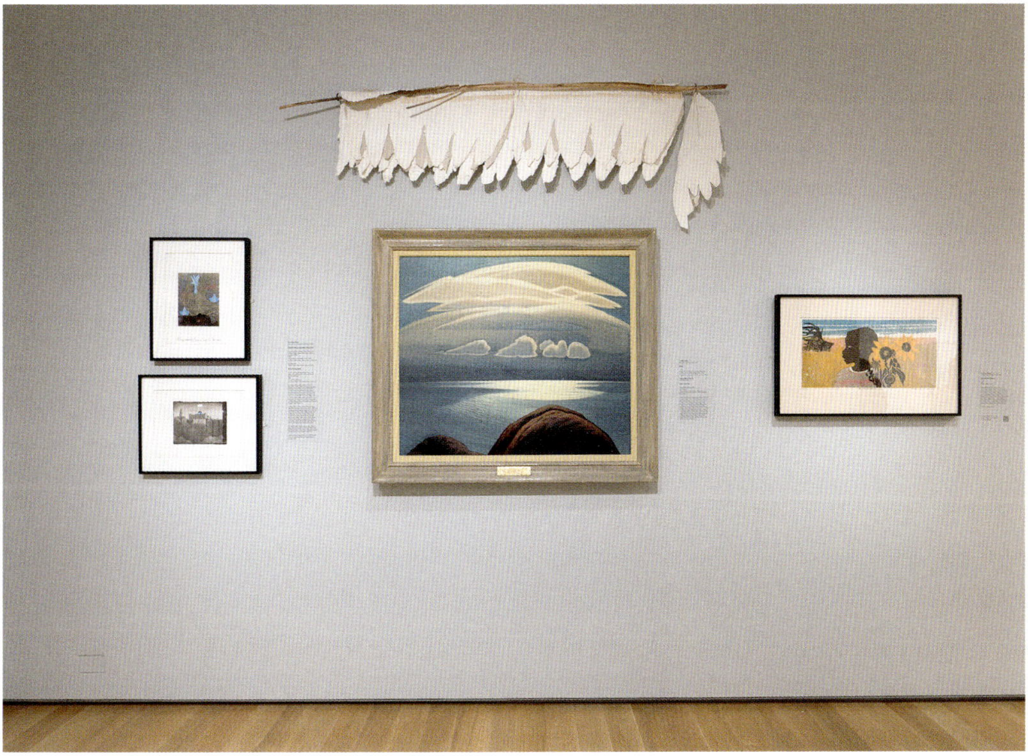

FIGURE 3.6 Installation view, "Power of Place," in *This Land: American Engagement with the Natural World*. (Left to right) Scherezade García, *Day Dreaming (Soñando despierta)*, 2010; Alex Guerrero, *Vista Psicotrópica*, 2010; Truman Lowe, *Wing*, 1965; Lawren Stewart Harris, *Lake Superior*, 1948–51; and Walter Williams, *Boy with Sunflowers*, 1965. Image by Rob Strong. © Hood Museum of Art, Dartmouth.

glimmer, brings a spark of life that is missing in Sloan's work. The Sloan is still a lovely picture of a moment and place in time. But the way that Karen and Sarah activated these objects together is much more illuminating than if you had just seen the Sloan isolated with Ashcan painters and other modernists who went to the Southwest in the 1920s, which is how those pictures are usually always seen, but not anymore.

MICHAEL W. HARTMAN Karen, you really highlight the importance of meeting audiences "where they are." Austen, could you also speak more about how "meeting audiences where they are" expands visitor experiences in the gallery?

AUSTEN BARRON BAILLY I think what *On This Ground* does, and what this trio of objects we just discussed foregrounds, is the importance of leading with great objects, great artists, great stories, and great quality. Meeting audiences where they are, to me, means prioritizing the visual engagement as the way to lead you deeper in. Seeing the outstanding objects that were selected for *On This Ground*, and then enhanced through these types of interpretations, is the great privilege and opportunity of any art museum. This object is what somebody made. And if it's really good, and you can reveal how and why—even if you have to hold it accountable to why it was revered in one moment and how it maybe has shifted in its significance but still holds aesthetic value—the object remains paramount.

KAREN KRAMER I love that—spoken like a chief curator! But I also wanted to say that for many of us, and certainly this is true for me, part of my curatorial practice is built on inviting and inciting change in the perception of Native art and culture. Meeting audiences where they're at, but then pushing them farther into a deeper and more nuanced understanding is what keeps me going. Putting that in conjunction with great art and artists is, as Austen said, one of the greatest privileges.

AUSTEN BARRON BAILLY What is so revealing to me when I reflect on the projects and evolution and things I've been drawn to in the field is that there is not always one primary way to tell a story or one single narrative. It's just not true. You have to be able to start stories and braid, looking at different perspectives and bringing them together.

KAREN KRAMER *On This Ground* is more about creating an additive experience than it is about adopting a revisionist approach. What I mean by that is we are not necessarily looking to reject dominant narratives about certain figures or moments in history in order to advance a particular agenda, be it political or social. But we do acknowledge that these traditional narratives are often one-sided. Instead, we add perspectives to these narratives that have often been excluded from art history, broader American history, and in a museum context. By asking the question "If the same stories are repeatedly told, whose stories are we missing?" we want to bring forward new ways of looking at the past. Being honest about America's past will help us all move toward a more empathetic future. We do this through artists, poets, scholars, and activists who demonstrate that multiple perspectives can coexist and that what we don't see in a work of art is sometimes just as important as what we do see. In this installation, we put the ongoing Wampanoag experience of colonization in direct dialogue with the Pilgrims. We look more closely at General George Washington's violent histories with the Catawba Nation and the Haudenosaunee during the American Revolution and subsequent directives as the first president and ask if we are ready to acknowledge new stories. *On This Ground* confronts the fear that some audiences have, or institutions have, that by telling different perspectives you're somehow revising history. I think that couldn't be further from the truth.

NOTES

1. This exhibition was on view at the Metropolitan Museum of Art from September 19, 2000, through January 7, 2001. For the catalog, see Catherine Hoover Voorsanger and John K. Howat, eds., *Art and the Empire City: New York, 1825–1861* (New Haven: Yale University Press, 2000).

2. Karen Kramer and Austen Barron Bailly, "Rebuilding a Framework: Native and American Art," Panel 1 of *Reenvisioning Histories of American Art*, Hood Museum of Art, Dartmouth College, April 7, 2022, https://www.youtube.com/watch?v=MkX6Ka7hyWc&t=2698s/.

3. This exhibition was on view at the Peabody Essex Museum from June 6 to September 7, 2015; the Nelson-Atkins Museum of Art from October 10, 2015, to January 3, 2016; the Amon Carter Museum of American Art from February 6 to May 1, 2016; and the Milwaukee Art Museum from June 9 to September 5, 2016. For the catalog, see Austen Barron Bailly, ed., *American Epics: Thomas Hart Benton and Hollywood* (Salem: Peabody Essex Museum, 2015).

4. This exhibition was on view at the Princeton University Art Museum from October 13, 2018, to January 6, 2019; the Peabody Essex Museum from February 2 to May 5, 2019; and Crystal Bridges Museum of American Art from May 25 to September 9, 2019. For the catalog, see Karl Kusserow and Alan C. Braddock, *Nature's Nation: American Art and Environment* (Princeton: Princeton University Art Museum, 2019).

PART II

REFRAMING COLLECTION PRACTICES AND CARE

4

Anya Montiel

REFLECTION AND REPRESENTATION

Native Art Acquisitions for the Fiftieth Anniversary of the Smithsonian's Renwick Gallery

"Art galleries must engage in a self-critical process
that recognizes the historical reasons for the underrepresentation,
misrepresentation, and exclusion of Aboriginal art."
Lee-Ann Martin (Mohawk), "Negotiating Space for Aboriginal Art"

More than twenty years ago, Mohawk curator and art historian Lee-Ann Martin offered an uncompromising proposition to art galleries and museums about the dearth of Indigenous art representation within their institutions. While she focused on the situation in Canada, the same statement could be extended to the United States today. If an art museum in North America excludes Native art from its galleries and collections, what narratives, then, are told to its publics; how is the museum fostering learning; and who is the museum truly serving? As a former curator at the Renwick Gallery in Washington, DC, and a curator of Native art, I will discuss how a half-century anniversary provided an opportunity for the Renwick to embark on a vigorous acquisition campaign, thereby adding more works by Native artists and other underrepresented groups into the permanent collection.

When the Renwick Gallery, a branch of the Smithsonian American Art

Museum known for contemporary American craft, approached its fiftieth anniversary in 2022, the curatorial team embraced the opportunity not merely to celebrate the gallery's history but also to envision its future while reflecting on the past and acknowledging the present. No one could ignore that this anniversary would be different. The exhibition planning occurred during the coronavirus pandemic as well as during nationwide protests calling for social justice and equity in the wake of the murders of Breonna Taylor, George Floyd, and Ahmaud Arbery. Likewise, the gallery is located steps from the White House in Washington, DC.

The resulting anniversary exhibition, *This Present Moment: Crafting a Better World*, curated by Dr. Mary Savig, the Renwick's Lloyd Herman Curator of Craft, highlighted "the role that artists play in our world to spark essential conversations, stories of resilience, and methods of activism . . . [and centered on] more expansive definitions and acknowledgments of often-overlooked histories and contributions of women, people of color, and other marginalized communities."[1] Before 2022, however, the Renwick wouldn't have been able to tell those stories. In 2019 the permanent collection numbered 2,196 works, and of those, two-thirds of the artists were men and over 90 percent were artists of European descent.[2] Native art consisted of only 12 works, or 0.5 percent of the collection. Those numbers fail to represent the history of American craft and artists working over the last fifty years. For the Renwick's fortieth anniversary, the exhibition *40 Under 40: Craft Futures* highlighted forty artists born since 1972 whose works blended "different attitudes, forms, styles, eras, materials, and methods of practice."[3] The selected artists demonstrated "the most engaging work of this generation . . . [and] highlight[ed] newly prevalent trends in the field."[4] *40 Under 40* was not a collections-based exhibition, but, strangely, not one of the selected artists was Native American.

Faced with Martin's request for accountability from museums and galleries, searching for a rationale for the absence of Native art and artists from an institution's curatorial and collecting priorities is necessary but can be challenging. In terms of the Renwick's collection and exhibition history, two conceivable reasons came from other Smithsonian curators. In 2002 art historian and former National Museum of the American Indian (NMAI) curator Jolene Rickard (Tuscarora) posited that "many see the formation of the National Museum of the American Indian as an opportunity for other art museums to shrug off their responsibility to include exhibitions focused on Indigenous art in their own spaces."[5] Rickard is referring to Public Law 101-85, which established the creation of the NMAI as part of the Smithsonian Institution in 1989. Previously, the NMAI was a private museum in New York called the Museum of the American Indian, with a vast collection totaling more than seven hundred thousand items from North, Central, and South America. The NMAI legislation authorized the operation of two museums, one in New York and the other in Washington, DC. Rickard wondered if other museums would view Native art as the purview of the NMAI only, instead of seeing its establishment as ushering in an era of Indigenous art renaissance.

Former NMAI curator Kathleen Ash-Milby (Diné) also investigated the state of Native art at other Smithsonian museums. She conducted interviews with two former Smithsonian curators and found that "one of the unintentional consequences of the creation of the NMAI was that staff working on Native art and culture projects at other Smithsonian museums witnessed the attrition of funding and postponement of exhibitions."[6] The establishment of the NMAI prevented or slowed other Smithsonian museums from collecting and exhibiting Native art. The NMAI, however, is not focused on art; it is a museum that features exhibitions about Native history, culture, and art. Ash-Milby also notes that the NMAI purchased few works of contemporary Native art in its early days.[7] In 2000, with the appointment of artist Truman Lowe (Ho-Chunk, 1944–2019) as the curator of contemporary art at the NMAI and then the hiring of curatorial research assistants, the museum featured more Native art exhibitions and acquired from those exhibitions.[8] Nevertheless, the other Smithsonian museums might have operated under the assumption (or the expectation) that the NMAI would handle anything related to Native art.

THE RENWICK HISTORY AND NATIVE ART

As mentioned previously, the Renwick collection included only twelve works of Native art at the inception of the planning for the fiftieth anniversary exhibition. Before explaining how the Renwick acquired those artworks, a brief history of the gallery is warranted. The Smithsonian opened the Renwick Gallery in 1972 as a showcase for "arts, crafts and design" under the supervision of the National Collection of Fine Arts (now known as the Smithsonian American Art Museum [SAAM]).[9] The gallery's namesake pays tribute to the building's original architect, James Renwick Jr. While known as the nation's museum for American craft, the Renwick takes an expansive definition of the term "craft." Instead of defining what is contemporary craft, its mission centers on "celebrating makers taking both innovative and time-honored approaches to their work."[10] The focus lies on the artists/makers and their techniques and materials. The current vision of the Renwick, however, marks a departure from its beginning.

When the Renwick opened to the public, the two-story building featured eight exhibitions. The themes of the inaugural exhibitions included furniture, glassworks, Pueblo pottery, European works from the collection of James Hazen Hyde, and four shows about American design and architecture. Since the Renwick was not established as a collecting institution, the exhibitions drew from other collections and artists. The Pueblo pottery exhibition, for example, highlighted Zuni and Acoma pottery from the collection of the National Museum of Natural History. The Renwick's first director, Lloyd Herman, organized and selected 116 exhibitions during his fifteen-year tenure.[11] Along with Pueblo pottery, the archives indicate that the Renwick featured the following Native art exhibitions: Northwest Coast boxes and bowls (1973), Kiowa and Kiowa-Apache painted tipis (1977), five generations of the Maria Martinez family (1978), Catawba pottery (1978), Native art from the Coe Foundation (1987), and Navajo weaving from the Denver Art Museum (1994).

In 1980 an act of Congress renamed the National Collection of Fine Arts to the National Museum of American Art, which held major implications for the Renwick. With a focus on American art, the Renwick, therefore, would highlight exhibitions of "American decorative arts and craft objects."[12] Collecting became part of the Renwick's mission the following year, with an emphasis on "post–World War II American crafts."[13] While the Renwick's exhibition history included international art, the collecting had been US-based. Herman also met with local craft collectors who then established the nonprofit organization the James Renwick Alliance in 1982 to advance the appreciation of American craft and to fund-raise for acquisitions.

While the Renwick wasn't officially a collecting museum until 1981, artworks had entered the collection previously. Of the twelve works of Native art, four entered the collection before 1972; two works date from the opening to 1980; and six were acquired since the shift toward becoming a collecting institution. In categorizing the twelve works according to medium, there are five pieces of pottery, four baskets, two pieces of jewelry, and one textile piece. If divided according to US regions, seven are from the Southwest, three from the Northeast, one from the Midwest, and one from the West Coast. Fortunately, all of the works have the names of the artists recorded, and all but two of the artists are women.

The four works that predate the Renwick Gallery are Pueblo pottery. They were under the purview of the National Collection (SAAM) until the establishment of the Renwick. In 1965 the National Collection purchased two ceramic bowls by Acoma Pueblo artists Lucy M. Lewis (ca. 1890–1992) and Marie Z. Chino (1907–1982). The next year the IBM Corporation gifted the museum two ceramic works by San Ildefonso artists Maria Poveka Montoya Martinez (ca. 1887–1980), Julian Martinez (1879–1943), and Santana Roybal Martinez (1909–2002). Pueblo pottery has been collected by museums and private collectors since the opening of the Santa Fe railroad in the late 1800s and then through the growth of tourism to the American Southwest. Moreover, the Smithsonian has been collecting Pueblo pottery since its early days. Folklorist Barbara A. Babcock explained that the Smithsonian's first collecting expedition in 1879 was for Pueblo pottery, and former Wheelwright Museum of the American Indian director Jonathan Batkin noted in 1987 that the Smithsonian had collected more than sixty-five hundred ceramics from both Acoma and Zuni pueblos.[14] The accession files do not indicate if the National Collection pursued acquisitions of Pueblo pottery or if there were ceramic specialists on staff.

In January 1972, during its opening month, the Renwick received another piece of Pueblo pottery. Lucy Kramer Cohen, a Native rights advocate and public health worker, brought a blackware bowl by Maria and Santana Martinez to the Renwick (hand delivered) for the permanent collection. She gifted it in honor of her late husband, Felix Cohen, the esteemed lawyer and legal scholar who authored *The Handbook of Federal Indian Law*. Kramer Cohen explained that her husband received the bowl as a gift from Maria's son Popovi Da. In the correspondence, she outlined her reason for the gift: "I know the Renwick has had many problems, financial and otherwise, but I am sure it is now at the beginning of a glorious career."[15] Most likely, Kramer Cohen was referring to the considerable costs associated with renovating the entire building from 1967 to 1972. The National Collection director, Joshua Taylor, responded to Kramer Cohen saying that the work "will be an important addition to the collection of American craft objects in the Renwick Gallery."[16] Despite not being a collecting museum, the museum staff gladly accepted gifts of artworks before 1981 and already focused its attention on American artists.

When Kenneth Trapp worked at the Renwick as its curator in charge from 1995 to 2003, four Native artworks came into the collection, two baskets and two pieces of jewelry. The works were not purchased directly from the artists but from small shops. In 1996 Trapp acquired a horsehair and abalone basket by Chumash artist Linda Aguilar from Pacific Western Traders in Folsom, California, one of the first Native art stores in Northern California. Then, while in Maine in 1998, Trapp bought an ash basket by Irene McDonald (Akwesasne Mohawk) from Maine Gathering, a store known for featuring the arts of Maine and the Northeast. Lastly, he acquired a silver and turquoise squash blossom necklace and earrings by Andy Cadman (Diné) from the Department of the Interior's Indian Craft Shop in Washington, DC, in 2002.

While Trapp paid for the Aguilar basket and Cadman jewelry through a museum account, he then found local donors to reimburse the Renwick and the works became gifts to the gallery. In the letter to the funders of the Aguilar work, Trapp noted that the basket "represents in part how I hope the permanent collection will develop" and continued that while Aguilar might not be as well known as "Dale Chihuly," he believed that the collection should "be as big as America is."[17] The letter reveals how Trapp envisioned the permanent collection to be expansive in terms of geography (California) and artists represented.[18] As for the McDonald basket, Trapp purchased it and then gifted it to the Renwick. Since he purchased the basket from a gallery and not the artist, Trapp wrote a letter to McDonald informing her that the basket was part of the permanent collection and was on view. He told her,

"[It] is a wonderful work of art that enhances the collection of American craft entrusted to the American people."[19] In both examples, Trapp used terminology demonstrating that he was building a national collection that highlighted artistic expressions across the country.[20]

ACQUISITION CAMPAIGN AND ACQUISITION PRIORITIES

The first dozen Native artworks in the Renwick collection consist of different mediums and represent various Native nations and regions of the United States, but after researching their provenance, it doesn't seem that Native art was part of the collecting plan. Moreover, the survey of the Renwick collection and its exhibition history revealed underrepresentation among many communities, not just Native people. There were few Black, Latine, and Asian American artists and artists with disabilities in the permanent collection. In the fiftieth anniversary catalog, Nora Atkinson, the Fleur and Charles Bresler Curator-in-Charge for the Renwick Gallery, remarked, "The Renwick's exhibition and collection program reflected (and often asserted) the primacy of the [craft] movement's dynamic male stars and the dominant narrative of its founding by artists coming of age under the GI Bill. Only four of twenty solo shows were devoted to women—and only one to a woman of color—in the museum's first decade."[21] The survey proved that an acquisition campaign was an essential component of the exhibition planning process.

In considering what to acquire for the fiftieth anniversary exhibition, the Renwick is in a unique position as being part of SAAM and the Smithsonian Institution. The Smithsonian has a policy of encouraging internal loans among Smithsonian units. Therefore, any future acquisition should not replicate artworks in other Smithsonian collections. Fortunately, the Smithsonian has an online collections database where Smithsonian collection holdings are listed to avoid duplications.[22] For example, the Renwick has 3 ceramics works by Maria Martinez, and the NMAI has 132 works by her. Since the NMAI has the most Native artworks made since 1972 among any Smithsonian unit, its collection was a point of reference.

The next priority would be acquiring works from living artists, which benefits the entire museum and its visitors. First, living artists can work with the curatorial, collections, conservation, and exhibit staff about the materials and techniques in their works while advising on how best to store, display, and care for them. Living artists also can assist the education and visitor services staff with interpretive strategies for their works. *Standards for Museums with Native American Collections* (published by the School for Advanced Research and the American Alliance of Museums) recommends that "the full breadth of Native materials considered for acquisitions includes contemporary work, reflecting the continuity of cultures."[23] Besides the benefits to staff, these artworks demonstrate to museum visitors that Native people are contemporary and not of the past. Even the first dozen Native artworks in the Renwick collection were acquired by living artists except one for one (Julian Martinez). Acquiring from living artists can create meaningful relationships and connections internally and externally.

Sometimes museums acquire collections of historic Native art, but there are ethical and legal considerations that museums may not understand. Those collections might not have clear provenance records, or perhaps the names of the artists were never recorded. When museums acquire historic Native collections, there is a responsibility to determine if those items have cultural sensitivities and restrictions or should be repatriated as per the Native American Graves Protection and Repatriation Act. More museums are understanding their responsibility toward ethical stewardship, defined as "a set of values and practices that promote historical reflection while directing museums to become agents of a more equitable and inclusive future. This entails building and nurturing respectful, open, and reciprocal relationships with descendant communities and other heritage stakeholders."[24] Museums need to understand the ethics around collecting practices and whether they have the institutional commitment and resources to engage in responsible stewardship.

Lastly, diversity was an acquisition priority. Especially for a national museum like the Renwick, geographic diversity is fundamental to conveying a variety of narratives and lived experiences. Some visitors erroneously believe that Native people live only in the American Southwest or on reservations. Acquisitions should include artists from different Native nations as well. While early Renwick acquisitions included pottery by Pueblo artists, other Native nations have ceramic artists and should be considered for acquisitions.

With these priorities and considerations in mind, acquiring artworks for the Renwick anniversary entailed using existing acquisition and endowment funds as well as submitting acquisition grant proposals and engaging in a vigorous gift campaign. The James Renwick Alliance (JRA), an independent nonprofit organization that assists with providing support to craft artists and museums, raised more than $157,000 for acquisitions from various donors. Their fund-raising efforts led to the acquisition of seven works, including the glass work *Safe Journey* (2021) by Preston Singletary (Tlingit).[25] In total, the fiftieth anniversary exhibition featured more than 130 new acquisitions, and the entire acquisition campaign brought 219 works into the collection.[26] Twenty-six works came through existing acquisition funds, and 7 arrived through endowment funds. Three artworks were purchased from grant funds, particularly the Smithsonian American Women's History Initiative Acquisitions Pool and the Smithsonian Latino Initiatives Pool. Gifts from collectors and supporters made up the majority of the acquisitions, including from collectors Judith Chernoff and Jeffrey Bernstein, who donated 43 pieces of sculptural wood art. The Renwick also instituted a fiftieth anniversary acquisitions committee that was cochaired by Myra J. Weiss, a member of SAAM's board of commissioners, and Carolyn Mazloomi, founder of the Women of Color Quilters Network, to advise when needed.[27]

NATIVE ART ACQUISITIONS

Out of the 219 new acquisitions, Native art represented 26 works, or nearly 12 percent.[28] While that percentage may seem small, it represents a start, not an ending, to increasing Native representation in the permanent collection. Since the opening of the anniversary exhibition in May 2022, more Native artworks have been gifted or promised to the Renwick. The 26 new acquisitions represent seventeen Native nations and the geographic regions of the Northeast, Southeast, Plains, Great Lakes, Southwest, West Coast, and Alaska. They include various mediums such as basketry, glass, ceramics, and textiles.

The Renwick acquired the first of those twenty-six artworks from the touring exhibition *Hearts of Our People: Native Women Artists*. Organized through the Minneapolis Institute of Art and curated by Jill Ahlberg Yohe and Teri Greeves (Kiowa), the exhibit demonstrated how women have long been the creative force behind Native art and featured more than 115 women artists. The exhibit opened at the Renwick in February 2020, and some of the exhibiting artists came to the gallery to speak about the exhibition and their artworks and to participate in press events. The curators and artists then led an exhibition tour for the museum staff and docents. The presence of the artists and the exhibition curators became an invaluable opportunity for the Renwick to become familiar with Native art.

The Renwick had not hosted an exhibit of Native art since the Navajo weaving exhibit in 1994 from the Denver Art Museum. Seeing the *Hearts of Our People* artworks in the Renwick's galleries and meeting the artists were integral to paving the way for acquisitions of Native art. Featuring more than one hundred artists in the exhibit, the staff saw a range of Native art and work in many mediums. SAAM director, Stephanie Stebich, expressed interest in acquiring available artworks from the exhibition. While much of the exhibition checklist came from museum collections, there were a few available works. The Renwick acquired *Sustaining Traditions—Digital Memory* by Kelly Church (Ottawa/Ojibwe/Potawatomi), who attended the opening (fig. 4.1).

Church is from an unbroken line of basket makers, and she and her family harvest and process the basketry materials for her work. *Sustaining Traditions—Digital Memories* is a basket that carries the past, present, and future teachings of this art. Woven with black ash and Michigan-sourced copper, the radiant green color alludes to the emerald ash borer, an invasive beetle that has decimated black ash trees in over twenty-three US states and two Canadian provinces.[29] When opened, the basket reveals a sealed glass vial with the carcass of the beetle along with a thumb drive containing directions on how to harvest and prepare black ash for weaving, in case those traditions are lost without access to healthy trees. As explained by Church and her daughter Cherish Parrish (Ottawa/Ojibwe/Potawatomi):

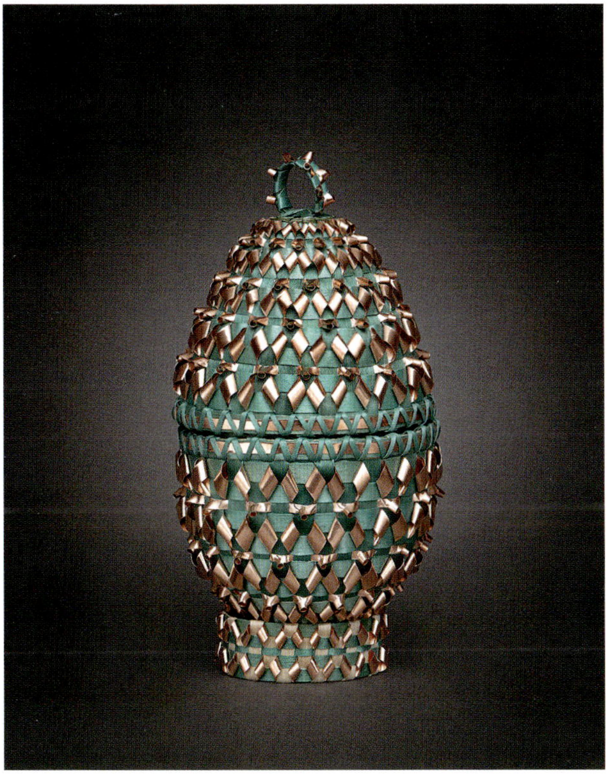

FIGURE 4.1 Kelly Church (Ottawa/Potawatomi, born 1967), *Sustaining Traditions-Digital Memories*, 2018. Black ash, sweetgrass, Rit dye, copper, vial EAB [emerald ash borer], flash drive, 9½ × 4½ in., Smithsonian American Art Museum, Museum purchase through the Decorative Arts and Crafts Endowment, 2020.49A-B. © Kelly Church.

> We must use not only the cultural teachings of our ancestors but also technology to help sustain our centuries-old basket-weaving methods. The world is fast forgetting how dependent we are on nature. No matter how little people think they use it, they are dependent on nature for their very lives.[30]

The Renwick has other baskets in its collection, including ones made of ash, and *Sustaining Traditions—Digital Memory* speaks directly to those older baskets while asking visitors to consider the health of our forests on future generations, especially basket makers. In the fiftieth exhibition catalog, Church echoes that sentiment, saying, "My weavings are records of moments in time. These records will serve as reminders of concerns we have today that need to be addressed for the benefit of future generations."[31] Her artwork demonstrates Indigenous knowledges of radiating responsibilities and relationships, expressed by Nishnaabeg scholar Leanne Betasamosake Simpson as "existence is ultimately dependent upon intimate relationships of reciprocity, humility, honesty, and respect with all elements of creation, including plants and animals."[32] Like the themes of the fiftieth anniversary exhibition, Church is calling for a "more relational and empathetic world.[33] The *Hearts of Our People* exhibition closed three weeks after opening due to the COVID-19 pandemic and never reopened. Nevertheless, it had a lasting impact on the Renwick, and the gallery went on to acquire artworks by two other artists, Shan Goshorn (Eastern Band Cherokee) and Carla Hemlock (Kahnawake Mohawk), in the exhibition.

When the secretary of the Smithsonian, Lonnie Bunch III, told a reporter in June 2020, "The job of a museum is not just to look back. It's to collect today for tomorrow," another area of urgency became documenting the current moment of the pandemic and calls for social justice.[34] One acquisition opportunity appeared when the *First American Art Magazine* organized the virtual art exhibition *Masked Heroes: Facial Coverings by Native Artists*, featuring 125 functional and artistic face masks by more than seventy artists. The magazine's editor, America Meredith (Cherokee Nation of Oklahoma), wanted to "celebrate the resilience of Indigenous peoples and help share the beauty that Native artists have created in the face of our shared crisis."[35]

Some of the featured artists offered their masks for sale, and the Renwick and the NMAI both hoped to acquire them from the exhibition. To avoid competing for the same masks, the two museums worked together. The curators consulted each other before acquiring, and the Renwick purchased three masks from the exhibition, including *Ononkwashon: a/Medicine Plants* by Marlana Thompson, a Mohawk bead artist and regalia maker from Akwesasne (fig. 4.2).[36] Beaded on black velveteen and lined with red flannel, the mask depicts strawberries, white pine, and cedar along with "C-19 [COVID-19], 2020" on the right side. The bottom row has three beaded skydomes, which represent prayers for her three children. She added a braid of sweetgrass on the bottom and inserted dried sage inside the lining. Thompson explained, "The pandemic will force many people to seek out our traditional teaching for gardening and harvesting foods and medicines. We should never forget

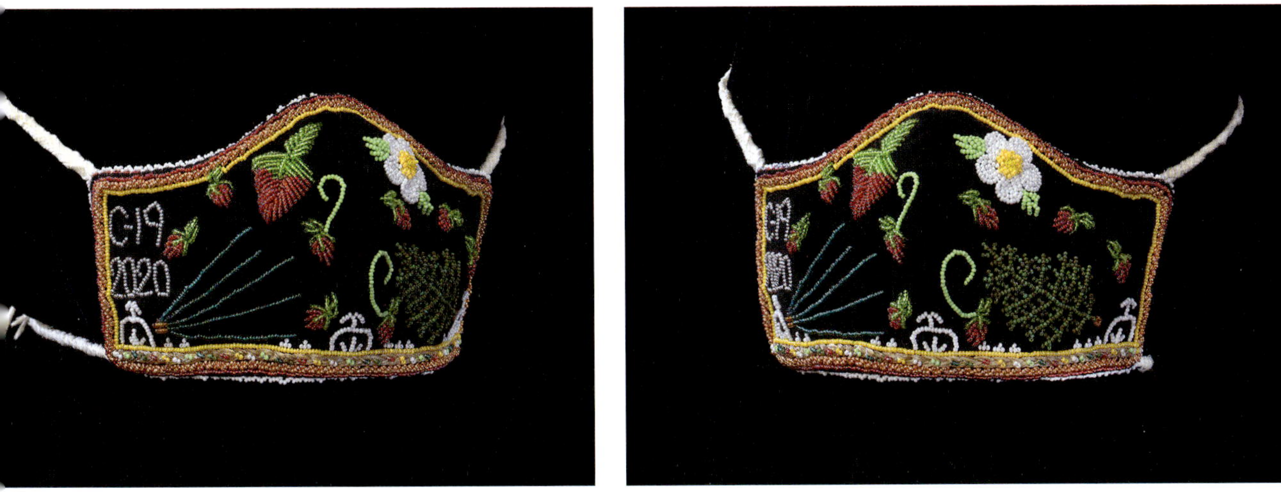

FIGURE 4.2 Marlana Thompson (Mohawk, born 1978), *Ononkwashon: a/Medicine Plants*, 2020. Black velveteen, red flannel, Czech seed beads, sweetgrass, sage, and leather, overall: 5 x 51¾ × 1⅞ in., Smithsonian American Art Museum: Museum purchase through the Kenneth R. Trapp Acquisition Fund; 2020.29.3. © Marlana Thompson.

what has happened."[37] Thompson's mask is another work that conveys Indigenous knowledges and relationships to the land. She incorporated images of and materials from medicinal plants, fruit, and trees that the Mohawk use for healing and health. Likewise, the mask is a testimony of her experiences as a mother during the pandemic. The Renwick acquired a total of eight masks, including works from Black and Asian American artists, and the NMAI acquired nine masks, including four from Indigenous Mexican and Canadian artists.

Since the Renwick is part of SAAM, I considered acquisitions that could be incorporated into the other museum location. For example, the SAAM building has a room dedicated to non-Native painters associated with the Taos Society of Artists, an organization of visual artists who depicted the landscape and people of northern New Mexico from 1915 to 1927. Often these artists exoticized and primitivized Pueblo people, which reflected the artists' prejudices. The oil painting *Summer in the Pueblo,* by Dorothy Brett (1883–1977), depicts four Pueblo women wearing shawls and long dresses, with three of them balancing water jars on their heads. The outline of their bodies mimics the shape of the nearby mesa. As scholar Barbara Babcock questions, "Why has a traditionally dressed woman shaping or carrying an olla, a water jar, become *the* metonymic misrepresentation of the Pueblo and why has Anglo-America invested so much in this image?"[38] Babcock then posits that these non-Native writers, artists, and art promoters "have been consistent in their refusal to see Pueblo women in their 'psychological, social, and colonial complexity.'"[39] The women have become silent, one-dimensional decorations for White audiences.

In response, I sought a work from a Pueblo artist that would communicate Indigenous perspectives and worldviews. The Renwick then acquired Virgil Ortiz's *Pueblo Revolt 2180*, a tall ceramic jar with four futuristic figures across its surface (fig. 4.3). Ortiz is from Cochiti Pueblo, an Indigenous (and matrilineal) nation in northern New Mexico. He is a storyteller whose artworks carry the history, lifeways, and continued resilience of Cochiti Pueblo people. Ortiz also builds futuristic worlds and characters, where knowledge of the past provides guidance for future generations. Ortiz's artwork fast-forwards to the year 2180, when Pueblo lands and people are under attack. That year is five hundred years after the Pueblo Revolt of 1680, a successful Indigenous revolution against Spanish religious and military persecution of Pueblo people in New Mexico. On one side of the jar, the female warrior Tahu, with her quiver and arrows on her back, leads the army. She is accompanied by figures such as Gliders, running messages across pueblos, and Translator, the army commander, communicating the events across time. Through this story, Ortiz promotes wider awareness of an underrecognized chapter in history while imagining a future of continued Indigenous resistance and resilience. Curator Karen Kramer commented that Ortiz's vision conveys the personal and universal at once with a fearlessness to address "five centuries of America's historical amnesia about Spanish contact, colonization, and genocide in the Southwest."[40] While artworks by both Brett and Ortiz depict Pueblo women, Ortiz's women lead their people and defend the land.

Along with the hope that an acquisition is displayed in different locations, there is a desire that an artwork will be incorporated into multiple exhibitions. One acquisition, a glass basket by Joe Feddersen, went from *This Present Moment* to another Renwick exhibition. Feddersen is a multidisciplinary

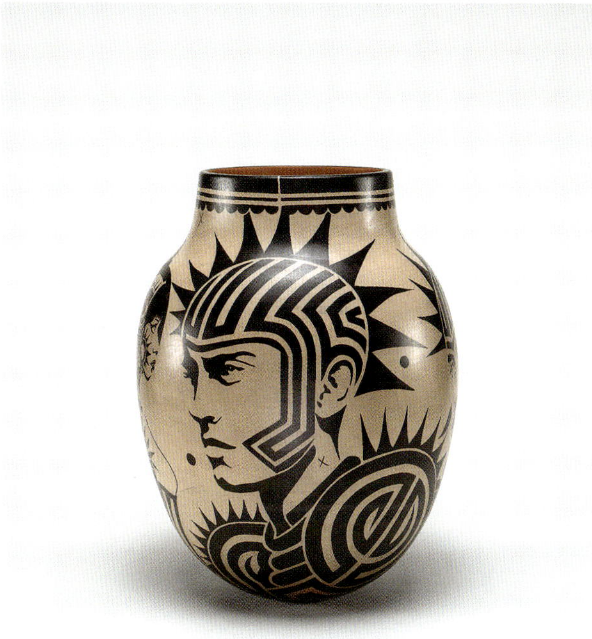

FIGURE 4.3 Virgil Ortiz (Cochiti, born 1969), *Pueblo Revolt 2180*, 2018–19. White bentonite clay with bee-weed (spinach) paint, 14⅝ × 12 in. Smithsonian American Art Museum: Museum purchase through the Kenneth R. Trapp Acquisition Fund; 2022.54. © Virgil Ortiz.

artist based in his homeland of Washington State who works in glass along with printmaking and basket making. He is Okanagan and Arrow Lakes, two tribes within the Confederated Tribes of the Colville Reservation. Feddersen is known for creating works in geometric patterns that reflect the environment and Indigenous Plateau basketry and glyphs. While he took a glass-casting course in graduate school, he did not reintroduce himself to the medium until twenty years later. At the time, he had been preparing for his 2003 solo exhibition at the NMAI in New York and considered presenting glass versions of the baskets he wove. Feddersen's friend, glass artist Cappy Thompson, introduced him to Preston Singletary, who assisted Feddersen in creating a suite of glass baskets, two of which are in the NMAI collection.[41] The Renwick acquired Feddersen's *Horses and Deer*, a 2020 glass "basket" featuring a lone deer surrounded by many horses (fig. 4.4). Feddersen explained that in parts of Washington State, wild horses have overgrazed the natural habitat, thereby threatening the livelihood of other species. The

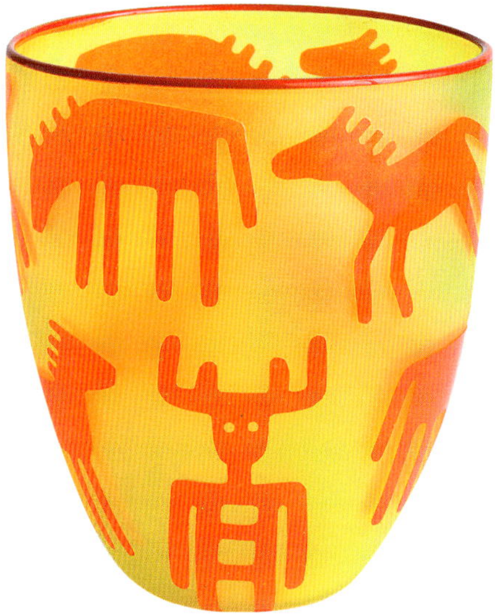

FIGURE 4.4 Joe Feddersen (Colville, born 1953), *Horses and Deer*, 2020. Glass, 13¼ in. × 11¾ in. × 10 in. Smithsonian American Art Museum: Museum purchase through the Kenneth R. Trapp Acquisition Fund; 2021.34. © Joe Feddersen.

basket's bright yellow background communicates additional urgency and alarm to the situation. According to Feddersen, his goal "is to create cultural assets for Plateau peoples, to contribute to *our* history. I want to do works that are of cultural significance and in the voice of my people."[42] Feddersen is communicating his worldview as a Colville tribal member and drawing attention to issues affecting his community.

After the fiftieth anniversary exhibition, Feddersen's *Horses and Deer* was added to the exhibition checklist for the 2023 Renwick Invitational. Since 2000 the Renwick has hosted an art invitational whereby jurors select four to six contemporary craft artists to showcase their works. The invitational is a popular exhibition that occurs every two to three years, and artists often create elaborate artworks that fill entire rooms.[43] A Native artist, however, had never been selected for the Renwick Invitational. When I brought that startling fact to the attention of the SAAM director, she proposed that the 2023 invitational include all Native artists. The jurors then selected Feddersen, along with artists Lily Hope (Tlingit), Ursala Hudson (Tlingit), Erica Lord (Athabascan/Iñupiat), Geo Neptune (Passamaquoddy), and Maggie Thompson (Fond du Lac Ojibwe) to participate.[44] Since *Hearts of Our People* closed to the public after three weeks, the 2023 Renwick Invitational enabled Native art to have a full run in the gallery. The effort hasn't gone unnoticed. In its review of the invitational, *Indian Gaming* magazine noted, "It is the latest example of the museum's commitment to highlighting contemporary Native American artists and Indigenous voices through acquisitions and exhibitions."[45]

CONCLUSION

Preparing for the Renwick's fiftieth anniversary provided an opportunity for the gallery to reflect on its past, rebuild the collection in the present moment, and envision its future through artworks that showcase "a multiplicity of perspectives and experiences."[46] Undergoing a major acquisition campaign required time, staff support and labor, financial resources, and trust among the team in the project's vision and staff expertise. The collections survey revealed significant gaps in terms of gender and artists of color, and although the acquisition campaign couldn't remedy every gap, the new acquisitions strengthened the content in the anniversary exhibition (and catalog). Also, the campaign created a ripple effect, with more acquisitions arriving, including a gift of Native jewelry.[47] The works by Native artists spoke directly to the existing collection, both at Renwick and SAAM, while providing new voices and narratives, drawn from Indigenous ways of knowing and relationships to the land.

NOTES

Epigraph: Lee-Ann Martin, "Negotiating Space for Aboriginal Art," in *On Aboriginal Representation in the Gallery*, edited by Lynda Jessup and Shannon Bagg (Ottawa: University of Ottawa Press, 2002), 244.

1. Mary Savig, *This Present Moment: Crafting a Better World*, Renwick Gallery of the Smithsonian Art Museum, website, 2022, https://americanart.si.edu/exhibitions/this-present-moment/, accessed March 23, 2023.

2. A collection inventory of the Renwick permanent collection was completed in spring 2019.

3. Nicholas Bell, "Craft Futures: A Generation at Hand," in *40 Under 40: Craft Futures* (New Haven: Yale University Press, 2012), 19.

4. Bell, "Craft Futures," 14.

5. Jolene Rickard, "After Essay—Indigenous Is the Local," in *On Aboriginal Representation in the Gallery*, edited by Lynda Jessup and Shannon Bagg (Ottawa: University of Ottawa Press, 2002), 118.

6. Kathleen Ash-Milby and Ruth B. Phillips, "Inclusivity or Sovereignty? Native American Arts in the Gallery and the Museum since 1992," *Art Journal* 76, no. 2 (2017): 18. An informal conversation with a former curatorial staff member from the National Museum of Natural History echoed Ash-Milby's findings.

7. Ash-Milby and Phillips, "Inclusivity or Sovereignty?" 18.

8. I was one of the curatorial research assistants for contemporary art under Truman Lowe. We, along with Rebecca Head Trautmann, worked on the *Continuum: 12 Artists* exhibition (2003–2005) for the New York museum and the *Native Modernism: The Art of George Morrison and Allan Houser* exhibition (2004–2005) for Washington, DC.

9. Kenneth R. Trapp, "Dedicated to Art: Twenty-Five Years at the Renwick Gallery," in *Skilled Work: American Craft in the Renwick Gallery* (Washington, DC: Smithsonian Institution Press, 1998), 15.

10. Renwick Gallery of the Smithsonian American Art Museum website, https://www.si.edu/museums/renwick-gallery/, accessed July 7, 2023.

11. Trapp, "Dedicated to Art," 18.

12. Charles J. Robertson, *American Louvre: A History of the Renwick Gallery Building* (Washington, DC: Smithsonian American Art Museum, 2015), 95.

13. Robertson, *American Louvre,* 95.

14. Barbara A. Babcock, "Mudwomen and Whitemen: A Meditation on Pueblo Potteries and the Politics of Representation," in *The Material Culture of Gender, The Gender of Material Culture* (Hanover, NH: University Press of New England, 1997), 260; and Jonathan Batkin, introduction to *Pottery of the Pueblos of New Mexico, 1700–1940* (Colorado Springs: Taylor Museum of the Colorado Springs Fine Arts Center, 1987), 30.

15. Lucy Kramer Cohen, letter (January 8, 1972), Renwick Gallery accession files, 1973.118.

16. Joshua C. Taylor, letter (January 10, 1972), Renwick Gallery accession files, 1973.118.

17. Kenneth Trapp, letter (March 28, 1997), Renwick Gallery accession files, 1996.83a-b.

18. Trapp acquired the Aguilar basket to be exhibited in the Renwick's twenty-fifth anniversary show, *The Renwick Gallery at Twenty-Five.*

19. Kenneth Trapp, letter (December 13, 1999), Renwick Gallery accession files, 1998.83a-b.

20. The twelfth artwork is a textile, *Edson's Flag* (2004), by Marie Watt (Seneca) from the collection of Driek and Michael Zirinsky. They gifted seven works, including the one by Watt to the Renwick in 2015.

21. Nora Atkinson, "A Foundation for the Future," in *This Present Moment: Crafting a Better World* (Washington, DC: Renwick Gallery of the Smithsonian Art Museum, 2022), 36.

22. The Smithsonian's Collections Search Center (https://collections.si.edu/search/) includes museum objects, archives, and library holdings.

23. "Standards for Museums with Native American Collections: A Guide to All Aspects of Work within Museums Holding Native Collections" (Santa Fe: School for Advanced Research, May 2023), 13.

24. "Ethical Stewardship," Peabody Museum of Archaeology and Ethnology, Harvard University, https://peabody.harvard.edu/ethical-stewardship/, accessed March 23, 2023.

25. "The JRACraft 50th Anniversary Acquisitions Fund Supports the Renwick Gallery of the Smithsonian Museum of American Art," *JRACraft News,* https://www.jra.org/jracraftnews/50th-renwick-anniversary-campaign/.

26. By June 2024, the Renwick had acquired more than three hundred new artworks for the permanent collection. The total is around 309 to 314 currently—not far from the number a year ago.

27. "Renwick Gallery 50th Anniversary Acquisition Campaign," Smithsonian American Art Museum, https://americanart.si.edu/art/new/renwick-50/, accessed March 23, 2023.

28. The new acquisitions also include roughly thirty works by Black artists, fifteen by Asian American and Pacific Islander artists, and twelve by Latine/x artists. There are artists who are mixed race and represent many communities.

29. It is believed that the emerald ash borer arrived in North America from overseas shipping crates in the 1980s.

30. Cherish Parrish and Kelly Church, "Sustaining Traditions," in *Hearts of Our People: Native Women Artists*, edited by Jill Ahlberg Yohe and Teri Greeves (Minneapolis: Minneapolis Institute of Arts, 2019), 304.

31. Kelly Church, "Artists Reflect: Kelly Church," *This Present Moment: Crafting a Better World* (Washington, DC: Renwick Gallery of the Smithsonian Art Museum, 2022), 108.

32. Leanne Betasamosake Simpson, *As We Have Always Done: Indigenous Freedom through Radical Resistance* (Minneapolis: University of Minnesota, 2017), 154.

33. Mary Savig, "This Present Moment," in *This Present Moment: Crafting a Better World* (Washington, DC: Renwick Gallery of the Smithsonian Art Museum, 2022), 43.

34. "Race in America: The Legacy of Juneteenth with Lonnie Bunch III," *Washington Post Live* (June 22, 2020), https://www.washingtonpost.com/washington-post-live/2020/06/22/transcript-race-america-legacy-juneteenth-with-lonnie-bunch-iii/.

35. "Masked Heroes: Facial Coverings by Native Artists," *First American Art*, April 26, 2020, https://firstamericanartmagazine.com/masks/.

36. The NMAI acquired five masks from the *Masked Heroes* exhibition.

37. Marlana Thompson, email correspondence with author, May 1, 2020.

38. Barbara A. Babcock, "Mudwomen and Whitemen: A Meditation on Pueblo Potteries and the Politics of Representation," in *The Material Culture of Gender*, edited by Katharine Martinez and Kenneth L. Ames (Winterthur, DE: Henry Francis du Pont Winterthur Museum, 1997), 261.

39. Babcock, "Mudwomen and Whitemen," 269.

40. Karen Kramer, "Foreword: Style reVOlution," in Charles S. King, *Virgil Ortiz: ReVOlution* (Albuquerque: University of New Mexico Press, 2021), 8.

41. Almah Lavon Rice, "Glass Is the Memory of Light: A Conversation with Raven Skyriver and Joe Feddersen," *El Palacio* (Fall 2021), https://www.elpalacio.org/2021/08/glass-is-the-memory-of-light/. The Renwick also acquired works by Singletary during the campaign.

42. Anya Montiel, "Joe Feddersen: Seeing the World Anew," in *Sharing Honors and Burdens: Renwick Invitational 2023* (Washington, DC: Smithsonian American Art Museum, 2023), 27.

43. Including the 2023 Renwick Invitational, there have been ten invitationals.

44. I selected Miranda Belarde-Lewis (Zuni/Tlingit) and Lara Evans (Cherokee Nation) to be jurors along with me for the invitational.

45. "New Native American Art Exhibition at the Renwick Gallery of Smithsonian," *Indian Gaming* (May 10, 2023), https://www.indiangaming.com/new-native-american-art-exhibition-at-renwick-gallery-of-smithsonian/.

46. "Smithsonian American Art Museum Acquires More Than 200 Artworks for Its Craft Collection," *East City Art* (May 17, 2022), https://www.eastcityart.com/art-news/smithsonian-american-art-museum-acquires-more-than-200-artworks-for-its-craft-collection/.

47. After the end of the anniversary campaign, the children of Native art collector Edie Fischer (1931–2021) contacted the Renwick about gifting their mother's jewelry collection. Fischer lived in Santa Fe and had purchased jewelry by Native artists over the years.

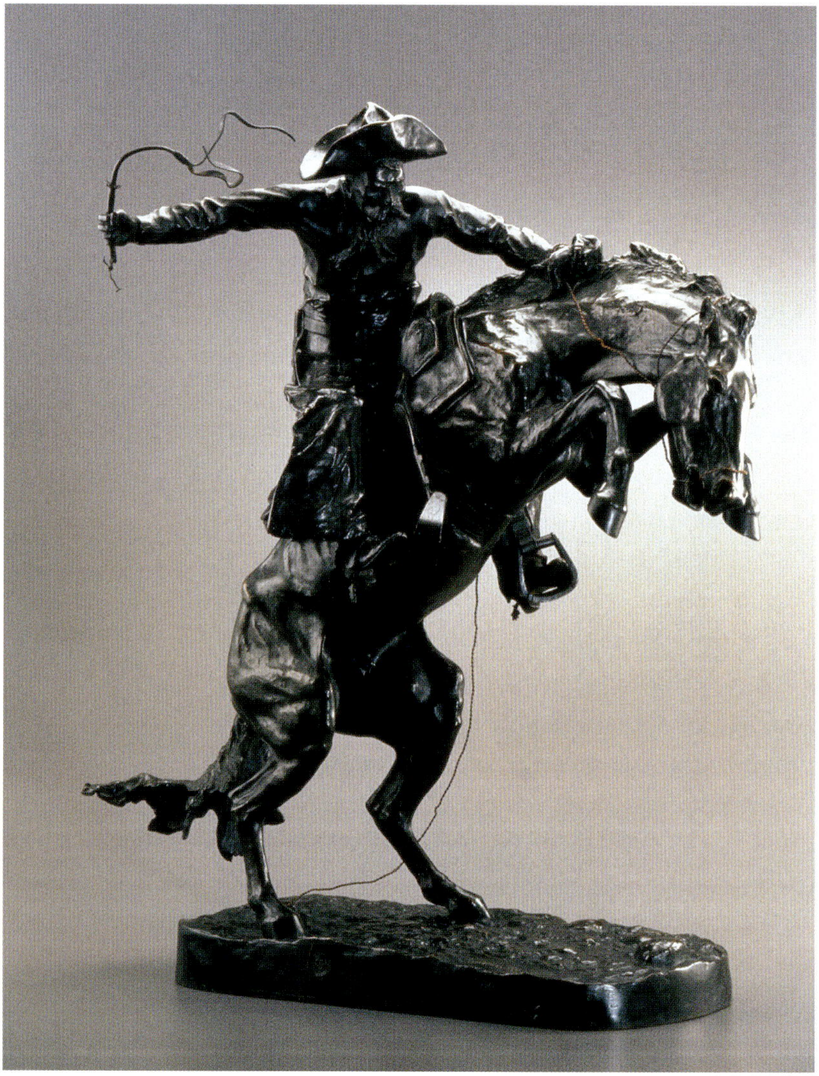

FIGURE 5.1 Frederic Remington (American, 1861–1909), *The Broncho Buster*, modeled 1895, cast ca. 1903. Bronze, 23⅜ × 19⅞ × 12¼ in. White House Collection, Gift of Miss Virginia Hatfield and Mrs. Louise Hatfield Stickney in memory of James T. Hatfield, 1973. © White House Collection/White House Historical Association.

5

Mindy N. Besaw

RECONTEXTUALIZING AND RECKONING HISTORIC AMERICAN ART

Frederic Remington's *The Broncho Buster* was an instant success in 1895. At the turn of the twentieth century, it was a national sensation and hundreds of copies were sold through Tiffany & Company. *The Broncho Buster* remains popular today and countless thousands of reproductions decorate living rooms and office buildings across the country (including the White House Oval Office) (fig. 5.1).[1] Despite its popularity and technical mastery, which pushed the boundaries of bronze casting to defy gravity, Remington's artworks, and other western subjects, fight for a place in the American art canon. Curators self-consciously grasp inclusion. When *The West in Bronze* was presented at the Metropolitan Museum of Art in 2013, Thomas Brent Smith declared, "This is a moment that shows Western American art's place within the larger canon."[2] But who are the arbiters of taste, and why does inclusion in the canon remain such a powerful benchmark even while museums across the country are working hard to undermine the canon and instead turn attention to underrecognized artists?

Remington is hardly an artist suffering from a lack of recognition, but critical and curatorial arguments about relevance point to a contemporary conundrum in museums and academia today. What do we do with artists like Frederic Remington and other White male historic American artists who can seem misaligned with efforts to diversify collections, focus on inclusion, and tell new stories? Remington held strong negative opinions about the influx of immigrants to the United States and was generally denigrating to women, yet his artwork holds a power separate from the artist's values. What is the role of scholars in addressing both? How do we find relevance for Remington, and his artwork, today?

Certainly, one approach is to dismiss or downplay the artwork and the artist as out of fashion. In 2020 *Boston Globe* critic Murray Whyte criticized museums for denying, or even deaccessioning, artwork that is seemingly irrelevant. "Museums make a record of taste as much as culture," he wrote; "their collections reflect the constant evolution of social priorities [from] one generation to the next. Excavating those things over time can be painful, deeply unflattering work, but that's the point: Moving forward without looking back invokes a willful blindness of convenience. As a society, we're not one thing, then another. We are the sum of it all."[3] Unfortunately, in the same article, Whyte rejected Remington as "amateurish and phony," "mediocre," an "embarrassment" and a "huckster." This dismissal allows Remington to remain underexamined, dismissing the artist's ongoing influence on American culture. Regardless, Whyte's insistence in looking back to face the present has merit.

What is the best approach? How can we meaningfully reexamine and recontextualize American art? The Metropolitan Museum of Art's American wing answered the call through interpretive "Native Perspectives" labels, published and presented online and in the galleries for the past five years. In the label for Remington's *The Broncho Buster*, Margaret Jacobs (Akwesasne Mohawk) writes, "The pieces seem to be everywhere, representing the epitome of what many believed a copy to be . . . —the last frontiersman and the master of a nation born out of wilderness, subsisting on an unsettled, magical land."[4] Jacobs directly counters period receptions of Remington's works, such as in an 1888 *Century Magazine* article where Remington and his collaborator, Theodore Roosevelt, defined the [White] cowboy as the *real* American. The cowboy is "the hero of rope and revolver," wrote Roosevelt, "as hardy and self-reliant as any men who ever breathed."[5] Beyond challenging these ideas of the West, Jacobs poignantly continues, "I do still wonder . . . why this artist, who lived so close to the Akwesasne Mohawk Reservation in upstate New York, traveled so far west to find his Native subjects? Maybe too many 'Indians' and not enough 'Cowboys' would have crushed his mythos of the American West."[6] Jacobs's label jabs at one of the problems with Remington's (and Roosevelt's) vision of the cowboy taming the Wild West—the West was not wild in 1895. Western lands had been settled thousands of years earlier by Indigenous peoples. As Jacobs astutely points out, Remington did not have to travel far from home in New York to meet Native peoples. Remington did, however, need to travel to find his *imagined* West of wilderness—one that he then transmitted to audiences around the country through his illustrations, effectively perpetuating an attractive and adventurous story of the wild and untouched West that continues to inspire and alure today.

Community voices and alternate interpretations offer useful insights into familiar objects, but to fully recontextualize historic American art, many tactics and approaches need to be made simultaneously. In the fall of 2024, Crystal Bridges presented the exhibition *Knowing the West*, the first major traveling exhibition to focus on the coexistence of art created in the nineteenth and early twentieth century by Native American and non–Native American artists. *Knowing the West* expands understanding of the nation's diversity by embracing and examining the American West as inclusive, complex, and reflective of diverse peoples who contributed to art and life in and about the West. The checklist includes textiles, baskets, paintings, pottery, sculpture, beadwork, saddles, and prints to flatten hierarchies that prioritize painting and sculpture in American art. To attempt a rebalance of a narrative dominated by European American artists like Frederic Remington, about two-thirds of the exhibition checklist comprises Native American artworks representing artists from thirty-five distinct tribes. Importantly, the exhibition development was collaborative and interdisciplinary. I am co-curating the exhibition with Jami C. Powell (Osage Nation), and the exhibition parameters, themes, and checklist are greatly informed by a curatorial advisory council of seven members.[7] While *Knowing the West* focuses on a specific region of the country, the exhibition offers a case study for ways to reconsider, rethink, and display American art.

LEARNING AND UNLEARNING

Knowing the West is the result of twenty years of my research and presentation of American art, and especially art of the West. It is informed by learnings and *un*learnings that have prompted observations, questions, and reflections that are worth sharing to both encourage others and to hold myself accountable. The role of a curator is changing. A specialty and focus in a particular area of art history is no longer enough. We must recognize expertise that comes through different ways of knowing. We must share space and platforms. We must sometimes step back and be a facilitator and an advocate not for ourselves but for others. We must seek out vulnerability and learn from it. This can lead to a new way of seeing American art.

I am trained as, and practice as, an Americanist. For years, I was immersed in art of the West and lived in Denver, Colorado, and then Cody, Wyoming. The exhibition *Frederic Remington: The Color of Night* traveled to the Denver Art Museum in 2003, where I absorbed the mystery and brooding of Remington's remarkable nocturn paintings completed in the last years of his life.[8] Later, in my position as curator of art at the Buffalo Bill Center of the West in Cody, I spent time with Remington's personal collection, which includes hundreds of objects the artist collected in the West and brought back to New Rochelle, New York, to create a "western environment" in his studio (fig. 5.2). The collection had been acquired by the Buffalo Bill Center of the West in the 1950s.

When the Remington Studio Collection debuted in Cody in 1959, Harold McCracken, the director of the Whitney Gallery of Western Art, described it as "representative paraphernalia, typical articles of dress and various memorabilia associated with frontiersmen and the Indians whom he portrayed." Some objects, according to McCracken, were "exceptionally fine examples of Indian costumes [and] cowboy gear."[9] Ironically, when the studio collection was moved from Remington's home town of Ogdensburg, New York, to Cody, Wyoming, McCracken called it "a most fortuitous circumstance" that the studio collection should come "back to the West," as if in homecoming.[10] This is an unusual claim considering the objects were acquired from Remington's home in New York, where they had been for more than fifty

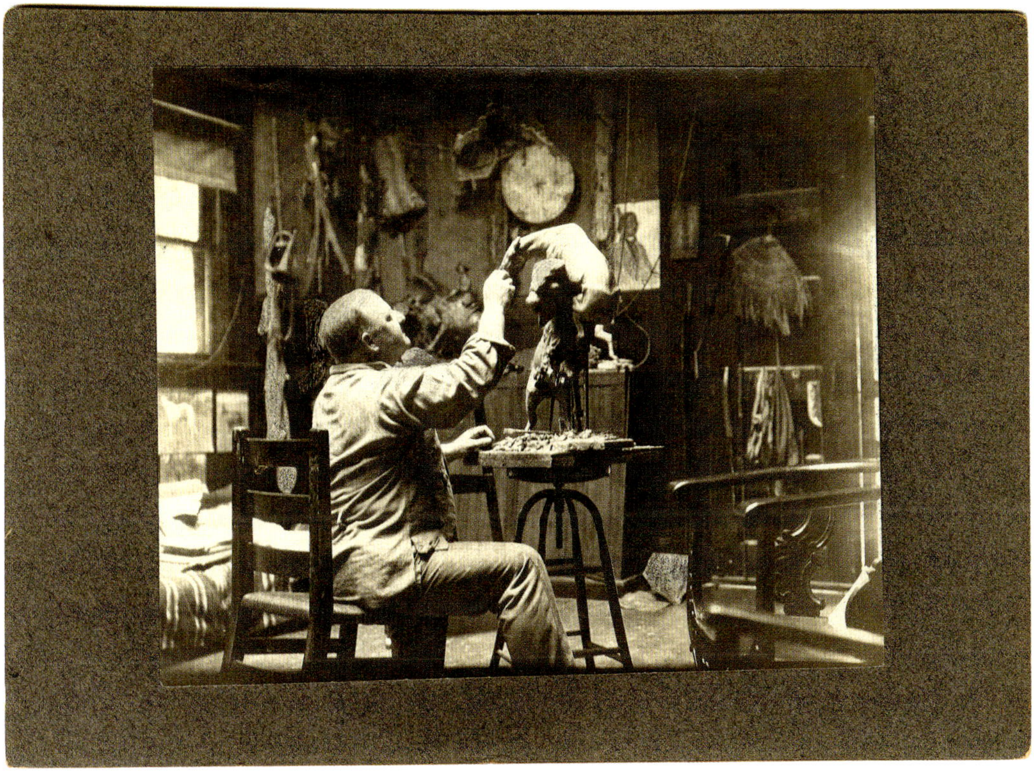

FIGURE 5.2 Frederic Remington (American, 1861–1909), sculpting *The Buffalo Horse*, 1907. Note the installation in the background of a bugle, shield, saddle, bow and arrow, and quiver. Image courtesy of the Frederic Remington Art Museum, Ogdensburg, New York. © Frederic Remington Art Museum.

years. Yet this "homecoming" makes more sense when considering the artworks and regalia made by Lakota, Cheyenne, Crow, Nez Perce, Blackfeet, and artists from additional Native nations across the US West (fig. 5.3). In that context, the objects did come home to the region where they were made and where their communities live today. The pamphlet published at the collection's debut presents a short essay about Remington, a chronology of his life, and numerous photographs of Remington. It does not, however, illustrate or describe a single object in the studio collection by any other artist, including Indigenous artists. The default narrative establishes a hierarchy that gives agency and authority to Remington as the artist/collector but erases the stories of the artists who made the objects he collected and valued.

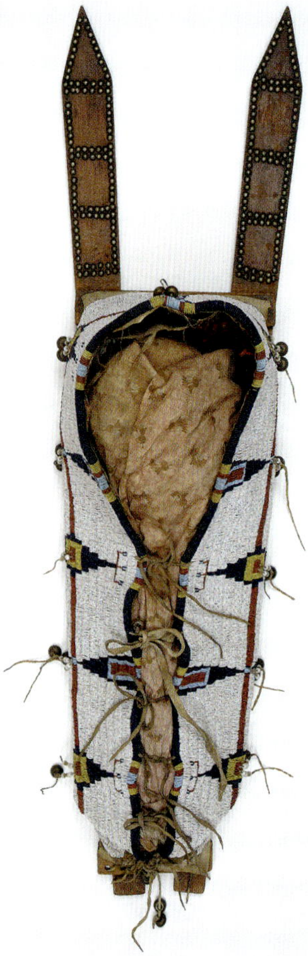

FIGURE 5.3 Cradleboard made by a once-known Cheyenne artist, ca. 1890. Muslin, wood, trade cloth, brass tacks, brass bells, beads, buckskin, 26 in. × 10½ × 6 in. Buffalo Bill Center of the West, Cody, Remington Studio Collection, Gift of the Coe Foundation, 1.67.400.

We must *un*learn the art historical training that defaults to and prioritizes dominant narratives rooted in colonialist ideologies and White supremacy. Imagine the rich stories that could be told of entanglement and encounters when Remington acquired the objects from the very people who lived the life he imagined and painstakingly recreated in his New York studio. Imagine the possibilities of discussing the objects fully within the context of the people and communities that created them and in letting the people from the community guide and control their narrative. In shifting the lens to value individual works made by Native American artists from the studio collection, Remington is decentered but also belongs to a more complex, and arguably more interesting, history. Exhibiting *The Broncho Buster* in dialogue with Native American artworks and cowboy gear reasserts and reintroduces the peoples whom Remington met on his travels.

UNLEARNING AND LEARNING THROUGH COLLABORATION

Collaborative exhibition development, inviting stakeholders into content creation, and listening to feedback on projects inspires a recontextualization of historic art. In 2016, when Crystal Bridges began planning for the reinstallation and reinterpreted the early American art galleries, we identified and spoke with stakeholder groups to inform the new presentation.

These stakeholders were regional community members with diverse social and cultural backgrounds and varying degrees of experience and familiarity with Crystal Bridges—from devoted museum members to the Marshallese residents who rarely visited the museum.[11] By this time, Crystal Bridges had been open for more than five years and had started to build a respectable reputation as a nationally focused American art museum. Despite our location in Bentonville, Arkansas, an important and defining characteristic of our museum, we denied our local place and presented canonical American paintings, sculpture, and works on paper from the colonial era to the present, largely from the northeastern United States.[12] The conversations with stakeholder groups encouraged and demanded new ways of presenting the collection to express relevance of the artworks. Stakeholders were ready for a broader definition of American art that presented complicated and textured stories, and they wanted to see themselves in the galleries. Through their encouragement, the reinstallation stepped out of a canonical comfort zone to make room for new ways of seeing, challenging the strictly chronological and art historical presentation of American art. Loans of Spanish Colonial paintings, folk art, Native American art, and decorative arts filled gaps in the collection. The new interpretation took a sociopolitical approach and focused on stories and contexts that offered complexity that previously had been simplified. Native American art was presented throughout the galleries "in conversation" with American art. In hindsight, however, while this was a good first step for Crystal Bridges, the "intervention model" of *inserting*, *including*, and *integrating* additional collections into the story of American art, rather than letting Native American and other underrepresented cultures *lead and guide* the narrative, still centers on a colonial approach.

In 2018, the same year the reinstalled galleries opened, Crystal Bridges presented the exhibition *Art for a New Understanding: Native Voices, 1950s to the Present*, highlighting Indigenous artists from what is now known as Canada and the United States whose paintings, sculpture, textiles, photographs, videos, and performances tell stories that are both intensely personal and broadly relevant. *Art for a New Understanding* argued that Indigenous artists reshape our understanding of contemporary art broadly. The focus on Native American art allowed for engagement with artists as well as Indigenous peoples in the region. As a co-curator on the project, with Candice Hopkins and Manuela Well-Off-Man, who were more knowledgeable about the subject, I acted as the primary contact for the museum's team as well as Crystal Bridges audiences and community. Working on this project deeply influenced my curatorial practice. Yes, I learned a lot about the artists in the exhibition, but I learned even more during the exhibition's development, especially through missteps and redirection. With the help of honest feedback from regional Native American people, I came to understand that local perspectives are essential, even with Indigenous members on the curatorial team; that Crystal Bridges needs to actively acknowledge its history and ongoing presence as a colonial institution occupying Native land; and that Native American community members need to be involved early in the process.

Kent Monkman's grand landscape painting *History Is Painted by the Victors* (2013) epitomizes my *un*learning based on the exhibition (fig. 5.4). The Americanist in me took great delight in Monkman's meticulously painted appropriation of Albert Bierstadt's *Mount Corcoran* (1876–1877, National Gallery of Art) as the setting for the scene populated with figures. Monkman based the nude figures swimming at the edge of the lake and lounging around the foreground on Thomas Eakins's photographic studies of himself and his students from the 1880s. Monkman's alter ego, Miss Chief Eagle Testickle, stands at the easel in the center of the canvas with her back to the viewers. Nude except for thigh-high pink platform boots, she glances over her right shoulder to meet the viewer's gaze with her paintbrush poised above the canvas. Monkman masterfully turned the tables on American art. The subject of Miss Chief's canvas is George Armstrong Custer and the Seventh Cavalry, who were defeated by Cheyenne and Lakota peoples at the Battle of Greasy Grass (otherwise known as the Battle of Little Big Horn) in 1876. The "history" is a relaxing and enjoyable moment days or hours before the soldiers' demise, while they commune with nature, uninhibited by clothing and the corruption of civilization. As the "victor" of the battle, Miss Chief literally creates the narrative that will soon unfold as the viewer watches, rendering her canvas in a style typical of Plains Indian hide painting. Monkman's clever use of American art draws attention to the assumptions and liberties taken by European dominant culture (and those of Americanists like me) through humor. Despite Custer's military loss, history books (and paintings) heroize him, and Monkman playfully draws our attention to these conflicting narratives. Seeing and acknowledging these assumptions can lead to correction and redirection.

Collaboration and partnerships across collections, and even museums, is another tactic to see American art anew. In 2020 Crystal Bridges organized a focused exhibition in collaboration with the Museum of Native American History (MONAH) in Bentonville called *Companion Species*, which I co-curated with Ashley Holland (Cherokee Nation). The small show included art by Native and non-Native artists and was comprised primarily of artwork from our two museums. It was inspired by Marie Watt's artwork in the Crystal Bridges collection by the same title, *Companion Species (Speech Bubble)* (fig. 5.5). The large-scale textile in the shape of a speech bubble, or megaphone, was made with the help of community members in Northwest Arkansas; Eastern Oklahoma; and Honolulu, Hawaii, in

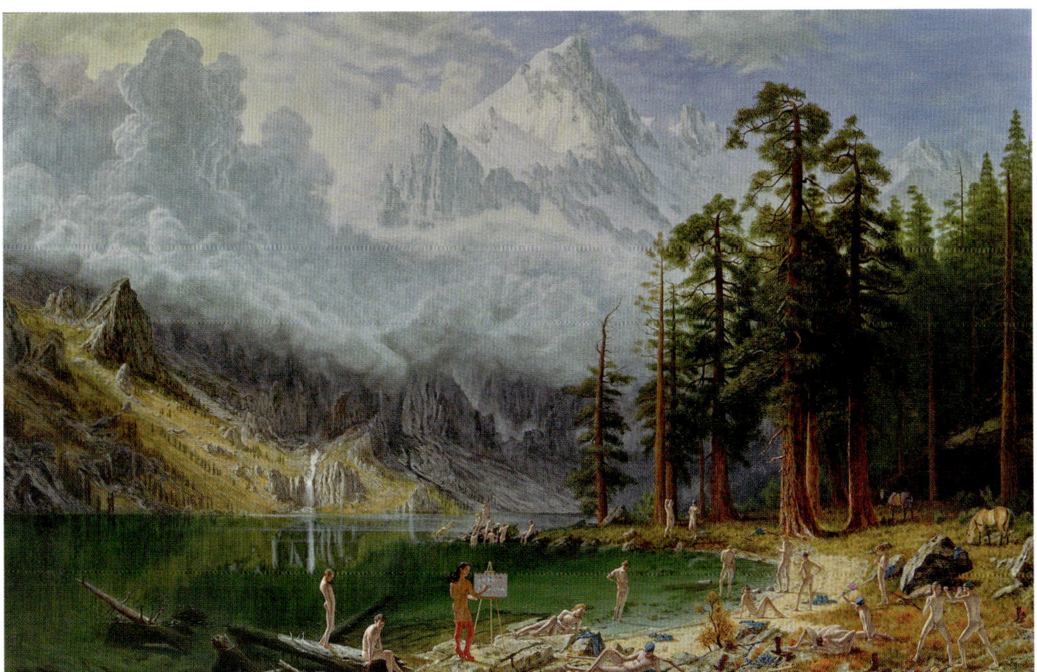

FIGURE 5.4 Kent Monkman (Fisher River Band Cree, born 1965), *History Is Painted by the Victors*, 2013. Acrylic on canvas, 72 × 113¼ × 1¼ in. Denver Art Museum: Gift from Vicki and Kent Logan, 2016.288. Image courtesy Denver Art Museum. © Kent Monkman.

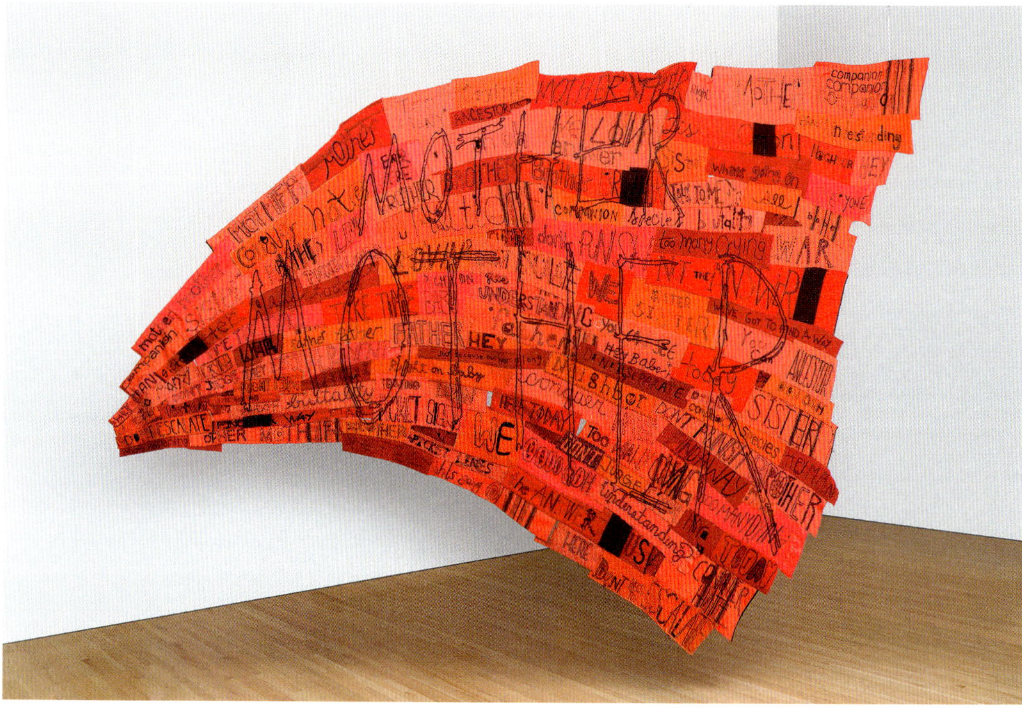

FIGURE 5.5 Marie Watt (Seneca, born 1967), *Companion Species (Speech Bubble)*, 2019. Reclaimed wool blankets, embroidery floss, and thread, 136⅝ × 198½ in. Crystal Bridges Museum of American Art. © Marie Watt.

the fall and winter of 2018–2019. Community members embroidered words on sections of reclaimed wool that were later sewn together by Watt in her studio. Words such as "neighbor" and "hate" mix with familial words like "mother," "grandmother," and "brother," which come from the lyrics to the 1971 Marvin Gaye song "What's Going On." Watt identifies with the way Gaye's song emphasizes relatedness and responsibility extending to all humans. As Watt points out, Seneca and Iroquois teachings emphasize the symbiotic relationships that humans have with the natural world, animals, and one another. Using relationships and storytelling as a backbone to the collaboration, teams from both Crystal Bridges and MONAH selected artworks and worked with two Indigenous community advisors to develop content. Unexpected conversations and visual comparisons between paintings by Norman Akers (Osage Nation) and Dorthea Tanning or Pablita Velarde

(Santa Clara Pueblo) and Louise Bourgeois helped to see the artworks anew. Working through collaboration—Watt's sewing circles and partnerships—are not typically the fastest or most productive way of creating a finished product, but the action of the creation reverberates and can build into something deeper and more meaningful. While the exhibition was short-lived, the collaboration across museums kindled valuable relationships.

Each of the case studies mentioned above uses different methodologies and approaches to better situate and contextualize historic artworks as well as museum and curatorial practices, but they also revealed challenges inherent in the systems in which we live and work. Museum databases, collections catalogs, and way-finding maps standardize, categorize, label, and simplify—much like a colonialist impulse to organize into taxonomies and categorize and establish hierarchies. The museum database and labeling standards do not always recognize multiplicities of identity, including tribal citizenship. Furthermore, American art collections are primarily White and male centered. This is a daunting fact. At Crystal Bridges, projections show that if we acquire fifty new artists per year, and half are ethnically or racially diverse, we will have only 35 percent non-White artists in our collection in twenty years. But it doesn't mean we should give up, because we can make a difference. There are outstanding and remarkable artworks to add to the collection and unexpected and new stories we can tell with the artworks we have.

We also choose our legacies. Temporary exhibitions offer museums a platform to acquire new art for collection. Crystal Bridges does not own a Remington bronze, but rather than seeking a sculpture for purchase and debut in *Knowing the West*, we acquired several prints and watercolors by Japanese American artist Chiura Obata (fig. 5.6). Obata immigrated to the United States from Japan in 1903, and while his artistic and professional career were unequivocally shaped by California, his watercolors and prints carry traces of his Japanese artistic training, reflecting a complex and transnational perspective on the landscape of the West. Obata visited Yosemite National Park and the Sierra Nevada Mountains in 1927, making over one hundred drawings based on his experience. A selection of the resulting prints from the *World Landscape Series* are included in the *Knowing the West* exhibition. Obata's compelling personal story as an immigrant artist navigating

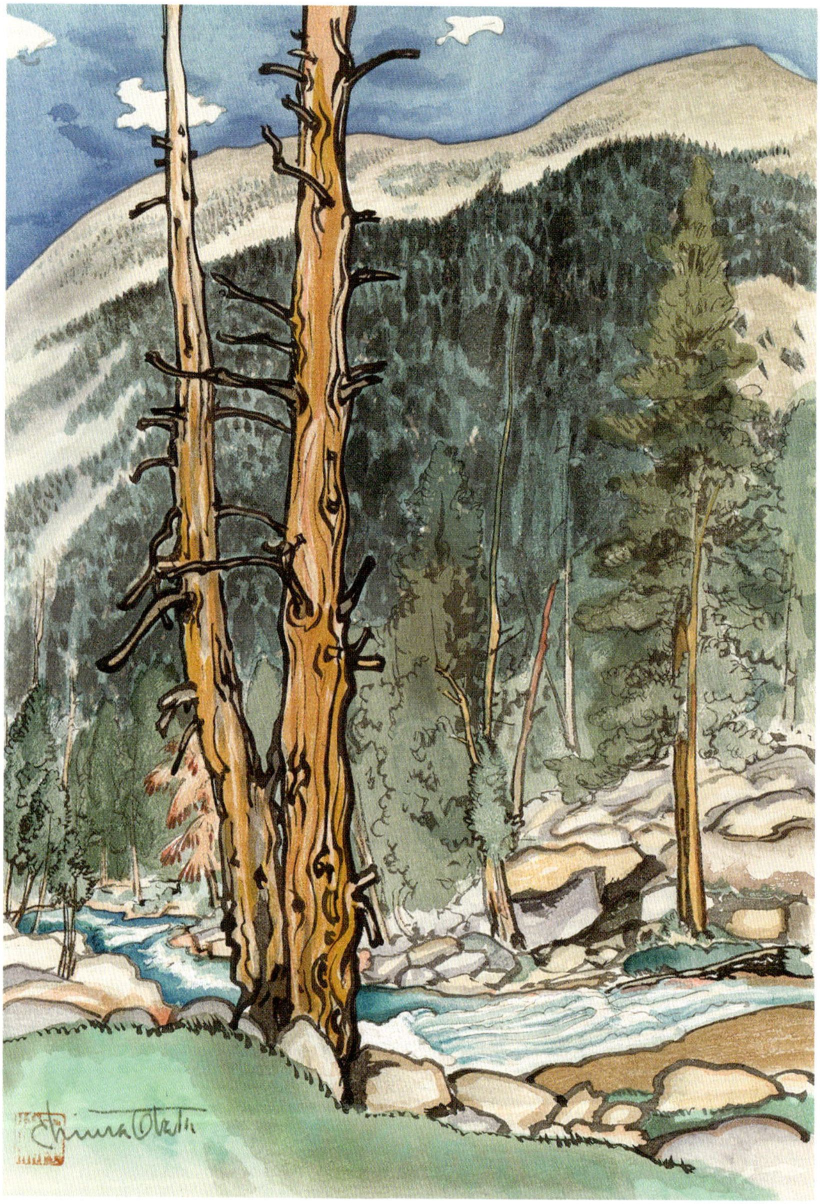

FIGURE 5.6 Chiura Obata (American, born in Japan, 1885–1975), *Upper Lyell Fork, Near Lyell Glacier* from *World Landscape Series "America,"* 1930. Color woodcut on paper, 15¾ × 11 in. Crystal Bridges Museum of American Art. © Estate of Chiura Obata.

anti-immigration laws and withstanding incarceration in Utah during World War II is also relevant to American art broadly. Some of Obata's drawings from the internment camp are now also in the Crystal Bridges collection.

RECKONING

In recontextualizing historic American art, I am interested in reckoning and interrogation to hold museums and curators accountable to their many audiences and stakeholders. Reckoning can add important layers of truth-telling to interpretation of artworks already in the collection, but truth-telling is not as simple as revealing troubling stories that are not always evident on the artwork's surface. More than thirty years ago, *The West as America: Reinterpreting Images of the Frontier, 1820–1920* (Smithsonian American Art Museum, 1991) was met with criticism and enraged audiences. The curatorial team for *The West as America* sought to "unearth a deeper, troubling story" behind images of westward expansion and to examine the myth and ideology that was part of the historical agenda hidden within the artworks.[13] The didactics and interpretation of the paintings were criticized as heavyhanded and preachy. Visitors felt talked down to and made to feel shamed for their beliefs. Headlines of reviews for the exhibition read "How the West Was Wrong in 'Images of the Frontier,' a Focus on the Negative" and "Old West, New Twist at the Smithsonian," with the subtitle "A museum's simplistic, preachy approach to history angers senators as well as historians and art critics."[14] The controversy surrounding the reinterpretation of European American images of the West highlighted just how deeply embedded the values and ideology were (and still are). The exhibition remains a cautionary example of potential consequences when values are challenged. Some members of Congress used the exhibition as a call to defund the arts and national museums in Washington, DC, which thankfully did not happen. Despite decades between then and now, political sensitivities about American mythologies and histories do not seem so different.

I believe we have obligations to truth-telling around American art, but we need to recognize that the tone and content is important. American history, especially the way it is interpreted and taught in schools, is an issue that elicits strong emotional reactions. Now more than ever, art museums need to be a space for dialogue and to provide opportunities for conversation and growth. In the exhibition *Knowing the West*, the tone that guides the interpretation is invitational, additive, and inclusive. We will learn together with the audience and not lecture or openly shame. Interpretive philosophies will acknowledge that audiences approach the West through many ways of knowing, and didactics and hands-on activities are intended to add layers of complexity to the visitor's initial ideas. Indigenous perspectives and other untold stories are prioritized throughout the exhibition.

To conclude, I return once again to Frederic Remington but this time his painting *Shotgun Hospitality*. Label text at the Hood Museum described the painting as a "psychologically-charged encounter between a shotgun freighter, who travels alone on the prairie transporting cargo, and three Plains Indians." It continues by asking the viewer to think about the mood and "palpable tension between the seated, but armed, freighter, and the three standing Native Americans—two of them armed." One interpretation of the scene fueled by the mythology of Remington's day assumes that the Plains men are the agitators, and the "hospitality" is not welcoming but, rather, ominous and used in the title ironically. The label concludes: "We are left to surmise this individual's critically important facial expression and the next exchange in this prairie encounter." But if we shift our perspectives, can we tell a new story?

This painting will be included in *Knowing the West*. If, instead, we ask the viewer, "Given the painting's title, who is hosting whom in this prairie encounter?" we provide a new opportunity to understand Remington's work and legacies of colonialism while countering the painting's previously prevailing narrative. A question like this rightfully reintroduces the idea that Remington's cowboy is on Indian land. Taken one step further, the label could also ask the viewer to consider if the cowboy's inquisitive look suggests that he is pondering a sale or trade proposed by the Native American men. If more context is provided and multiple possibilities are suggested, object labels can create an invitation for viewers to critically engage with an artwork while shifting and reframing predominant narratives. Actively engaging the viewer through the possibility of complex interpretations embraces entangled histories while incorporating multiple ways of knowing and storytelling. At the same time, placing this painting in a gallery where it is outnumbered by Native American art objects introduces these ideas more fully within the space. When artworks made by Nellie Two Bear Gates (Iháŋkthuŋwaŋna Dakhóta, Standing Rock Reservation), Nampeyo (Hopi-Tewa), Bear's Heart (Cheyenne), and the many Native American artists whose names are no longer known outnumber paintings and sculptures by Remington and Albert Bierstadt, and when Native makers are centered, the predominant narrative within the gallery shifts. Historical entanglements that engage in truth-telling and more fully reckon with the complicated realities of the past can recontextualize American art.

When we step back, let go of the canon, and embrace new ways of seeing and thinking, American art gets messy. But there are also exciting things that can happen when we incorporate new contexts and ways of knowing. Share the floor, encourage others, and find untold stories to inform the present and critically engage academics, museum professionals, and museum visitors to enter dialogues with one another. Look to colleagues and collaborators and recognize expertise in unexpected places, such as community stakeholders. Recontextualizing and reckoning with the past is a promising path forward.

NOTES

1. *The Broncho Buster* in the White House collection is often associated with Theodore Roosevelt. Another cast was given to Roosevelt by the Rough Riders in 1899, although that cast is not the same one as in the White House collection, which was added only in the mid-twentieth century. Until recently, when President Biden redecorated, *The Broncho Buster* had been a prominent feature in the Oval Office, no matter the current political party sitting in office. See Margaret Carrigan, "Art History Fact Check: Trump Mixes Up Teddy Roosevelt with an Anonymous Remington Cowboy," *Art Newspaper*, June 29, 2020, https://www.theartnewspaper.com/2020/06/30/art-history-fact-check-trump-mixes-up-teddy-roosevelt-with-an-anonymous-remington-cowboy/.

2. Thomas Brent Smith, quoted in Carol Kino, "Esteem for the American West," *New York Times*, October 27, 2013, F17. Thayer Tolles, who co-curated the exhibition, said the point of the exhibition was to emphasize "that Western art should be considered in the mainstream."

3. Murray Whyte, "At Portland Museum of Art, Two Painters Are a Mythic Mismatch," *Boston Globe*, October 28, 2020.

4. Margaret Jacobs, "Frederic Remington, *The Broncho Buster*," for "Native Perspectives," Metropolitan Museum of Art American Wing, https://www.metmuseum.org/about-the-met/collection-areas/the-american-wing/native-perspectives/, accessed August 7, 2023.

5. Theodore Roosevelt, "Ranch Life in the Far West," *Century Magazine* 35 (February 1888), 505, 502.

6. Jacobs, "*The Broncho Buster,*" Metropolitan Museum of Art.

7. The advisory council for *Knowing the West* included Dr. Kirsten Pai Buick, Christina E. Burke, Laura F. Fry, Michael R. Grauer, Dr. Michael Hartman, Dr. Chelsea Herr (Choctaw Nation), and Dr. Scott Manning Stevens (Akwesasne Mohawk).

8. See Nancy K. Anderson, *Frederic Remington: The Color of Night* (Washington, DC: National Gallery of Art, 2003).

9. Harold McCracken, "Frederic Remington's Studio," in *The Frederic Remington Studio Collection, Whitney Gallery of Western Art, Buffalo Bill Historical Center* (New York: Galleries Press, 1959), n.p.

10. McCracken, "Frederic Remington's Studio," n.p.

11. More than fifteen thousand Marshallese live in Northwest Arkansas and surrounding communities, the largest concentrations of Marshallese peoples in the continental United States. Marshallese Educational Initiative, https://www.mei.ngo/marshallese-in-arkansas/, accessed September 7, 2023.

12. The accompanying collections catalog published at the opening of the museum in 2011 was *Celebrating the American Spirit: Masterworks from Crystal Bridges Museum of American Art* (Crystal Bridges Museum of American Art in association with Hudson Hills Press, 2011). The jacket summary emphasizes the "unfolding story of the United States" and the museum's collection offering a "superb overview of American art . . . [to] rival that of the best museums in the country."

13. William H. Truettner and Nancy K. Anderson, *The West as America: Reinterpreting Images of the Frontier, 1820–1920* (Washington, DC: National Museum of American Art, 1991).

14. Benjamin Forgey, "How the West Was Wrong in 'Images of the Frontier,' a Focus on the Negative," *Washington Post*, March 18, 1991, D1; Michael Kimmelman, "Old West, New Twist at the Smithsonian," *New York Times*, May 26, 1991, H1.

6

Layla Bermeo / Roger Paul

FEKE'S *KINCEMOSS*

Collaboratively Rewriting a Colonial Painting

ROGER PAUL *(Passamaquoddy/Wolastoqey), Wabanaki Educator and Language Keeper* The Museum of Fine Arts, Boston, is a renowned institution to much of the world. Not my world. I grew up on various reservations in [the] northeastern US and the Canadian Maritimes. I never learned English until I was forced to, by Sister Mean . . . err, Jean Marie, at the age of six. That world has always been out of reach for those of us who were not descendants of colonizers. So when I noticed an email from the museum, I purposely ignored it. I wanted nothing to do with that horrible shrine of brutal colonization that curates nothing more than exploitation of Indigenous peoples throughout the world, merely for the illusion of prestige and profit.

LAYLA BERMEO, *Kristin and Roger Servison Curator of Paintings, Museum of Fine Arts, Boston* Roger ignored my emails for weeks. I reached out to him in the fall of 2020 as part of *Translating American Stories*, a new initiative to bring multilingual labels into the permanent collection galleries of the Art of the Americas Wing (the Wing) at the Museum of Fine Arts, Boston (MFA). By offering English-Español texts in past special exhibitions of Latin American art, we had learned that many of our visitors, even those who spoke only English, experienced connections to artists' voices and original contexts of the works. We saw how bilingual labels could function visually, as well as interpretively. As we worked from home during the COVID-19 pandemic, unable to physically access our galleries or audiences, *Translating American Stories* became our attempt to rethink the collections from afar—if we couldn't move the objects, then perhaps we could at least change the stories we told about them.

Translating American Stories focused on six iconic works in "Boston on the Eve of Revolution," a gallery filled with representations of historical figures like John Singleton Copley's portraits of Paul Revere and Sam Adams. This gallery remains the space that we most want to change but also the most challenging to change (fig. 6.1). Boston-area schools have long focused on these objects in their American history curricula, and in the creation of this gallery leading up to the opening of the Wing in 2010 there was an enormous sense of pressure to uphold a traditional, Patriots-versus-Tories narrative. We wondered if multilingual interpretation could reorient our displays

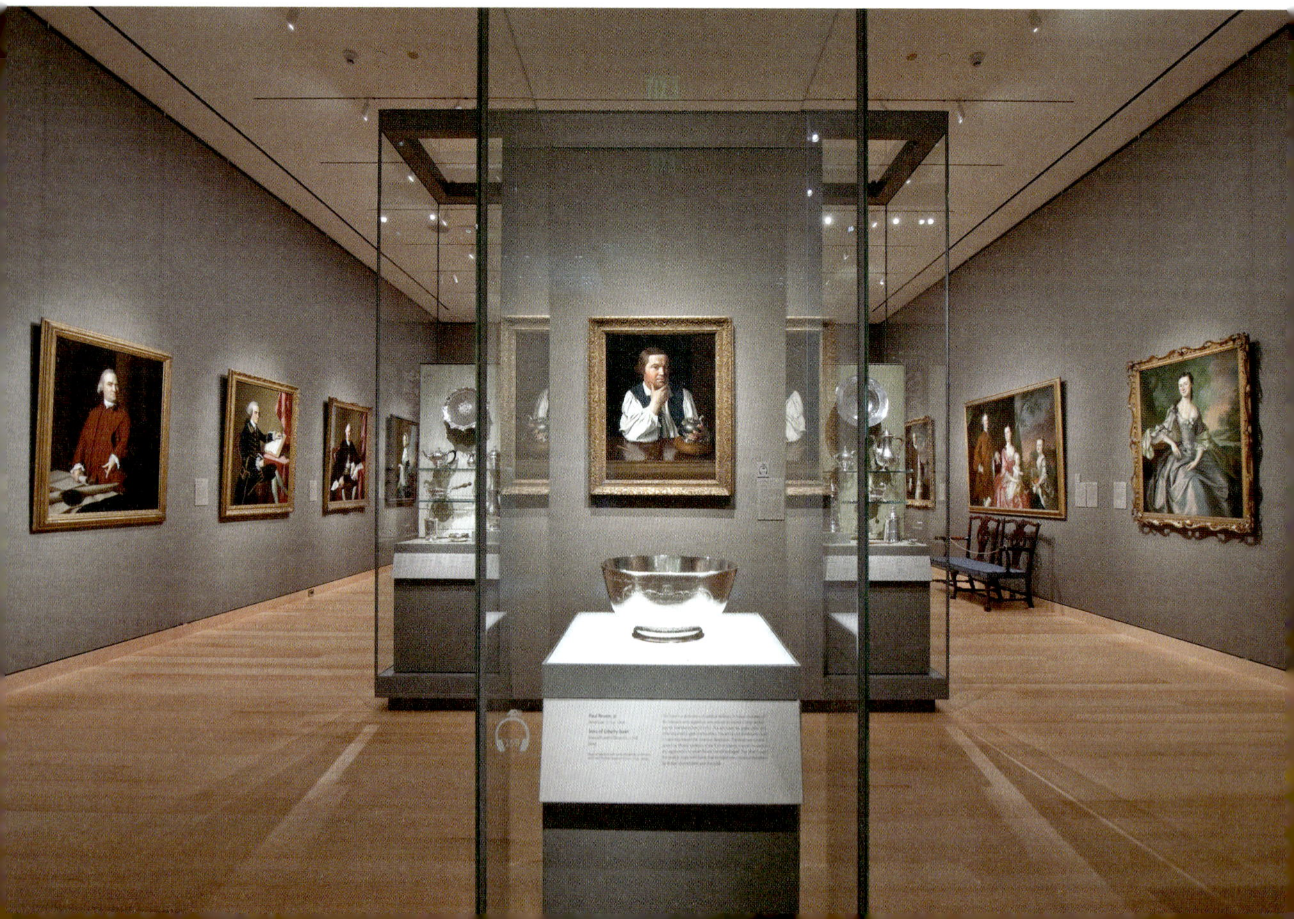

FIGURE 6.1 Installation view, Carolyn A. and Peter S. Lynch Gallery (132) in 2010. © Museum of Fine Arts, Boston.

away from standard heroic tales of the Revolutionary War and help us draw out lesser-known histories of these colonial objects often obscured beneath shining surfaces, including their reliance on the labor of enslaved African and Indigenous peoples. Could labels in different languages better describe the international journey of Revere's famed *Sons of Liberty Bowl*, made from silver mined in the Spanish colonies and modeled after a Chinese vessel? Would text in Kreyòl (Creole) enable our Haitian visitors to see their own histories in a refined desk and bookcase designed by cabinetmaker George Bright but carved from mahogany extracted by enslaved workers in Saint-Domingue? To explore these questions, we organized a convening of community leaders and solicited feedback from bilingual MFA staff, offering modest honoraria for their advice. Considering where we are, we decided to include labels not only in Spanish, Kreyòl, Mandarin, and Brazilian Portuguese, but also in an Indigenous language that could bring attention to the long life of the land that the MFA now occupies.[1] We needed Roger's help. But initially he wanted nothing to do with us.

This essay focuses on the creation of a single bilingual label (figs. 6.2–6.3). As we sat with the invisibility of Native art and stories in "Boston on the Eve of Revolution," we confronted the limitations of our collection and raised questions about the works that we do have—oil paintings, high-style furniture, and silver made for White colonists. With scant Indigenous art related to the Revolutionary period, could we begin to shift the narrative of this gallery by presenting a colonial work from an Indigenous perspective, showing connections between Native and non-Native worlds? While most colonial objects are implicated in histories of stolen land, few directly represent it, and one of the only images of water, hills, and sky in "Boston on the Eve of Revolution" appears in the background of Robert Feke's portrait of Isaac Winslow (fig. 6.4). Rather than devoting the label to the central figure (Winslow, whose family colonized Maine, is depicted in three different paintings in our collection), we hoped to draw attention to the landscape at which he points, using a local Indigenous language to describe its significance.

As with many museum initiatives that seek to reach audiences from diverse backgrounds, we knew that in order to be successful, this label had to be created collaboratively. I was fortunate to work closely with Tess Lukey

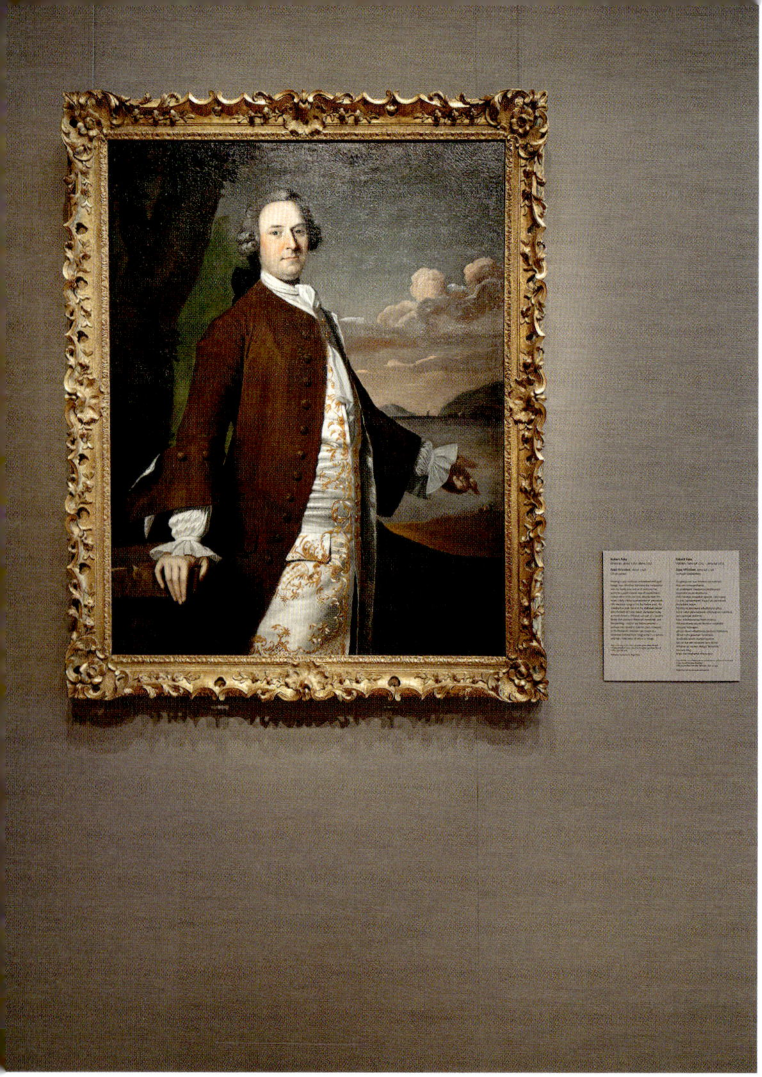

FIGURE 6.2 *left* Installation view, featuring bilingual gallery label for Robert Feke, *Isaac Winslow*, 1748. Oil on canvas, 50 × 40⅛ in. Gift in Memory of the sitter's granddaughter (Mary Russell Winslow Bradford, 1793–1899): 42.424. Image by Maggie Loh. © Museum of Fine Arts, Boston.

FIGURE 6.3 *below* Bilingual gallery label for Robert Feke, *Isaac Winslow*, 1748. Image by Maggie Loh. © Museum of Fine Arts, Boston.

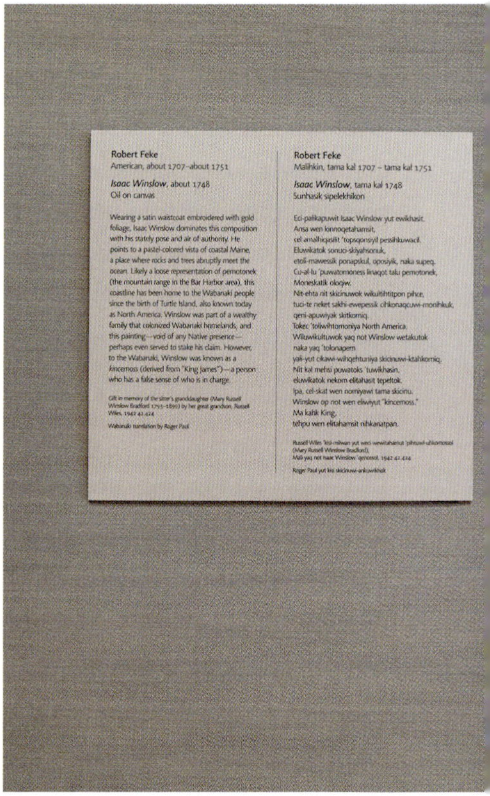

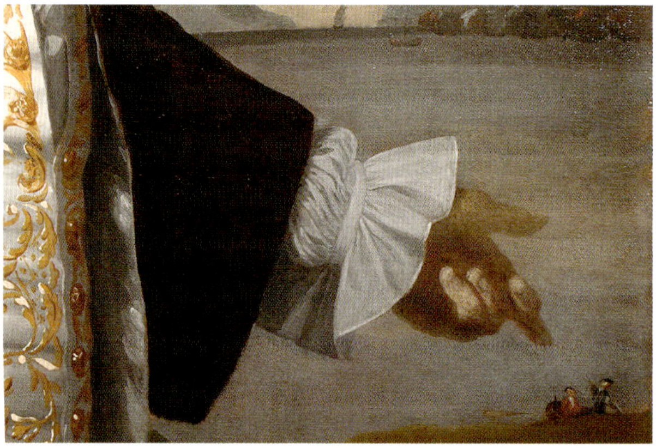

FIGURE 6.4 *left* Detail, Robert Feke, *Isaac Winslow*, 1748. Image by Layla Bermeo. © Museum of Fine Arts, Boston.

(Wampanoag Tribe of Gay Head Aquinnah), then a curatorial research associate in the Art of the Americas department and a student of the Wôpanâak language. Chris Newell (Passamaquoddy), who, at the time, was the first Wabanaki director of the Abbe Museum in Bar Harbor and a participant in our initial *Translating American Stories* convening, recommended that Tess and I reach out to Roger Paul, a deeply respected language keeper from his community. Even after Roger refused to respond to our messages, Chris maintained that he would be the best partner for this project and facilitated an introduction on our behalf. In the many pressing conversations about the importance of collaboration within museums, the sharing of authority, and the welcoming of many voices, there remains comparatively little discussion or acknowledgment regarding the ambivalence that our knowledge partners often experience and the uneasiness of working within the very spaces that have excluded or exploited them. As Roger's personal reflections within this essay reveal, outside experts can carry with them not only traumas associated with our specific museum but also traumas inflicted by institutions in general.

Our label for Feke's portrait, written in English and Wabanaki, is one small example of how we wrangled with this uneasiness together and built a relationship as well as a new framework for understanding a painting, eventually creating something that made us and Roger proud.[2] The yearlong process of writing a single, 127-word label demonstrates the time, openness, and reciprocity required to care for both our collections and our collaborators. In addition to documenting some of our journey, this essay hopefully provides a model for creating bilingual museum interpretation beyond considerations of present demographics, instead recognizing deep histories of our surrounding places and their peoples.

CHANGING EXPECTATIONS, PERSPECTIVES, AND PROCESS

ROGER PAUL: I had nothing but anger and outrage toward the MFA, especially since I had helped chaperone a recent visit of tribal elementary students. We were guided to a gallery in the basement that housed Indigenous artifacts, and right at the entrance we were faced with Maya burial urns! As a member of our repatriation committee, the evidence of these people digging up our ancestors and displaying their funerary objects to greedy and selfish capitalists, for their viewing pleasure, was just too much for me. I immediately expressed my shock and disgust at their ignorance of such a heinous act. To which I got the reply, "There are no bodies inside." I was beside myself. How can you speak to such callous and cruel attitudes? I tried not to ruin the trip for our students, but my silence and obvious anger were evident. It didn't get any better when the guides were so proud to showcase their Egyptian mummy gallery. Even the principal tried to calm me by saying, "At least they are not Indigenous." I began to get physically sick and had to leave the building and wait for them outside. I could take no more of the subjugation porn on display. So suffice to say, I was not impressed by an email from them. I merely trashed it and all the following emails.

Shortly thereafter I got a call from Chris Newell, a fellow tribal member whom I've known for almost his entire life. I always answer his calls. He is a shining star from my tribal community who has followed well in his father's footsteps as an ambassador of our Passamaquoddy people to the rest of the world. His father, Wayne Newell, was one of the elders in my community who mentored me in my formative years. Chris was aware of my avoidance of the emails from the MFA. He spoke about the project that they were working on, intending to showcase a more diverse perspective. I expressed my approval of his collaboration with them, hoping it would help them to see beyond their imperialistic blinders. He asked if I would be involved. I would never hesitate to be a part of anything Chris is doing, based on the knowledge that if he is involved, it can only be a good thing. This was different; how could I possibly work with an institution that I despise? I told him that I would not be able to hide my disgust and that his diplomatic skills were much more suited for this. He assured me that they were okay with my honesty and were willing to work with me to share my input on the project. I went ahead and agreed to talk to them, thinking that they would sense my contempt and it would be over.

I prepared myself to be respectful but honest. The two young women I met were POC [people of color] and seemed very pleasant. Although it helped ease my anger a bit, I initially saw it as a plot to manipulate me. One of them was a Wampanoag tribal member, and it brought to mind a scenario a few years back in Washington, DC. The Smithsonian Institution was going to allow some spiritual leaders, Wampanoag included, to go to their offsite prison . . . err, facility, to let us do ceremonies with our ancestors. When I boisterously complained to them about their holding tens of thousands of our ancestors hostage, they sent a couple of Indigenous youth interns to talk to us before they allowed us access. The youths' mission seemed to be to assure us that the institution has ours, and our ancestors', best interests at heart. These poor youths had no idea that the institution was using them to try to manipulate us, which angered us even more. We never did get to go to the facility, but that's a story for another day.

Preparing myself for an obvious manipulation from the MFA, I proceeded with caution when meeting with them. I was waiting to hear the propaganda from the Wampanoag member about how the MFA was a concerned ally and any other manipulative jabber. I was pleasantly surprised when they actually seemed genuine, and, surprisingly, they agreed that the MFA needed to be more inclusive. Still with my guard up, I listened to what they were proposing. It sounded good, but was it for real? They went on to explain about themselves, the other people involved, and what they hoped to accomplish. I sensed a real goal to break through the iron curtain protecting the colonizer narrative.

Not completely on board yet, I made it clear that I would be honest about my, and what I considered to be my ancestors', viewpoint. They seemed delighted and began to explain their initiative. I was to describe a colonial painting from the standpoint of an Indigenous person connected to the land depicted and to present this perspective, which was entirely omitted, on the label in an Algonquian dialect. It all seemed too good to be true, but I agreed to move forward.

LAYLA BERMEO: As Tess and I described our *Translating American Stories* initiative to Roger and other contributors, we emphasized that we were not asking them to simply translate words that curators wrote. Instead, we sought to work with them to create completely new content and incorporate narratives previously left out of our galleries. This process moved away from the practice of displaying a single object with two labels by different authors, as we had done in our past exhibition, *Collecting Stories: Native American Art* (2018–2019). While such an approach can literally present multiple points of view, it can also suggest a hierarchy between the museum's "official" interpretation and a secondary voice. What would happen if we tried to write one label together?

We also considered how we could invite contributors to share their honest perspectives, knowledge, and language skills without overburdening them with tasks that are related to our training but not theirs. In order to offer some of the tools that we use for writing labels, we arranged sessions in which we looked closely at the works of art together, discussing their most striking visual qualities. We circulated readings and asked our contributors which histories of the objects were most important to include in the text and what they would change about the current label. Curators took on the responsibility of drafting the new labels but workshopped every word with the contributors before they translated them into Spanish, Kreyòl, Mandarin Chinese, Brazilian Portuguese, or Wabanaki. As they translated the texts, which were proofread by an additional group of linguists, we encouraged them to avoid directly translating English words and to use terms and phrases that would be most natural to speakers of these languages. They also added, reorganized, and edited the English text to better capture certain concepts in their languages and to make them more accessible to their communities.

Roger seemed to enjoy conversing with Tess and me about the contexts of *Isaac Winslow*, including historian Ian Saxine's work on the eighteenth-century Maine frontier, but he initially had little to say about the painting itself.[3] Completed during the artist's mature phase, this portrait exemplifies Feke's talent for depicting ambitious colonists as they wanted to be seen. Winslow's gaze is steady and confident, his body so inflated that his silk waistcoat folds into wrinkles around his full belly. Gold embroidery dances across his elongated torso, curling into whimsical floral patterns that contrast with the swaths of solid brown that make up his jacket. While one hand is firmly planted on a stone pedestal, the other turns in a soft gesture, pointing to the water, land, and tiny figures in the background. Feke's compositions and color palette, which combine swollen forms and sharp details, would become so influential in the British colonies that later historians of American art would refer to him as "the first native-born genius."[4] Roger, however, did not agree with this assessment. He spent much of our video call talking around the painting, admitting that this style of historical portraiture simply was not interesting to him. He gave polite but noncommittal answers to direct questions about the image. He insisted on referring to Feke as "Fake." Finally, I offered a scenario, suggesting that he imagine that his family walked into the MFA and saw this painting on the wall. What would he want them to know about it? Immediately, he replied, "I would want them to know that he's standing on our land."

Contemporary scholars agree with Roger that the people and places rendered invisible in Feke's paintings are critical to understanding the artist's work. In her analysis of the transatlantic networks that shaped eighteenth-century objects, Zara Anishanslin describes his portraits as "lovely colonial-made things that contain hidden histories of the dark ugliness beneath the building of empire."[5] Although he worked within the conventions of European portraiture, borrowing poses from prints, Feke did not simply copy British sources; as Anishanslin argues, he incorporated distinctively local props and landscapes into his paintings to emphasize his sitters' imperial identities within the context of the colonies. Of Feke's many portraits of the merchant class, *Isaac Winslow*, she writes, best demonstrates this aspect of his work.[6] After marrying the heiress Lucy Waldo, Winslow joined his father-in-law's land speculation group, Kennebec Proprietors, which aggressively settled the Wabanaki homelands around the Kennebec River in Maine. Set against hills that recall *pemotonek*, the coastline near Bar Harbor, Winslow's powerful figure stakes his claim to this land, represented as devoid of any Native presence. Roger understood how the painting and its ongoing display at the MFA functioned as a tool of dispossession, but looking at Winslow's puffed-up body and slight knowing smile, he also saw something else. "He looks like a *kincemoss*," Roger said. "Someone who thinks he's in charge but really is not."

As Tess and I began drafting the new label for *Isaac Winslow* based on Roger's observations, we knew that we needed to focus on two issues: the land and the *kincemoss*. Thinking of her own homeland of Noepe (Martha's

Vineyard), Tess lyrically described the landscape in the painting as "a place where rocks and trees abruptly meet the ocean." We tried to combine art historical description with language representative of Roger's perspective, at one point changing the phrase "since time immemorial" to the more specific "since the birth of Turtle Island" at his suggestion. When the three of us reached a consensus on the English version of the label, Roger began the process of translating it into language that would be most accessible to Wabanaki people, which includes the Passamaquoddy, Wolastoqey (Maliseet), Mi'kmaq, and Penobscot communities. He rearranged phrases and reorganized the text to create a different rhythm, consulting with other language keepers and revising his selection of words. But the term *kincemoss* makes the final point in both the English and Wabanaki texts.

Derived from "King James," *kincemoss* emerged from cultural mixing and contact between Wabanaki and English-speaking peoples and therefore appropriately unites our two labels. The repetition of this term not only offers the same information to visitors from different backgrounds, but it also mobilizes a Wabanaki concept to unlock meaning within a colonial painting. Early in the process, critical theorist Homi Bhabha, then the MFA's curator in residence, had encouraged us to seek out exactly these moments of overlap, to investigate how the act of translation could freshly illuminate works of art for speakers of both languages. He maintained that if English speakers read one label and Wabanaki people read the other, without the two texts informing each other, then our project would essentially be incomplete. As they worked with us to create labels in Spanish, Mandarin Chinese, Kreyòl, and Brazilian Portuguese, our contributors expressed similar goals. They engaged deeply with the histories of Copley's portraits and Revere's silver but also thought about how tone and turns of phrase from these languages could make the new labels vibrant and accessible to visitors, particularly those who have long felt unwelcome in museums. Although Roger is a professional linguist working in Maine, we recruited the majority of our contributors from our own staff as a way to draw on local talent and emphasize the racial and cultural diversity that already exists within the MFA.

As institutional leaders race to create programming that will be relevant to underrepresented audiences, their first instinct is often to look outside of the museum. While external visions can productively disrupt staid patterns of display and interpretation, such an approach also overlooks the many people from diverse backgrounds working in security, maintenance, food service, and other departments that require workers to cultivate intimate knowledge of the museums' spaces and visitors. In addition to our colleagues from other curatorial departments, *Translating American Stories* included contributors from learning and community engagement, senior associates, development, and information technology, as well as local artist Chanel Thervil, who recently had been commissioned to create a community art project at the MFA.[7] We came together throughout the process—on Zoom and in person, as a large group and in smaller teams focused on specific objects—to divide responsibilities, discuss the works of art in the "Boston on the Eve of Revolution" gallery, and share our experiences. These gatherings looked notably different from our typical meetings about creating content or reinstalling galleries, as they included multiple Black, Latine, and Asian American colleagues from different generations and backgrounds. This inclusive process not only avoided tokenizing colleagues from communities often underrepresented in museums but also created a working environment that actively facilitated new ways of looking at art, developing interpretation, and reaching wide audiences.[8] Although Roger did not work in the building with us, these meetings influenced his experience, demonstrating new possibilities for belonging.

CREATING ANOTHER, PARALLEL WORLD

ROGER PAUL: As we met on more occasions and with more people, I began to feel confident and grateful to be considered on this endeavor headed by Layla and Tess. They were legitimately trying to include the true diversity and heart of the Americas into the stuffy old European-based MFA.

Not caring if the museum would actually follow through with this endeavor, I wanted to be a part of what, to me, sounded like a wonderful project. With all the amazing people involved, the sense of fellowship and comfort overtook the doubt and distaste I had for the MFA. Layla and Tess posed the question of what I wanted my people to know about this painting, and they gave me license to express my honest opinion. Knowing that I carried in my heart the thoughts and feelings of thousands of years of attempting to be erased by the colonizer culture, I had so much to say. I also had to present it in a way that would honor my heritage and not be ungracious. As difficult as it was to hide my aversion, I feel thankful that the spirit of my ancestors guided me to complete the assignment that was kindly offered to me by Layla and Tess. I was so thankful that they were pleased with my contribution and that I could help them to successfully bring their revolutionary ambitions to fruition.

LAYLA BERMEO: It took nearly a year to write, translate, proofread, design, and print the new labels for six works of art in "Boston on the Eve of Revolution." Additional months were required to record and transcribe the multilingual labels for our audio guide, which visitors can access through the MFA mobile app. And then we needed special signage and online materials to notify our audiences about these resources, which tacked on additional time. Conceiving of ways to speed and scale up this initiative, and to more fairly compensate contributors for their work, continues to be a challenge for us. However, we know that the investment of time—the hours spent looking at art together, compromising on the content, disagreeing about word choice, proofreading different languages—is also what makes these labels powerful. They embody the multifaceted experiences of their authors and call out to new audiences. The English-Wabanaki label particularly relies on efforts that reach far past our own moment. It is indebted to the work of Roger's ancestors, who passed down and protected their language despite constant threats of erasure through colonialism. Their time and dedication made possible this label, as Roger's skillful translation has been shaped by his elders and mentors.

In the introduction to *Kuhkomossonuk Akonutomuwinokot: Stories Our Grandmothers Told Us*, the late Wayne Newell wrote, "Bilingual text gives readers an opportunity to appreciate the language of Passamaquoddy storytelling and to understand how the language creates another, parallel world."[9] Like Newell's book, Roger's label for *Isaac Winslow* creates an invitation to enter a parallel, Wabanaki world. His participation in our *Translating*

American Stories project demonstrates the immeasurable generosity of Indigenous educators who continue to welcome and share knowledge with non-Native people, working through the lingering pain of their ancestors and themselves. His words situate us on Wabanaki land, and from there we can see an American history different from the one that we thought we knew so well.

ROGER PAUL: In closing, I must admit that I hope Wayne Newell would also be very appreciative that I applied his years of guidance to create such a cordial but stern label.

NOTES

1. The Museum of Fine Arts, Boston, stands on the homelands of the Massachusett people, a site that has long served as a place of meeting and exchange among different nations. The Massachusett and their neighbors, the Wampanoag, have historically spoken an Algonquian language. Under the direction of jessie "little doe" baird, the Wôpanâak Language Reclamation Project (WLRP) has established the mission to return language fluency to the Wampanoag Nation. We reached out to the WLRP at the beginning of the *Translating American Stories* initiative and understood that, at the time, study and use of the language was restricted to members of the community.

2. Although "Wabanaki" typically refers to four tribes (Passamaquoddy, Wolastoqey (Maliseet), Mi'kmaq, and Penobscot), and not to a language, Roger Paul uses this collective term to describe his text at the MFA. An expert in multiple languages, Roger has intentionally used words that will be accessible to Wabanaki people from different backgrounds.

3. See, for example, Ian Saxine, "The Performance of Peace: Indians, Speculators, and the Politics of Property on the Maine Frontier, 1735–1737," *New England Quarterly* 87, no. 3 (2014): 379–411.

4. Wayne Craven, *Colonial American Portraiture: The Economic, Religious, Social, Cultural, Philosophical, Scientific, and Aesthetic Foundations* (Cambridge: Cambridge University Press, 1986), 281. Versions of this phrase continue to appear in biographies of Feke.

5. Zara Anishanslin, *Portrait of a Woman in Silk: Hidden Histories of the British Atlantic World* (New Haven: London: Yale University Press, 2016), 240.

6. Anishanslin, *Portrait of a Woman in Silk*, 238–40.

7. In addition to contributing to the translation of the Krèyol label for the George Bright desk and bookcase (about 1770–85), Chanel Thervil also created an artistic response to the object. Her bilingual poem "Mahogany/Kajou," read by Haitian linguist Jean Lesly René, can be accessed on the MFA mobile app.

8. In developing our process for *Translating American Stories*, we drew on the format of the MFA's Table of Voices program. Founded in 2019, Table of Voices actively collaborates with Boston community members to offer more expansive and accessible interpretations of the stories and works presented at the museum. Contributors are invited to join a cohort of peers who are deeply familiar with a project's subject matter. Groups give candid feedback, often pushing MFA staff to complicate traditional narratives and participate in an integrated practice of curatorial work, design, interpretation, and community outreach. Recent exhibitions, such as *Hear Me Now: The Black Potters of Old Edgefield South Carolina* (2023) and *Toshiko Takaezu: Shaping Abstraction* (2023–24), were deeply shaped by Table of Voices, and the program will continue to inform curatorial projects across the MFA. *Translating American Stories* prioritized the perspectives of MFA staff members from diverse backgrounds who are typically excluded from creating content, and this model of internal collaboration has, in turn, informed Table of Voices and similar convenings. *Guarding the Art*, the 2022 exhibition curated by members of the security department at the Baltimore Museum of Art, offers a particularly compelling example of the type of internal collaboration previously overlooked by major museums.

9. Wayne A. Newell and Robert M. Leavitt, eds., *Kuhkomossonuk Akonutomuwinokot: Stories Our Grandmothers Told Us* (Robbinston, ME: Resolute Bear Press, 2021), ix.

PART III

INTERRUPTING COLONIAL STRUCTURES

7

Kirsten Pai Buick

"GUESS WHO'S COMING TO DINNER?"

The Aesthetic and Curatorial Politics of Invitation and Interruption in Imperial Museums

When the National Gallery, London, opened *Kehinde Wiley: The Prelude* in 2022, it was with great fanfare. Billed as the artist's first collaboration with a major UK gallery, the installation included five paintings and one six-channel digital film in his exploration of European Romanticism. Wiley, a US artist, has gained renown for his acts of substitution as he takes famous, grand-manner paintings and replaces the White European subjects with Black subjects. The surprising combination of familiar contexts that now feature prominent Black figures where one was expecting Napoleon or St. Anthony or the Three Graces strikes audiences as evocative and fresh. The Black youths are themselves recognizable for their style and their solemnity as they seem identifiable with a global hip-hop culture or, more ominously, for their presence on the evening news as victims or witnesses to police violence levied against them and their communities. Moreover, curators and collectors remain enchanted by the tension between two recognizable tropes: one belonging to high art and the other to urban street culture, here meeting and merging in a painting or a sculpture by Wiley.

Comparisons could be made between the practices of Wiley and those of Fred Wilson in how they engage the narcissism of imperial museums. Wilson, a conceptual artist, is given access to the totality of a collection—from archives to objects—and, using the tools of museum display, reorganizes, relabels, and reinstalls portions of a collection, which, as a result, are transformed under his curatorial activism. What Wilson does on a grand scale, whether it is the Accademia in Venice or the Allen Memorial Art Museum at Oberlin College, Wiley does with a single and singular work of art. Both artists offer critiques of the histories they reference. While Wilson's critique is one that encompasses institutions of collecting and display, Wiley's intervention opens questions around canon formation and the histories of art and criticism that solidify masterpieces and masters. Nevertheless, the question begs itself: How effective is institutional critique when the invitation is fulsome and eagerly extended? And here it is important to make a sharp distinction between Wilson and Wiley. The spaces that Wilson solicits, or those that extend an invitation to him, understand that they either will be changed forever by his interruptions or betray the promise of what he offers. Wiley's interruption, on the other hand, is both more complex and yet less so. His "grand manner" substitutions keep the "Old Masters" relevant and bring them back to the table of culture. In that way, Wiley's work functions like a segment of a mirror for the self-absorption and vanity of empires. Museums are the mirrors of empire, made up of looted artifacts and ritual objects hoarded within imperial centers and displayed among the works of sanctioned and named artists who give structure and coherence to empire through their artist academies and schools, their critics and historians.

Museums play a crucial role in the project of reenvisioning American art across disciplinary and geographical boundaries. Using case studies, this chapter explores the aesthetic and curatorial politics of three imperial museums as revealed in how and under what circumstances they extend their invitations. What is ultimately revealed is how they plan to remain relevant in an era that vigorously questions our monuments and engages in a level of institutional critique unmatched in any point of history. Their resistance to self-examination and true change creates a distorting and distracting feint around ideals of openness and accessibility.

INVITATION

My ambivalence around Wiley's engagement with the shibboleths of empire crystallized when I was invited by the National Gallery to be part of the programming for *The Prelude*.[1] Wiley had been given the freedom to choose the work most inspirational to him from the National Gallery's vast collection and to build an exhibition based on the work. Wiley selected Caspar David Friedrich's painting *Wanderer above the Sea of Fog* (ca. 1817) and, more broadly, the theme of the sublime in landscape representation. He cast Black Londoners in the film created to accompany the exhibition, even taking them on a trip to Norway to explore its mountains, fjords, and glacial landscapes.[2] Chris Mugan, writing for ARTUK.org, compares Wiley's challenge to the lack of diversity in so-called Western art to the works of Kara Walker and Kerry James Marshall—"so-called," I argue, because Wiley, Walker, and Marshall are all "Western" artists, but here it is a term used to distinguish "White" from "non-White." Walker's and Marshall's focus on figural subjects is given a new twist by Wiley, who, according to Mugan, instead centers on the "classic masterpieces" of the "landscapes of the Romantic movement."[3] Mugan then gives a textbook description of European Romanticism:

> On show are a set of paintings and one film, all inspired by the movement of European Romanticism that developed alongside changing ideas in thought, music and literature from the late eighteenth century and dominated cultural life for the next fifty years or so. . . . Romanticism had a particular impact on the field of landscape painting, thanks to a striving for spirituality and a return to nature in the face of growing industrialisation.[4]

Later in the article, Mugan also acknowledges this as a time of imperial expansion among European nations with their involvement in the slave trade and penetration into India, North and South America, as well as the Caribbean. But a more direct connection is not made between empire and the aestheticization of landscape. Still, any such awareness of the connection between empire and aesthetics seems absent in the museum's invitation to me. As elaborated upon by the director of public programs, Wiley's exhibition "looks at the 'Wanderer,' the icon of romanticism of the anonymous lone traveller seeking extreme experiences and disrupts this by placing a Black woman within this role."[5] Specifically, I was asked to lecture remotely for about forty minutes followed by a Q&A on what they conceived as "the Black Sublime," speculating excitedly that the National Gallery may have innovated the term for its exhibition. The parameters of my lecture were then outlined for me in the form of a question: Might I be able to address "black representation with reference to American sublime landscape painting including Winslow Homer's work during/after the American Civil War and his treatment of the black figure within marine painting, and how this relates to the slave trade and forced migration?"[6] My question for Wilson and Wiley must now also be mine: How effective can institutional critique be when the invitation is not only fulsome and eagerly extended but also defined and circumscribed by the institution itself?

As a scholar whose work increasingly focuses on constructions of identity through spatial relations and the various articulations of landscape (e.g., property, beautiful/sublime/picturesque, wilderness, west, frontier, ecology, etc.), I had and have serious issues with the uncomplicated racial qualifier appended to "the Sublime," as it already carries significant implications for the far-flung territories of European fantasy, Othering, and empire. In 1757 the Anglo-Irish politician, economist, and philosopher Edmund Burke (1729–97) published *A Philosophical Inquiry into the Origins of the Sublime and Beautiful*, in which he configured the Sublime to exist as a self-contained idea, discretely circumscribed and independent of the Beautiful.[7] Burke developed a field of aesthetic psychology separate from his predecessor John Locke (1632–1704), who linked the science of taste to the foundation of morals.[8] For Burke, the Sublime was characterized by qualities of "the masculine"—powerful, vast, infinite, magnificent, terrible, obscure, and so on. The Beautiful, in contrast, encompassed "the feminine" in its delicacy, grace, elegance, smoothness, sweetness, smallness, passivity, and so on.[9] Through Burke's formulation, we can already glean the imperial hardening of gender itself into two self-contained constructs that are discretely circumscribed and independent of each other. The concept of "the Picturesque" was introduced later by Uvedale Price (1747–1829) in 1796 to function as a mediating point of discourse between the Sublime and the Beautiful, and Price related it directly to landscape representation.[10] Characterized by roughness and irregularity, the Picturesque blended but left perfectly distinct the two contrasting categories of Sublime and Beautiful.[11] Price, following Burke, posed the three categories as originating in two fundamental human instincts: self-preservation and society.[12] There was a racial component to the three ideologies as well. Significantly, within Burke's formulation of a science of the passions, slavery/enslavement/the slave trade was not separate nor distinct phenomena. Burke was opposed to the slave trade and later to slavery itself because it perverted the natural right of self-possession and was incompatible with the obligation of self-mastery.[13] Moreover, as the categories became codified in landscape representation, there were implications for who could occupy those spaces according to gender, class, labor, and race.[14]

Ultimately, the National Gallery's invitation was one that relied on the careful forgetting of how empire used such constructs as Sublime, Picturesque, Pastoral, Wilderness, Frontier, and Beautiful to aestheticize, make recognizable, define, and carve out empire. Instead, they invited a US art historian of African descent (me) to ruminate, via American imperial landscapes, on the work of a US artist of African descent (Wiley). In this way, Great Britain's imperial designs remained firmly in the past according to what was asked of me. Nevertheless, I did counter their invitation with an alternative narrative, writing:

> I do teach an upper division course on US landscape representation, and we do delve into the commodification of the sublime, first looking at Europe in the 18th century and disaster tourism to Mt. Vesuvius and then to the 1823 disaster experienced by the Willey family in the White Mountains of New Hampshire. Eric Purchase writes about it in his stellar book *Out of Nowhere: Disaster and Tourism in the White Mountains*.[15] An enterprising soul opened the Willey house for domestic tourism, which was tourism's unofficial launch in this country. From there we talk about how the concept of "providence" plays out and the idea that experiences of the sublime follow on the heels of someone else's disaster. We then watch two

> documentaries—*Fatal Flood of 1927* [italics added] and Spike Lee's on Hurricane Katrina. There is indeed a racial aspect (and a classed one and gendered) to the sublime and how it configures its own borders—think about former President Trump throwing rolls of paper towels to survivors of the hurricane in Puerto Rico, which reinforced to other ignorant US Americans that Puerto Rico was not part of the US. Kehinde Wiley's offering is actually closer to Mary Shelley's depiction of the monster among the picturesque as she relies on the experiences of the "un-monstrous" and Wiley the "un-Black" to complete their pictures and to question their own status. Frankly, £240 is not enough to seriously think through the Wiley and Homer paintings.[16]

My counteroffer was dismissed with a polite "thank you" for the promptness and frankness of my reply, with the observation that my work sounded very interesting and the hope that I could make it to the National Gallery on some sunny day.[17] Ironically, Friedrich's painting is on the cover of the Dover Thrift Edition of the novel *Frankenstein* (figs. 7.1a, b, and c).

INTERRUPTION

The National Gallery's invitation to me was one that could only envision a critique of empire that matched American artist (Black) to American empire to American art historian (also Black). Wiley, ultimately, never left the United States despite immersing himself and his models in the world of Friedrich within the context of Great Britain's National Gallery. Additionally, I was given no opportunity to engage the Sublime and empire at its originary source of Great Britain. Finally, the tittering emphasis on "the Black Sublime" reveals the nature of Wiley's interruption and who is presumed to be "looking." It is not Wiley's Black figure who pays as much studious attention to the landscape as Friedrich's figure; it is not the subject embedded in his landscapes. Instead, the presumed observer is the viewer in the gallery (White and European) into whose familiar landscape the site and sight of a Black figure bisects, disrupts, and interrupts the fantasy of an unknown yet to be

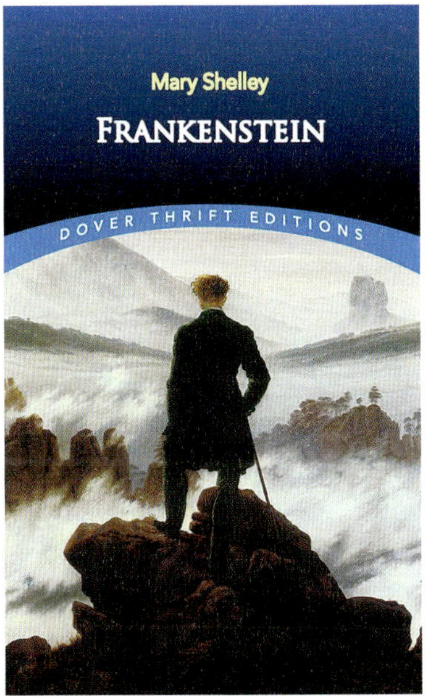

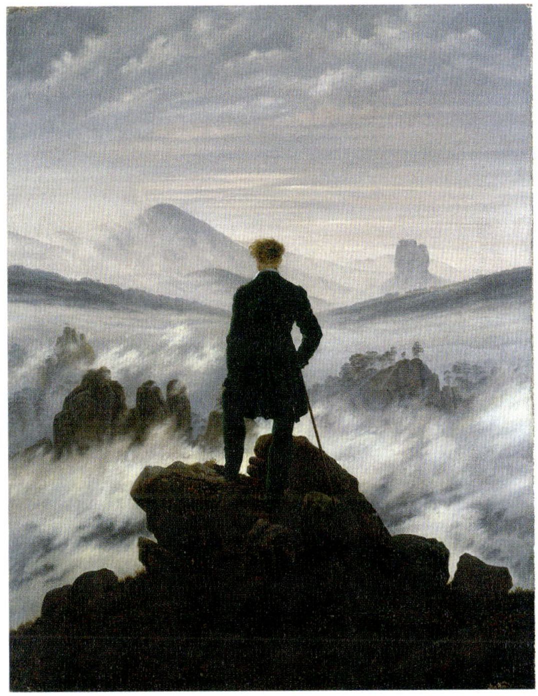

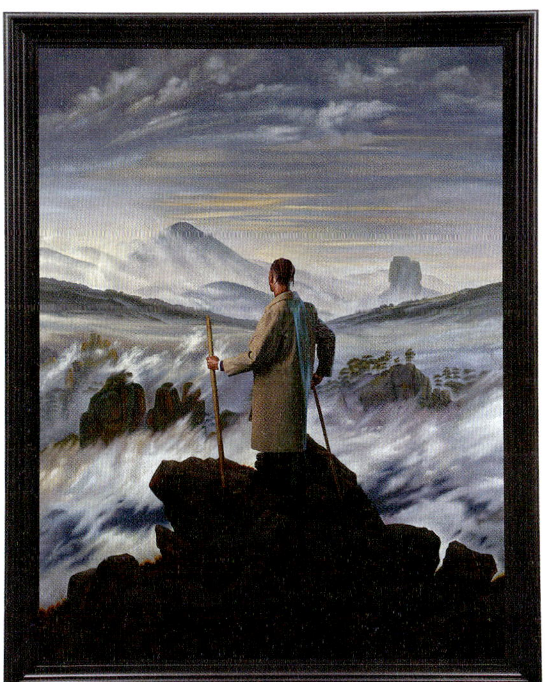

FIGURE 7.1A *above left* Cover of Mary Shelley's *Frankenstein*, Dover Thrift Editions, published 1994. (Middle) Caspar David Friedrich. *Wanderer above the Sea of Fog*, about 1817. Dover Thrift Editions.

FIGURE 7.1B *above right* Caspar David Friedrich (German, 1774–1840), *Wanderer above the Sea of Fog*, ca. 1817. Oil on canvas, 37⅓ × 29½ in. On permanent loan from the Foundation for the Promotion of the Hamburg Art Collections. Hamburger Kunsthalle. Photo: Elke Walford/Art Resource, New York.

Figure 7.1c. Kehinde Wiley (American, born 1977), *Prelude (Babacar Mané)*, 2021. Oil on linen, 152½ × 120 in. Image courtesy of the Rennie Collection, Vancouver, and Stephen Friedman Gallery, London. © Kehinde Wiley.

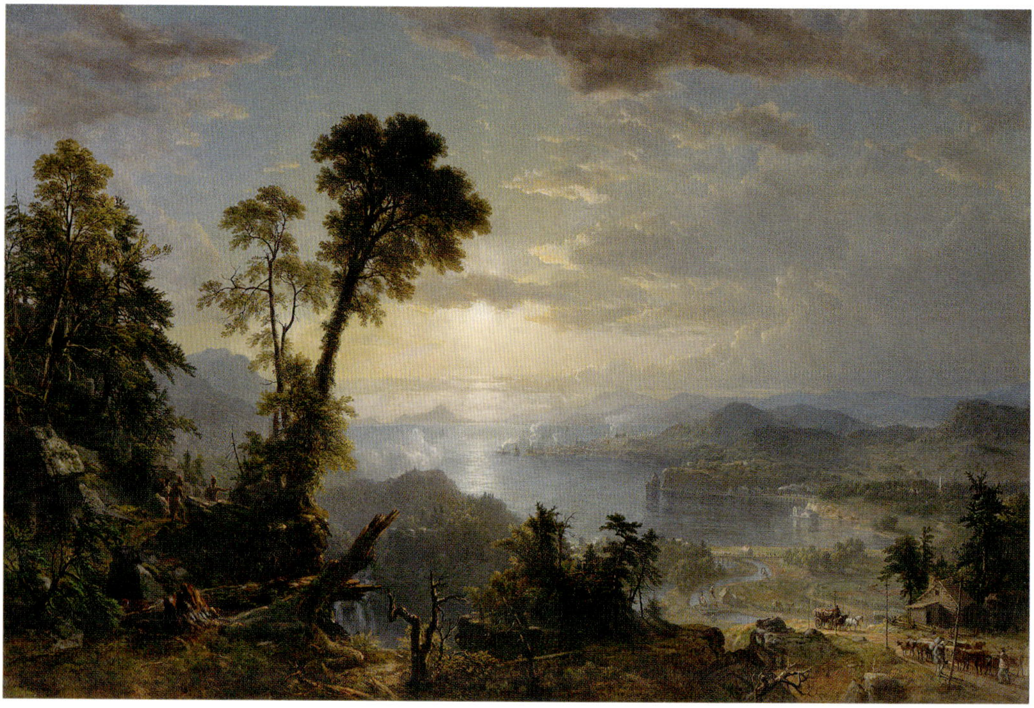

FIGURE 7.2 Asher B. Durand (American, 1796–1886), *Progress (The Advance of Civilization)*, 1853. Oil on canvas, 48 × 72 in. Virginia Museum of Fine Arts: Gift of an anonymous donor, 2018.547. Image by Travis Fullerton. Image courtesy of Virginia Museum of Fine Arts.

discovered and conquered. Wiley and Wiley's figures are Frankenstein's monster.

As institutions reenvision American art, interruption of common narratives has become a popular methodology, especially on gallery walls. One example will suffice in which an imperial US museum uses Indigenous art to "interrupt" nineteenth-century landscape painting: the reinstallation of one of the galleries at the Virginia Museum of Fine Arts (VMFA), which houses one of the most iconic images of nineteenth-century American landscape representation—Asher B. Durand's *Progress* of 1853, presented as an anonymous gift to the museum in 2018 (fig. 7.2). Museums like the VMFA benefit from curators like Leo Mazow, Louise B. and J. Harwood Cochrane Curator of American Art, who is willing to challenge the old narratives. He considers the hiring of the museum's first curator of Native American art, Dr. Johanna

Minich, a positive move, and he shares his galleries with her and speaks enthusiastically about her ongoing intervention in the gallery of iconic US landscape representations.[18] But how much are curators like Minich being asked to perform as Wilson or Wiley figures in the museums that hire them? How sustainable a practice is this for the museums and for the curators?

Museums must walk a fine line with their audiences. And so we find soft, inoffensive language on the gallery label "American Land, American People" that reduces racialization, extermination, kidnapping, poisoning, rape, lynching, infanticide, and murder to "trauma":

> AMERICAN LAND, AMERICAN PEOPLE
>
> In the hopes of offering a more complete narrative of American art and cultural history, VMFA will being displaying combinations of Euro-American and Indigenous works in this gallery.
>
> Spanning the period from the late 1800s through the 1920s, four paintings—by Asher B. Durand, Thomas Moran, Frederic Remington, and Walter Ufer—communicate long-held assumptions about the American landscape as a site of celebration, nostalgia, and, often, exploitation. These works both preserve in paint and romanticize a quickly vanishing wilderness.
>
> Two works by Indigenous artists Dyani White Hawk and Jaune Quick-to-See Smith tackle head-on the carefully crafted messages of Euro-American landscape paintings. While not landscapes themselves, they raise opposition to these socially sanctioned and culturally reinforced narratives.
>
> Where the compositions by Durand, Moran, Remington, and Ufer elaborate on the prevailing expansionist ideology of the time, White Hawk's and Quick-to-See Smith's works point to the selective histories presented in American landscape painting in the first place. Both sets of works, however, remind us that land is much more than the soil beneath our feet. It is the inspiration for scenes of incredible beauty and a reminder of the trauma of displaced people.[19]

Text and image battle in these contexts. The relative urgency of the label is belied by the seeming serenity of Durand's painting, and artistic convention will always win because it is the most legible and coherent within our epistemologies of looking versus reading versus abstraction. The power of Durand's painting to override words as well as abstraction is there to be witnessed on the walls of the gallery.

Installed by Minich across the room from Durand's *Progress* is Dyani White Hawk's (Rosebud Sioux, b. 1976) color lithograph *Trust and Loss* from 2013 (fig. 7.3). White Hawk incorporates a 1929 newspaper advertisement selling lands from her own reservation, made possible by the breaching of the Dawes Act of 1887, which broke up communal tribal lands and placed them in "trust." Also installed in the gallery is Jaune Quick-to-See Smith's (Salish/Kootinai, b. 1940) *War Torn Dress* of 2002 (fig. 7.4). Quick-to-See Smith uses the powerful metaphor of the war shirt, torn and bloodied and soiled, cut in half with the words "Your God" and "My God" printed above and below the forced horizon line (the vivisection) that divides Native American land and people. Nevertheless, within the space of this nineteenth-century gallery of landscape paintings, we must ask, Does the work of Indigenous artists interrupt or answer the viciousness of empire, or are the works a mirror that throws us back onto the beauty and convention of landscapes like the seeming benignity of Durand's *Progress*? Enough about me; now you say something about me.

It is my contention that what curators and museums demand of First Nation artists simply is not up to the task of interrupting imperial narratives, because as you move around the galleries and those spaces dedicated to British colonial and US art (the American Galleries), it is back to business as usual. It is like spectacle, the musical numbers that would suddenly erupt in the middle of the film, after which the narrative would resume. Nineteenth-century US landscape representation was merely one of the tools in what historian Karl Jacoby descried as "the era of extermination."[20] Landscapes provided a conventional gloss over murder and dispossession; they are therefore irredeemable despite juxtapositions of contemporary Indigenous art and the hiring of Indigenous curators. First Nations artists and First Nations curators know. This is not historical trauma. The damage is ongoing

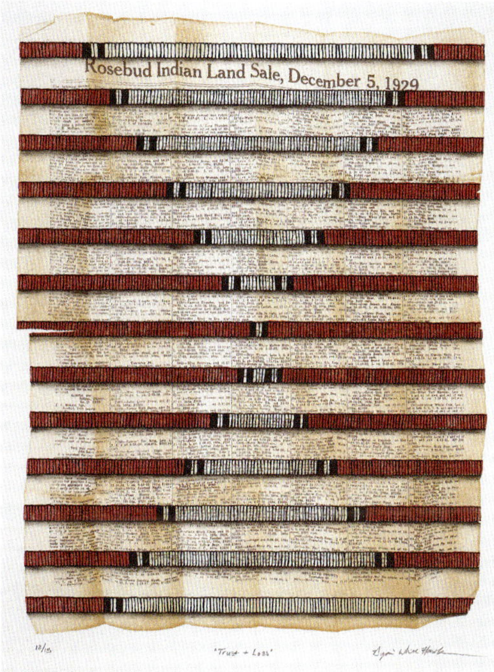

FIGURE 7.3 Dyani White Hawk (Sicangu Lakota/American, born 1976), *Trust and Loss*, 2013, color lithograph, 30 × 22 in. Virginia Museum of Fine Arts: Funds provided by Margaret A. and C. Boyd Clarke and Aldine S. Hartman Endowment Fund; 2020.154. Image by Travis Fullerton. © Virginia Museum of Fine Arts.

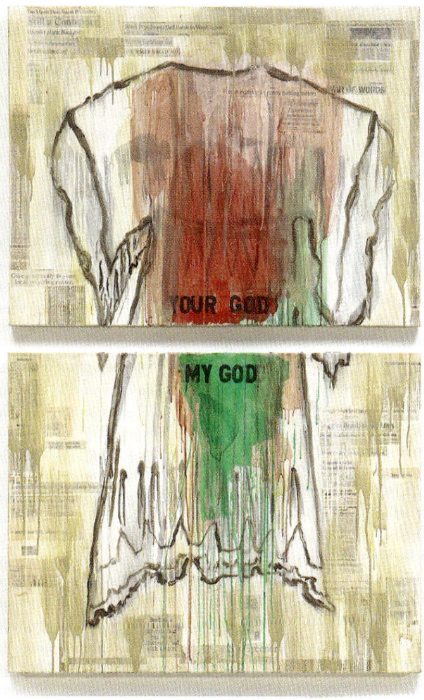

FIGURE 7.4 Jaune Quick-to-See Smith (Salish/Kootenai/American, born 1940), *War Torn Dress*, 2002, mixed media on canvas, 78 × 48 in. Virginia Museum of Fine Arts: Arthur and Margaret Glasgow Endowment; 2018.353a-b. © Virginia Museum of Fine Arts.

and exceeds any and all representational strategies. Through proximity to historical works of art within the gallery and the new focus on ecocriticism, Indigenous art within these contexts functions to absolve the old horrors of nineteenth-century landscape representation. While the hope is for critical interruption, Indigenous art in these spaces keeps the "Old Masters" relevant and brings them back to the table of culture so that figures like Thomas Cole, for example, can be described shockingly as a "proto-environmentalist."[21] The "invitation" is thus to the old specters of empire who reenter and reemerge on the backs of First Nations people. There is no need to guess who's coming to dinner when you already know. Oh, it's you.

UNINVITED: A THIRD CASE STUDY AND A CONCLUSION (OUT) OF SORTS

In the summer of 2010, my sister and I had the privilege of touring the Detroit Institute of Arts' (DIA) exhibition *Through African Eyes: The European in African Art, 1500–Present* with the show's curator, Nii Quarcoopome, curator and department head of Africa, Oceania, and Indigenous Americas at the DIA. Before becoming a curator and later deputy chief curator at the DIA, Quarcoopome (who is Ghanaian) was an assistant professor of African art at the University of Michigan. It was there, as a graduate student, that I met him, and he became one of my most important mentors. Ostensibly, the idea of Africans looking at Europeans and at the European diaspora does not seem controversial. However, the exhibition traveled to only one venue after leaving Detroit. Only the Nelson-Atkins Museum of Art, in Kansas City, was brave enough to accept the exhibition, because apparently the art world in the form of American imperial museums was not ready to see the results of Africans looking back. A sense of the exhibition's controversy is conveyed in a review by Holland Cotter for the *New York Times* titled "The Exotic in the Eyes of African Beholders." Cotter writes:

> Once upon a time black Africans saw white Europeans as supernatural beings. They were wrong. Whites saw blacks as savages. They were wrong. Flip those identities around. Still wrong. Shake things up,

> though, and eliminate the identities altogether, and you start to get right. Mr. Quarcoopome shakes things up.
>
> His show—modest in size, with fewer than 100 works, it feels underscaled in the institute's cavernous galleries—concludes with a contemporary section that combines images of ordinary Africans modeling trendy global haircuts ("French Style," "Tokyo Old Joe," "Watusi") and portraits of Elvis Presley; Puff Daddy; Queen Elizabeth II; Félix Houphouët-Boigny, former president of Ivory Coast; and Barack Obama.
>
> These images are all part of a tradition of African art that has for centuries looked at, evaluated and selectively embraced the West. That tradition is represented by a show organized by an African and installed in a great museum designed on European models and built by white Americans. And that museum is in a great city that is now predominantly African-American.
>
> Who would have imagined, even just a few years ago, that such histories and energies could have been found in art that most of us never knew existed? Enough to say that if you get a thrill from seeing things you've never seen and thinking thoughts you've never thought, Detroit is a good place to be these days.[22]

Like the National Gallery's "Black Sublime," Cotter's reference to an "African Beholder" is just as controversial . . . to them: "*Who would have imagined, even just a few years ago, that such histories and energies could have been found in art that most of us never knew existed?*" The issue turns on the Black Beholder in both Wiley's case and in the case of the objects amassed by Quarcoopome. Black and Indigenous Beholders, despite their invitations, are disruptors who interrupt the looking dynamics of empire by returning the gaze. Notwithstanding the art world's trepidation, the DIA was selected as a winner in the American Association of Museums' Twenty-Fourth Annual Excellence in Exhibitions competition for 2012 for *Through African Eyes*. But part of the story remains untold.

To conclude the exhibition, Quarcoopome commissioned Isaac Otchere, also known as Azey (b. 1964), to represent the historic election and inauguration of Barack Obama in 2008 (fig. 7.5). Otchere, who is from Kumasi in Ghana, helps us to understand one African artist's perspective on his own diaspora through one painting. In a bit of mischief, Otchere makes the bald spot of Chief Justice John Roberts the vanishing point of his composition. Despite this bit of humor, the painting is filled with significant people and events that makes it reminiscent of earlier works, like Charles White's 1942 mural *Five Great American Negroes.* At the very center is the swearing in—the moment that Obama takes the oath of office—as the culminating event of the work. On the top left is the long campaign, from the hard-fought primary to win the nomination against Obama's formidable opponent, Senator Hillary Clinton, to the debates with Senator John McCain. At the center left, Otchere depicts the Obama campaign's mastery not only of sloganeering but also of technology; I think we all remember that moment in the football stadium when Obama gave the number to text your donations. Flashing on the Jumbotron, the number allowed people in the stadium and those who were watching the event on television to donate instantaneously. The combined fund-raising by the Obama and McCain campaigns made this election the first billion-dollar race for the presidency. On the bottom left, Otchere portrays the night that Obama won, and while it was an American election, the celebration that Otchere depicts takes place in Africa. Above President Obama's head is the White House, and in the sky is a clock whose shape is defined by a rainbow, reinforcing the sense of hopefulness and the "about time–ness" of the election of the first African American president of the United States. On the top right, a group of figures from US history celebrate the election. James Meredith is there; in 1962 he was the first African American student admitted to the segregated University of Mississippi. When Meredith tried to enter, Mississippi's governor tried to stop him. That led to violence on the Oxford campus. US attorney general Robert Kennedy sent five hundred US marshals to take control, and days later Meredith was allowed in the school. Though he faced harassment during his time at the school, he graduated with a degree in political science. He raises his fist in triumph. The bust of Meredith placed in his honor at Ole Miss continues to be a site of controversy. In 2014 the statue was once again vandalized with a noose

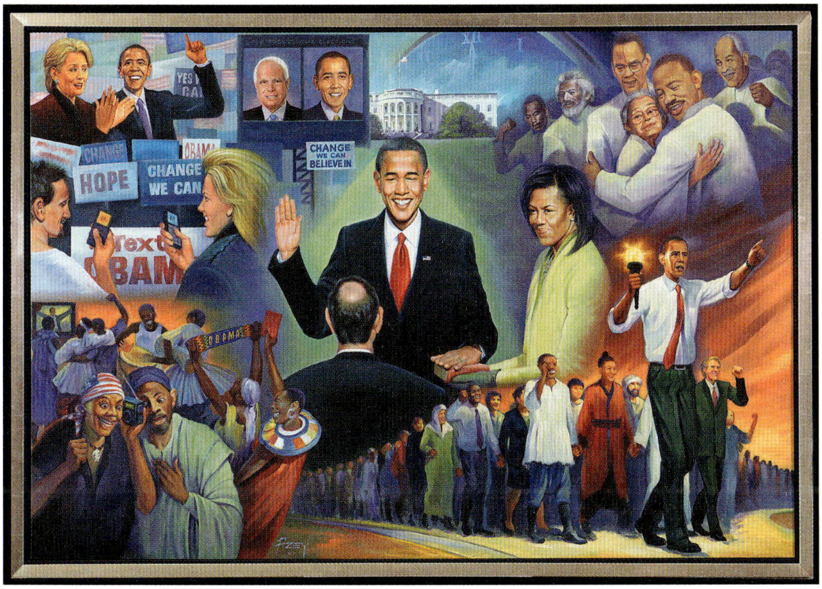

FIGURE 7.5 Isaac Otchere Azey (Ghanaian, born 1964), *The Election of 2008*. Oil on canvas, 48 × 71 in. Image courtesy of private collection. © Isaac Otchere Azey.

placed around the statue's neck.[23] Next to Meredith is Frederick Douglass and then Malcolm X. Embracing with joy are Rosa Parks and Martin Luther King Jr. Behind them is Justice Thurgood Marshall, who served as the first African American justice of the US Supreme Court from 1967 until 1991. At the bottom right, President Obama carries a torch and leads humanity toward the future. It is a triumphant image and, as I intimated before, a fascinating look at how one African artist understands his own diaspora.

Despite Otchere's acclaim, the painting of the election of 2008 was removed from Quarcoopome's exhibition. Its exclusion prompts several questions: Why was the painting removed? What made the painting so objectionable? What could the painting have added to the overall narrative of the exhibition? In its place was another work by Otchere, the significantly titled *One World Hair Studio*, which features P. Diddy, Will Smith, and Barack Obama (fig. 7.6). While the three figures ostensibly represent hair-styling options, they once signified men whose fame stretched beyond the United States and whose talents and fortune rendered them figures to

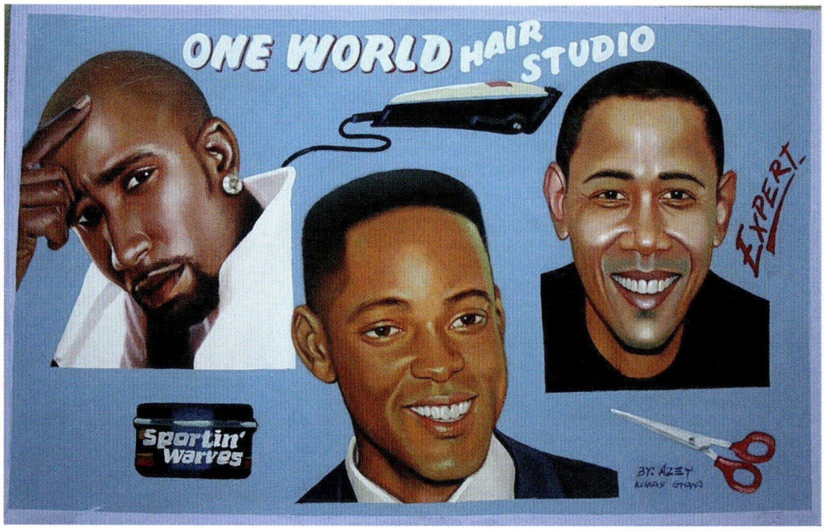

FIGURE 7.6 Isaac Otchere Azey (Ghanaian, born 1964), *One World Hair Studio*. Oil on canvas. Dimensions unknown. Private collection. © Isaac Otchere Azey.

emulate. Furthermore, the designation "One World" is a clear nod to the power of the African Diaspora. I would argue that the election painting and the hair-styling painting convey similar messages about that power. And each registers something that surprised even the curator—that is, the gradual disappearance and significance of Europe and its diaspora in the visual culture of Africa.[24]

While both paintings, created by the same artist, convey similar messages, the excuse of aesthetics was used against only one painting—the election. Similar messaging, yes, but also only one was an offense to those who were still resentful of Obama's win. By choosing the hair studio over the election, the DIA reduced Obama to a celebrity whose only impact was a surface one related to style rather than Otchere's exuberant reflection on Obama's historical and geographical importance as the first Black president of the United States of America. Alternately, the hair studio painting put Obama safely back in Africa and an African barbershop, a celebrity whose style could be modeled and selected for an African man's next hairdo. Style politics triumphed over Obama's impact on American and global politics.

CONCLUSION

This chapter has been a reflection on invitations, interruptions, and monsters among the picturesque, on considering what is allowed and thus invited into imperial spaces. As we reenvision American art, we can use the previous case studies to speculate on all the exhibitions and opportunities that are not allowed entry, or even to exist, and what is lost to us as a result. We have rushed to deploy art and art history as absolving agents—dissolving and dis-solving agents—in our redemptory installations in imperial museums. It is my contention that we don't need to describe Thomas Cole as a proto-environmentalist; it is an unnecessary designation that exposes the absolving perception of environmentalism and conservationism—both of which are ideologies that are rarely, if ever, contradicted by the racism and nationalism that subtends them. It was November 30, 2021, after all, when Prince William found himself at the center of controversy while speaking at the Tusk Conservation Award ceremony in London, where, with an array of Africans behind him, he said that the increasing pressure on the African continent's "wildlife and wild spaces as a result of human population" was presenting "a huge challenge for conservationists, as it does the world over."[25] In other words, there are too many Africans in Africa. What does it mean to celebrate histories of conservation in what Karl Jakoby described as the era of extermination? Furthermore, the juxtaposition of the labor of Indigenous curators and artists to the original violence of colonization crystallizes the power of form over rhetoric, exposing the potential of ecocriticism and environmentalism to become the continuation of a kind of expansion that once again argues for the erasure (by any means necessary) of Indigenous inhabitants because they disrupt imperial sight lines. The categorization of Kehinde Wiley's vision as "the Black Sublime" speaks to this invited disruption, where momentary interruption is the price of renewed relevance and absolution for the real monsters of empire.

NOTES

1. To be clear, the National Gallery's invitation would not have been my first opportunity to explore Wiley's work. I teach Wiley in my classes; and I contributed a brief essay to the Brooklyn Museum's catalog for the exhibition *Kehinde Wiley: The New Republic.* See Kirsten Pai Buick, "Cameroon Study," in *Kehinde Wiley: The New Republic,* edited by Eugene Tsai, 106–107 (Brooklyn: Brooklyn Museum and Prestel, 2015).

2. Kehinde Wiley Studio, The Prelude, Exhibitions, https://kehindewiley.com/exhibitions/the-prelude/, accessed August 1, 2023.

3. Chris Mugan, "Kehinde Wiley: Radically Rethinking Romanticism at the National Gallery," ARTUUK.org, January 7, 2022, accessed August 1, 2023, https://artuk.org/discover/stories/kehinde-wiley-radically-rethinking-romanticism-at-the-national-gallery/.

4. Mugan, "Kehinde Wiley."

5. Dr. Christina Bradstreet, courses and events programmer, National Gallery, London, email message to author, January 11, 2022.

6. Bradstreet, email message to author, January 11, 2022.

7. Edmund Burke, *A Philosophical Enquiry into the Origins of Our Ideas of the Sublime and Beautiful* (London: Printed for R. and J. Dodsley, 1757).

8. Richard Bourke, *Empire and Revolution: The Political Life of Edmund Burke* (Princeton: Princeton University Press, 2015), 86–88.

9. Burke, *A Philosophical Enquiry*, unpaginated.

10. Uvedale Price, *An Essay on the Picturesque as Compared with the Sublime and the Beautiful; and, on the Use of Studying Pictures, for the Purpose of Improving Real Landscape* (London: J. Robson, New Bond Street, 1796).

11. Sidney K. Robinson, *Inquiry into the Picturesque* (Chicago: University of Chicago Press, 1991), 17.

12. Bourke, *Empire and Revolution*, 90.

13. Bourke, *Empire and Revolution*, 371.

14. See the discussion of "The Picturesque" in John Dickie, *Darkest Italy: The Nation and Stereotypes of the Mezzogiorno, 1860–1900* (New York: St. Martin's Press, 1999), 83–119. See also John Barrell, *The Darkside of the Landscape: The Rural Poor in English Painting, 1730–1840* (Cambridge: Cambridge University Press, 1980); and Ann Bermingham, *Landscape and Ideology: The English Rustic Tradition, 1740–1860* (Berkeley: University of California Press, 1986).

15. Eric Purchase, *Out of Nowhere: Disaster and Tourism in the White Mountains* (Baltimore: Johns Hopkins University Press, 1999).

16. Author email message to Dr. Christina Bradstreet, courses and events programmer, National Gallery, London, January 11, 2022.

17. Dr. Christina Bradstreet, courses and events programmer, National Gallery, London, email message to author, January 12, 2022.

18. Dr. Minich left the VMFA in 2022. As of September 2023, this position has not been filled.

19. Gallery label at the Virginia Museum of Fine Arts, 2021.

20. Karl Jacoby, "The Broad Platform of Extermination: Nature and Violence in the Nineteenth Century North American Borderlands," *Journal of Genocide Research* 10, no. 2 (2008): 249–67.

21. William L. Coleman, "An Interview with the Curators of Thomas Cole's Journey: Atlantic Crossings," *Panorama: Journal of the Association of Historians of American Art* 4, no. 2 (2018), https://journalpanorama.org/article/an-interview-with-the-curators-of-thomas-coles-journey-atlantic-crossings/. The statement was made by Elizabeth Mankin Kornhauser, one of the curators for the Metropolitan Museum of Art's Thomas Cole exhibition in 2018. "When we set out to explore Cole's journey, we honestly didn't know what we'd find. I feel like all of our suspicions have come true: that his tours of England and Italy were unbelievably rich and important. I have posed the question, 'Had Cole not had his early British roots, had he not seen the horrors of the Industrial Revolution, then gone on this Grand Tour to learn about art of the past, contemporary landscape art and techniques, immersed himself in the ruins of a past civilization, and then come back and taught all this to his students, particularly Church and [Asher B.] Durand, would there ever have been a national school of landscape art and the so-called "Hudson River School"?' I actually question whether that would have come about: his role was so important in imparting all this at the right moment to the young Church, to the mature Durand, and they took it and ran with it. The other thing we learned is that Cole really probably is the first proto-environmental artist in America."

22. Holland Cotter, "The Exotic in the Eyes of African Beholders," *New York Times*, April 15, 2010.

23. "Noose Tied around Statue of James Meredith, Civil Rights Icon," *CBS News*, February 19, 2014, https://www.cbsnews.com/news/noose-tied-to-ole-miss-statue-of-james-meredith-civil-rights-icon/.

24. Nii Quarcoopome, interview by author, February 18, 2024.

25. Nick Duffy, "Prince William Says Human Population Growth in Africa Is Harming Wildlife," *inews*, November 23, 2021, https://inews.co.uk/news/prince-william-human-population-growth-africa-harming-wildlife-1315378/.

8

Hazel V. Carby

IMAGINING OTHERWISE

In 1972 I began my career as the only Black teacher at a high school in the London borough of Newham. London ranks as the world's top city for the ultra-wealthy, for their investments and lifestyle prospects. Newham, only five miles east, has one of the highest poverty rates and lowest life expectancy rates of all London boroughs and is the most ethnically diverse district in England and Wales.[1] The kids in my class didn't go to art museums, theaters, or concert halls because "Culture" was the preserve of people with the plummy, cut-glass diction of the British Culture. They feared being forcibly ejected by museum guards for not obeying mystifying rules of etiquette they had never been taught. They also didn't travel to central London or camp or hike in the countryside, believing these spaces and activities were reserved exclusively for the predominantly White, wealthy, educated elite. So I took them camping and hiking, to concerts, to theaters and art museums. Leading the way, I hoped, would demonstrate that I, and they, were not intruding. Initially excited to leave their neighborhood, all sense of adventure died when my pupils confronted the visual representations of White, Eurocentric, colonial, imperial culture. Though I was unable to protect them (or myself) from the pain of our encounters, we all persisted: through talking about and sharing our reactions to what we saw and heard, we eventually made tentative claims upon the spaces into and through which we moved.

As a professor at elite universities in the United States, first at Wesleyan and then at Yale, I have ushered generations of young people across the thresholds of art museums into spaces they were reluctant to enter. The reasons for their reluctance varied: some felt they had never acquired the arcane knowledge or language necessary for art appreciation; others declared that art museums were "spaces of White supremacy," housing objects that were of no relevance to their lives or imaginations and that colonized or flatly denied the truths of their existence.

All art museums must reckon with the history of their role in actively maintaining and reproducing the mythologies and ideologies of Eurocentric art history and perpetuating imperial and settler colonial domination through curated practices of violent racist humiliation. I have traveled to art museums all over the United States and returned home to write letters protesting their relegation of Black and Indigenous art to marginal spaces and anthropological interpretation; I protest because I remain invested in the transformative power of art and the pedagogic potential of art museums. Entering some of them is like walking through the syllabi of conventional, Eurocentric art history courses, but others prompt me to wonder if they have been influenced by the research and teaching of scholars, particularly scholars of color, who are not art historians but whose work contests racialized and gender-normative ways of knowing in profound ways. If such engagement has the potential to support the decolonization of curatorial practices and collections, is it possible for art museums to learn from and avoid the errors we have made as professors in our academic struggle to institute insurgent, antiracist counter histories?

Within the United States, research and scholarship on ethnic, Indigenous, racialized, and gendered cultures and histories has gained a presence on college campuses, nurtured by Asian American, Black, Indigenous, Latine/x, and gender-nonconforming faculty and their allies who have established academic departments and programs, created centers, and supported consortiums. This extraordinary collective intellectual effort has been undermined by an ignominious lack of financial support from university administrations who have also failed to establish equity in the representation of Black, Brown, Indigenous, and nonconforming gendered bodies among the teaching staff.

Despite the pernicious racism of educational institutions, it is undeniable that these new fields of knowledge stand at the forefront of curricular innovation, challenging and transforming settler colonial understandings of the past and present to build a more just and equitable future. If this work has made little impact on the structure of higher education and remains marginal to the mission of universities to train future leaders, for those of us at universities with art museums, it has been important to ally with curators and directors who are committed to the process of decolonization and have expanded and diversified their collections. At Yale I urged students to study the complex historical and formal relations between forms of literary and visual culture. When I realized that some students were viewing objects digitally in order to avoid entering the Yale Art Gallery, I moved my seminars into art gallery classrooms, where my students had direct engagement with individual art objects. The art gallery provided financial support for acquisitions and for bringing Black artists to campus; with the help of their staff, I was able to curate study galleries designed for African American studies courses.

Having been involved in the creation of administrative units for alternative fields of knowledge, particularly the institutionalization of Black studies; the study of race, ethnicity, and migration; and for gender and sexuality studies, I am concerned that forms of interdisciplinary thinking and learning that originally sought to transcend and transform traditional disciplinary boundaries and measures of worth, of inclusion and exclusion, have instead adopted these measures and instituted canonical thinking as a means to gain institutional recognition. Despite claims of institutional commitments to diversity emanating from university administrations, their practice is to encourage and maintain siloed fields, departments, programs, and centers in constant competition with one another for the crumbs of resources they parsimoniously distribute. Silos of knowledge narrow visions of who can be included in "we," abandon the possibility of multiple affiliations and solidarities, of "standing with" and alongside in favor of singular modes of belonging. Disciplinarily bound borders and ontologically exclusionary concepts anchor ethnically and racially organized fields of knowing and new forms of silencing. Can the process of decolonizing the practices and collections of university art museums transcend these boundaries and divisions between formations of knowledge that have become siloed in university departments?

Writing about environmental racism, degradation, and ecological catastrophes as continuing legacies of the settler colonialism threatening Indigenous existence and Black and Brown well-being has led me to ask if we have paid an unacceptable price for the curricular enrichment and enlargement of our historical particularities. How do we think across these histories and place them in relation to each other? In what ways are we restrained within the confines of siloed fields of knowledge? Are we cultivating monocultures: fields organized into discrete ontological formations that limit our imaginative capacity to engage with the complexities of relationality, of historical convergence as well as divergence? If we remain immersed within gated communities of circumscribed knowing, each cultivating its own vocabulary and developing discrete historical and conceptual frameworks, do we remain blind to the necessity not only of thinking *across* human and nonhuman disciplinarily bound borders of knowing but of the possibilities of imagining otherwise without boundaries?

Racialized image making has become an important activity for universities that suffer our intellectual existence within restraints that ensure that our ability to fundamentally contest dominant formations of knowledge is domesticated and pacified—in short, colonized. University administrations shamelessly exploit images of our physical presence to their own advantage. Their websites representing themselves as bastions of racial equality, adopting the terms "diversity," "equity," and "inclusion" (or "belonging") as credentials for self-promotion. Akin to corporate "greenwashing," "fostering inclusion and diversity" is *not* a commitment to end structural racism or an agreement to decolonize academic institutions by unearthing, confronting, and acting to repair the violence and violations of settler colonialism and racial capitalism.

This "white noise" of diversity, equity, and inclusion continuously assembles, reassembles, and delivers platitudes in frequencies that convey negligible amounts of information. The undercurrent is the recruitment of personnel by administrators and executives of universities and corporations who require bodies of certain colors, shapes, and visual features to fit into an invented jigsaw of diversity. These bodies thus "become sites of the extraction of surplus value . . . something that can be calculated and recombined."[2] The key word in this process of selection is "fit" because the incorporation of bodies that carry "diversity" must not disrupt the field lines of their vectors of power: their presence must enrich institutional definitions of community and social order; diversity must not disrupt or unbalance the preservation of the corporate university's central function, the dissemination of Eurocentric, settler colonial forms of knowledge, and power structures that secure our permanent marginalization. Commitments to diversity and inclusion function as tactics of colonial pacification that nurture the soil from which Native informants can be harvested.

As Darby English argues, art can enable students to think very deeply about the politics of exclusion and difference, and "it has often been the case that art offers the richest insights into what moments of emergency—like ours—actually do to subjects of a culture."[3] Artists have long drawn upon imaginings of futurity as a force that can galvanize action leading to profound systemic change. Within and across the Americas, settler colonialism has resulted in bleak and truncated futures, in threats of annihilation for Africans and Indigenous peoples who, regarded as less than human, have been beaten, humiliated, imprisoned, lynched, raped, shot, starved, whipped, bartered as chattel, exploited as units of energy, herded into slave ships, dispossessed, corralled onto reservations, and discarded as waste. However, this unmitigated and genocidal brutality failed to eradicate visions of futurity, of international solidarity and dreams of communal possibility.[4] These ideas concerning knowledge, power structures, futurity, and solidarity informed my work as a Roth Distinguished Fellow during the 2021–22 academic year at Dartmouth College. When I visited the Hood Museum of Art, I hesitated when I reached the threshold of the first gallery of *This Land: American Engagement with the Natural World*. On the surface, the title *This Land* appeared neutral, typical of the cautious announcements we expect from art galleries and museums, which have to be wary of the financial consequences of offending influential patrons. The source of my hesitation was the difficult, contradictory relationship I have with "this land" and with the label "American." Both terms are usually taken for granted, a form of common sense that is deployed to erase or silence histories fraught with contesting geopolitical claims of boundaries, belonging, and exclusion. I feel unsettled in and by "this land." Always circumspect, I walk lightly on its soil, refusing to become rooted. For most of my career, my academic affiliations have been tethered to universities and colleges in the United States, but my work is not tied to the nationalist tendencies and exclusionary conceptual boundaries dominating American and African American studies.[5] On the contrary, my scholarly, imaginative, and political commitments range across the histories, literatures, and visual cultures of the multifarious Black and Indigenous communities of the Caribbean, Europe, and the Americas. It matters that I make this distinction between a formal affiliation and a critical imagination, though "distinction" is, perhaps, a word inadequate to describe what I have experienced as a profound geopolitical rift. So I paused with my hand on the door, took a deep breath, and steeled myself to be alienated from the assumptions of affiliation simultaneously embodied in and disguised by "This Land" and "American."

We should be outraged by art museums, catalogs, and courses in art history that continue to reenact narratives of Manifest Destiny in their accounts and exhibitions of American art.[6] This narrative, a legacy of settler colonialism, insists that the story of a young nation is captured in the work of the landscape paintings of a group of European American artists working in the romantic tradition led by the Englishman Thomas Cole. Beginning in the mid-nineteenth century, the Hudson River School, as they came to be collectively known, painted the American landscape as encounters with the sublime, rendered as pristine "Nature," and untouched "Wilderness." The chronology adopted for this lineage traces American "expansion," from the earliest portrayals of the forest, lakes, and hills of New England to Albert Bierstadt's monumental paintings of the American West as a frontier ripe for settlement, without regard for the violence and violations of colonialization borne by Black and Indigenous peoples whose labor shaped the land.[7]

This Land, a collaboration between Hood curators Barbara J. MacAdam, Jami C. Powell, Thomas H. Price, Morgan E. Freeman, and Michael W. Hartman, replaced the temporal, exclusionary settler colonial ways of seeing with powerful alternative modes of interpreting and refusing its legacy. The

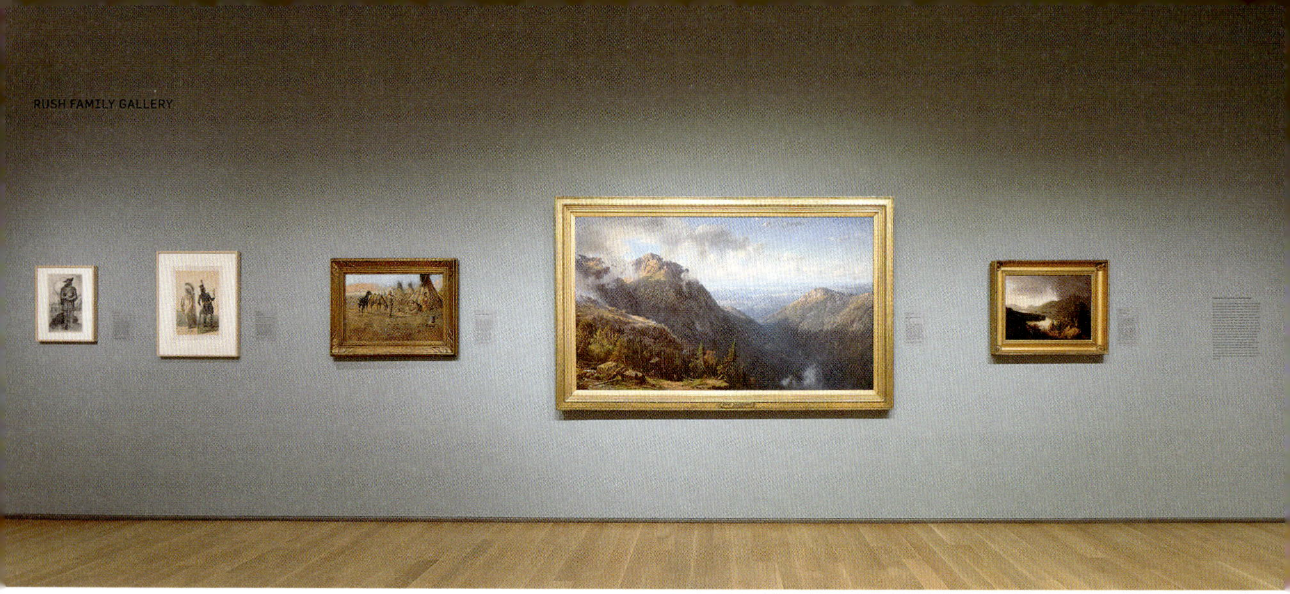

FIGURE 8.1 Installation view, "Expansion, Encounter, and Exchange," in *This Land: American Engagement with the Natural World*, featuring (left to right) Régis François Gignoux, *New Hampshire (White Mountain Landscape)*, about 1864 and Thomas Cole, *View on Lake George*, 1826; both of the Hudson River School. Image by Rob Strong. © Hood Museum of Art, Dartmouth.

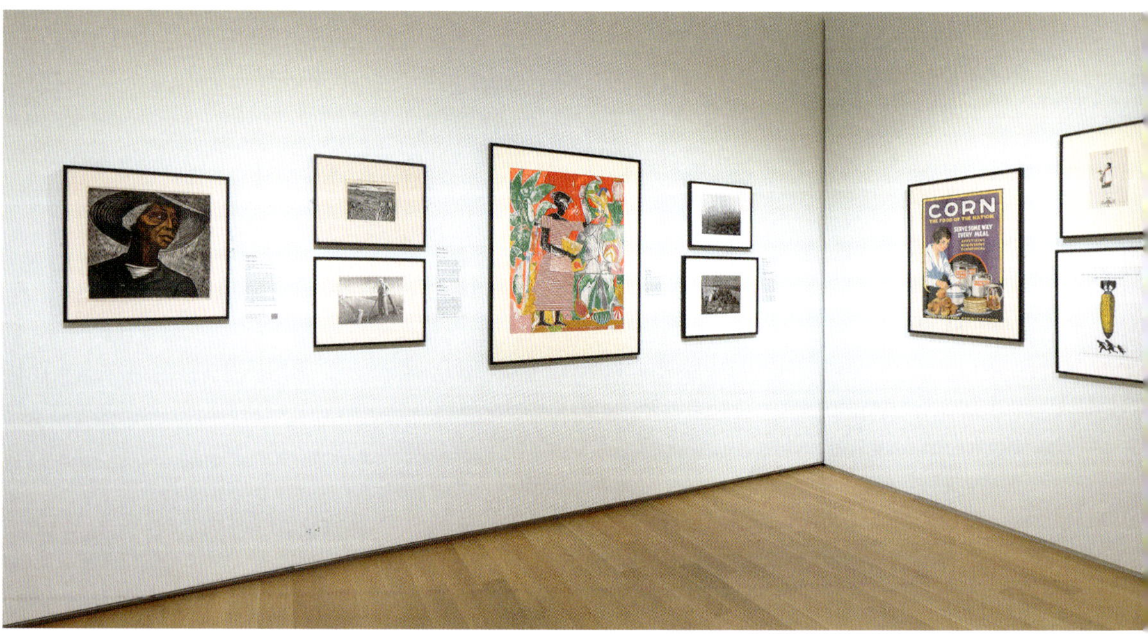

FIGURE 8.2 Installation view, "Sustenance," in *This Land: American Engagement with the Natural World*. Image by Rob Strong. © Hood Museum of Art, Dartmouth.

exhibition included "not only Euro-American, African American, Latin American, and Asian American works but also, for the first time, traditional and contemporary Native American works hung alongside . . . early to contemporary 'American' art."[8] In addition to the inclusion of a multiplicity of peoples and their art forms, the imaginary geopolitical boundaries of land were expanded beyond the United States. Jami C. Powell, the first curator of Native American art at the Hood Art Museum, is an impressive and effective advocate for the transformation of the curatorial practices, collections, and spatial layout of art museums.[9] She argues that the work of museums should be "celebrating the creative expression and knowledge . . . that comes from populations around the globe."[10]

There were multiple forms of engagement with the legacies of settler colonialism in the exhibition, in its variety of modes of information, overall design, and spatial layout: in wall labels, panel texts, audio and video files; in the placement of objects in thematic galleries whose spatial relations revealed complex and contending stories; and through creative, imaginative alternative narratives of the past and present of the human and nonhuman inhabitants of "this land" revealed in the passage between and through galleries.

The romantic settler colonial tradition of landscape painting representing nature as pristine, or untouched, was not ignored or glossed; rather, its ideologies were opened to question and subtly undermined. Thomas Cole's oil painting *View on Lake George* (1826) and *New Hampshire (White Mountain Landscape)* (about 1864) by the French painter Régis François Gignoux, also of the Hudson River School, were placed next to each other (fig. 8.1). But on the opposite wall, as if in direct contradiction of these two paintings, were artworks that did not separate nature from the human and human activity. Gathered under the theme of "Sustenance," a series of artworks including Vincent Smith's *Down on the Farm* (1966, woodcut on paper), Romare Bearden's *In the Garden*, from the portfolio *Prevalence of Ritual* (1974, screen print on wove paper), and George Tice's *Cornfield and Farmhouse* (negative 1966; print 1989, gelatin silver print) "explored the complexities of food acquisition in relation to necessity, abundance, nourishment, and labor" and the "specialized ecological knowledge that communities hold and how those knowledges sustain our lives" (fig. 8.2). I have a vivid memory of the

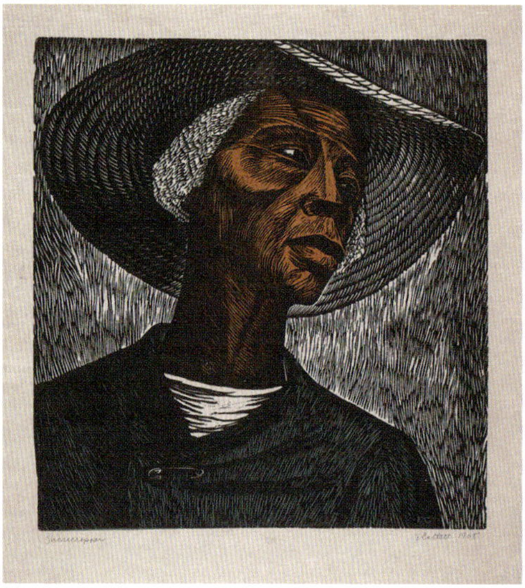

FIGURE 8.3 Elizabeth Catlett (American and Mexican, 1915–2012), *Sharecropper,* about 1952 (key block), 1968 (color blocks and this impression). Color linocut, 22 × 21 in. Hood Museum of Art, Dartmouth: Purchased through the Mrs. Harvey P. Hood W'18 Fund; 2012.62. Image by Jeffrey Nintzel. © 2024 Catlett Mora Family Trust/Licensed by VAGA at Artists Rights Society (ARS), New York.

placement of Elizabeth Catlett's linocut *Sharecropper* (1952, 1968), an extraordinary evocation of a proud and dignified figure looking directly at the viewer and positioned to stare defiantly across the gallery at Cole's and Gignoux's works: a powerful condemnation and refusal of the romantic tradition of American landscape painting that dehumanizes as it erases the people who worked and shaped it (fig. 8.3).

It is the first objects we see as we enter an exhibition that set the context and establish the lines of curated storytelling that unfold in subsequent galleries. From the outset, the artwork in the first gallery of the exhibition unsettled and disrupted conventional, settler colonial histories and visual representations of "American Engagement with the Natural World," for the lands of North America were immediately revealed to be sites of contestation embattled (fig. 8.4). The White Buffalo Calf Women March took place on November 27, 2016, at Oceti Sakowin Camp, in the No Dakota Access Pipeline Movement, described as "The largest Indigenous uprising in North America in recent memory."[11] In this painting of the event, Yatika Starr Fields realizes the intimate connections between past and present and between the physical and spiritual aspects of women leading Indigenous movements: the Women's March evokes the strength and power associated with the sacred story of the White Buffalo Calf Woman.

Through bold color and shading, Fields recreates unity, solidarity, and solidity, while the folds and shadows in the skirts produce movement and momentum. There is power, strength, determination, and purpose in these bold strokes and shapes, capturing an unwavering forward march of resistance

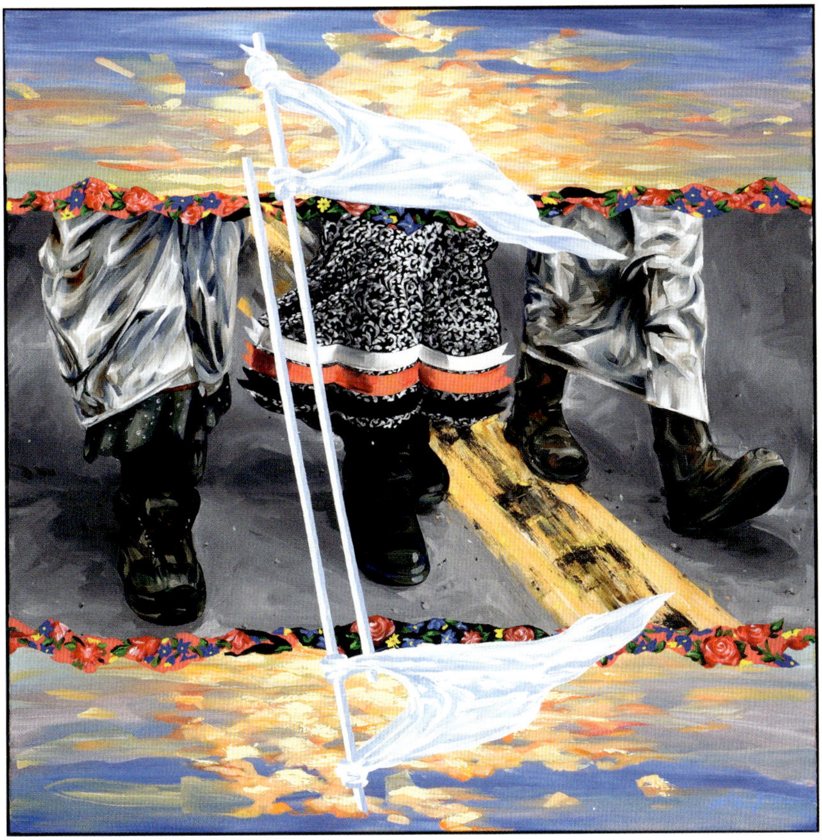

FIGURE 8.4 Yatika Starr Fields (Cherokee/Creek/Osage/American, born 1980), *White Buffalo Calf Women March*, 2017. Oil on canvas, 60⅟₁₆ × 60⅟₁₆ in. Hood Museum of Art, Dartmouth. Purchased through the Alvin and Mary Bert Gutman 1940 Acquisition Fund; 2018.24. Image by Jeffrey Nintzel. © Yatika Starr Fields.

and refusal down the center of a road, which is both a particular location and an act of recall, the historical and cultural memory of the many, many roads trodden by Indigenous peoples in protest. Yes, this is a specific historical moment and movement, but the solidity of boots on the ground project commitment to the long haul, behind and ahead. The landscape is segmented with two skies, top and bottom, each culminating in a chain of flowers that separates the skies from the road while also embracing and honoring the marching legs and feet on tarmac. Two white flags on staves connect the three segments in testimony to the multiple dawns and sunsets through which these three figures have marched before and will continue to march into the future. Landscapes entice, inviting viewers to locate themselves in relation to what they see. *White Buffalo Calf Women March* encourages a lowering of the gaze, a consideration of the ground occupied by the viewer, the land on which she stands and walks; in what direction, toward what end, and with what pace and determination? Settler or colonized, the viewer is implicated either way and with these questions is propelled into the exhibition.

This Land was not only a response to the sublime landscapes of American romantic painting, but in this first gallery its selection of art photography was a passionate and compelling rejection of the Edward Curtis anthropological delusions of vanquished, vanished, or vanishing Indigenous subjects that settler visitors may harbor. On the contrary, the artists here are concerned with the creation of counternarratives and modes of storytelling, and each creates their story within an alternative, counter landscape.

Josué Rivas is a photographer whose self-description is as a visual storyteller and educator working at the intersection of art, journalism, and social justice. Rivas says, "The intention of my work is to create a safe space for Indigenous peoples to tell their own story through photography and public art. By making our own image and exploring our identity, we develop a better sense of who we are. As we reclaim our narrative, we defend what is most sacred to us, our story."

Included in the exhibition are two photographs taken by Rivas in 2016 at Standing Rock from his much larger *Standing Strong: Awakening* series (fig. 8.5). Rather than narrating how opposition to the Dakota Access Pipeline (DAPL) galvanized people into particular protest actions, the focus in the first photograph is the community that was built over time from and through the practice of resistance. It is a quiet, contemplative, intimate portrait of a community embedded in, and deeply tied to, the land it seeks to protect. The second photograph shows the aftermath of the destruction of the encampment, though the proclamation "Indigenous Sovereignty protects land—air—water" remains standing (fig. 8.6). Law enforcement used armored vehicles, automatic rifles, acoustic weapons, water cannons, concussion grenades, attack dogs, pepper spray, beanbag bullets, riot gear, and other offensive military weapons and equipment against organizers and

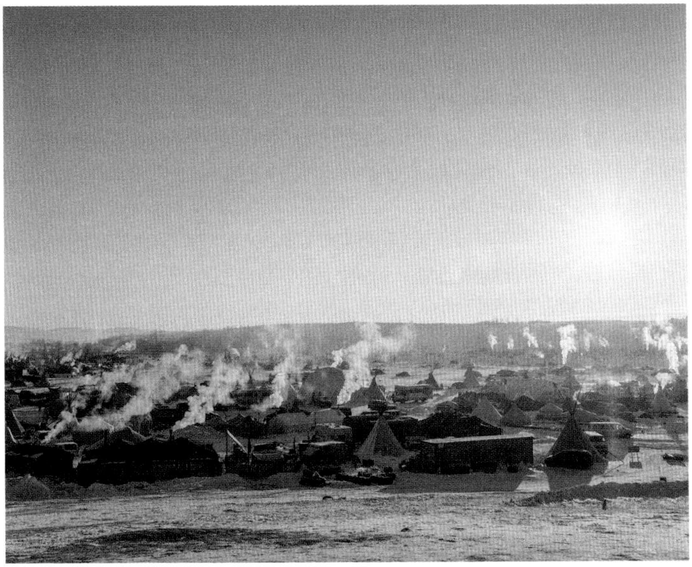

FIGURE 8.5 Josué Rivas (Mexica/Otomi, born 1989), *Untitled* from *Standing Strong: Awakening Series*, 2016 (negative), 2020 (print). Archival inkjet print, 16 × 20 in. Hood Museum of Art, Dartmouth: Purchased through the Anonymous Fund #144; 2020.8.2. © Josué Rivas/INDÍGENA.

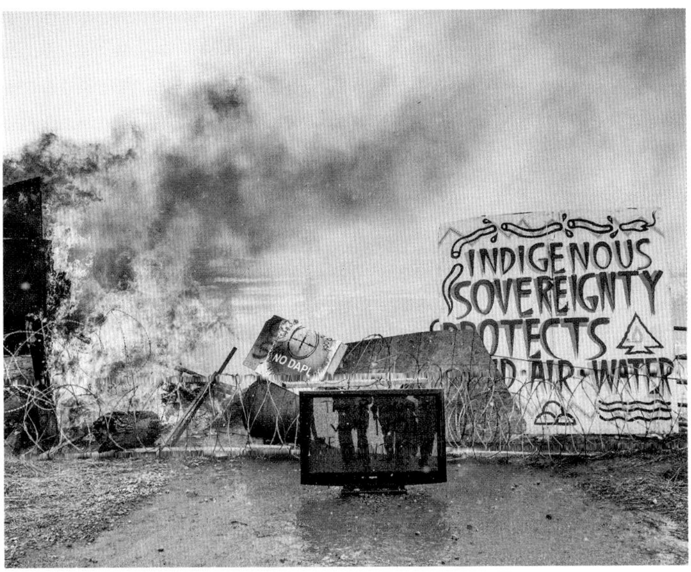

FIGURE 8.6 Josué Rivas (Mexica/Otomi, born 1989), *Untitled* from *Standing Strong: Awakening Series*, 2016 (negative), 2020 (print). Archival inkjet print, 16 x 20 in. Hood Museum of Art, Dartmouth: Purchased through the Anonymous Fund #144; 2020.8.1. Image by Jeffrey Nintzel. © Josué Rivas/INDÍGENA.

water protectors. This highly militarized response to Indigenous groups and their allies peacefully protesting the Dakota Access Pipeline violated constitutional rights to free speech and peaceable assembly and the Fourth Amendment's prohibition against excessive use of force and unreasonable seizures and searches.

Here, in the Rivas photograph, the story is not *only* the aftermath of violence and violation but also what remains, what will *not* be broadcast in the United States. Written by hand across the television screen placed in front of the rolled barbed wire are the lyrics of Gil Scott-Heron's "The Revolution Will Not Be Televised," the final lines of which are:

> The revolution will be no re-run, brothers
> The revolution will be live.

Rivas sees himself as collaborating with the community, seeking to build a body of work in which he is deeply invested, with the aim of preserving the stories from Standing Rock for future generations, stories that speak, as he insists, "from an ethical place not an extractive place." Indigenous activists and their allies from Nigeria to Australia and New Zealand, from Alberta to Ecuador and across the Amazon, are leading the fight against powerful mining and oil corporations who can summon military and militarized police to protect their interests. Forging alliances and strong bonds of solidarity in social movements is essential in the face of the planetary crises of global warming, ecocide, extractionism, and all other forms of the continuing colonial, racialized, and gendered violence integral to the economies of capitalist exploitation and degradation.

Placed a few paces to the left of Josué Rivas, was Cara Romero's fine art photograph, *Oil Boom*, a landscape that exposes what is beneath the surface evidence of the fossil fuel industry (fig. 8.7). The machinery of oil extraction and transmission of energy is confined within a narrow band of sky: oil derricks, pump jacks, fencing, and power lines are solid dark shapes set against a sunset or sunrise, east or west, standing on a surface layer of dark soil. What is below, out of sight, is that which most urgently needs to be exposed to the light to be recognized and acknowledged.

The photograph portrays a complex entanglement with extraction.

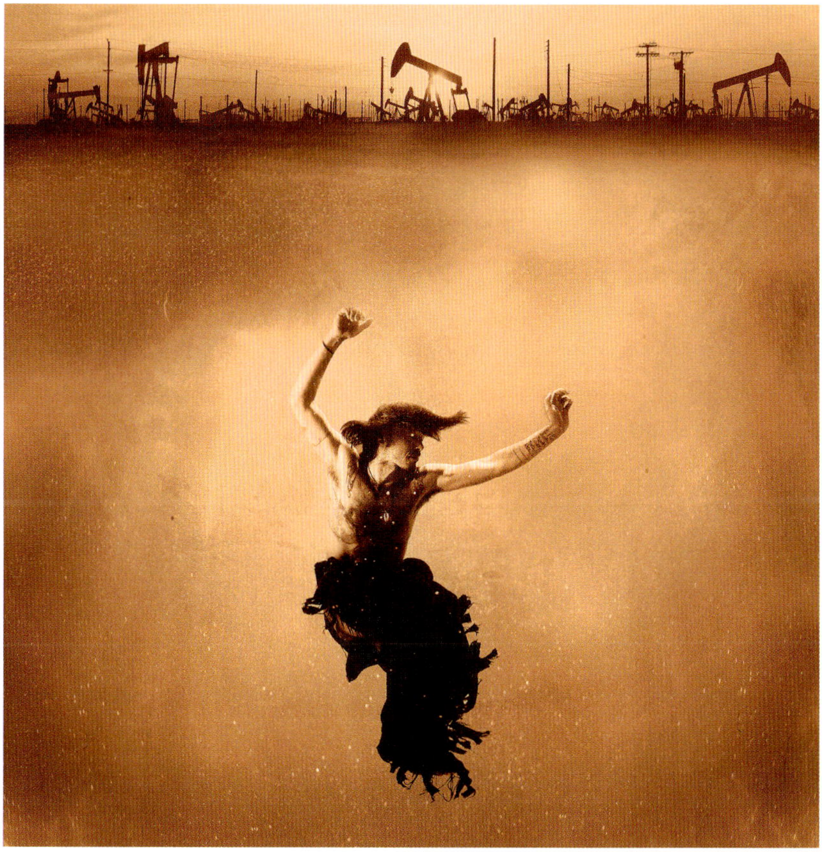

FIGURE 8.7 Cara Romero (Chemehuevi/ American, born 1977), *Oil Boom*, 2015. Archival pigment print, 44¾₁₆ × 44⅛ in. Hood Museum of Art, Dartmouth: Purchased through the Sondra and Charles Gilman Jr. Foundation Fund; 2019.78.2. © Cara Romero.

Romero uses light to create a liquidity and ambiguity. Cannupa Hanska Luger, the artist, is Romero's model for this photograph. There is a suggestion of movement but is it up or down? Is their body floating, or drowning, or about to surface? A thick shadow, evocative of the black snake of Lakota prophecy and realized in the Dakota Access Pipeline, runs from the back of the figure's head, wraps around their neck, and descends down to the center of the chest, thickening around the lower part of the body and legs, making it impossible to swim. Beneath the torso, the knees are bent as if sitting encased, wrapped in viscous crude. Is this figure being extracted, or is it being discarded as waste, the nonprofitable residue, from extraction? Is crude a weight? A burden? It is certainly fibrous—threads are torn—the edges are ragged, edges like that of a heavy fabric. The halo of light darkening at edges of the frame adds a spiritual or sacred quality to the figure: sacrificial, collateral damage. It is as if the figure is captured in slow motion, like that of a beautiful dancer.

The pendant, reflecting light and other white marks, suggest bubbles, pockets of air, plankton, smaller and denser in formation at the top left, break up or break down the solidity of pigment. The beams of light suggest sunlight, solar, atoms, and power coming from above. The lines of light and shadow behind the machinery of extraction, which are horizontal, become vertical streams below and cradle the body, but is this a descent or a rebirth? Romero's atmospheric palette of color and light creates a full spectrum of liquid amber that contrasts with the heavy solidity of black crude.

The ultimate mark of power may be its invisibility:[12] We are encouraged to believe that what is below is subordinate to, less consequential than, the visible structures of power.[13] Romero's *Oil Boom* exposes the buried/silenced history of dispossession, exploitation, and Indigenous genocide. Romero's art not only recovers this history but also brings it to light, into the present, a strong Indigenous presence.

Undergraduates have become adept at excavating the soil of academic entanglement with the corporate world to find the oil seeping under the foundations and investments of their universities. I hoped the artwork of Yatika Starr Fields, Josué Rivas, and Cara Romero, in the first gallery of the Hood Museum, would encourage Dartmouth students and faculty and alumni to reflect upon the partnership between the college and Arthur L. Irving, the sole owner of Irving Oil, the fossil fuel company that donated the lead gift of $80 million for the establishment of the Arthur L. Irving Institute for Energy and Society.[14] The Irving Oil Refinery in Saint John, New Brunswick, is the largest oil refinery in Canada, producing a range of products including gasoline, diesel, heating oil, jet fuel, propane, and asphalt: more than 80 percent of its production is exported to the United States; its petroleum refining is the largest emitter of greenhouse gas in New Brunswick; and the company ranks eighteenth in the top one hundred dirtiest emitters in Canada.[15]

As stated on their website, the mission of the Arthur L. Irving Institute for

Energy and Society at Dartmouth is "to advance an affordable, sustainable, and reliable energy future for the benefit of society," while behind the scenes Irving Oil trades in death, dispossession, and destruction in the name of sustainability. Their commitment to "Inclusivity, Equity, and Justice" states that they know their focus on "preparing future energy leaders . . . is embedded in the struggles for more just and equitable futures for our students. Sustainable energy futures in the U.S. and abroad," they continue, "require leadership that includes Black, Brown, Indigenous, and other people of color and other marginalized groups." Their responsibility, they conclude, is to "actively contribute to the realization of these futures."[16] Seemingly unaware that the rather awkward phrase "Black, Brown, Indigenous, and other people of color" actually describes most of the peoples of the world, are they ensuring our future or burying/silencing the history of dispossession, exploitation, and Indigenous genocide that Romero's work exposes?

Extraction from Canada's tar sands has caused destruction so vast and deep it challenges the existence of land and people. Oil companies have replaced Indigenous people's traditional lands with mines that cover an area bigger than New York City, stripping away boreal forest and wetlands and rerouting waterways that are sources of sustenance, of life. The Alberta tar sands have become synonymous with global climate change: their production process also wreaks destruction across a huge region of North America's boreal forest. Tailings ponds, which now hold more than 1 trillion liters of toxic waste and growing, are a by-product of the tar sands industry and an environmental catastrophe.[17] Toxic chemicals pollute fragile boreal forest; leak into major rivers; and penetrate the skin, veins, and flesh of humans and other than humans, rendering people and life itself dispensable, disposable waste.

In October 2017, in the face of fierce opposition from Indigenous peoples, like those portrayed in the artwork of Yakita Starr Field and Josué Rivas, TransCanada, the company behind the Keystone XL pipeline in the United States, abandoned a plan for a pipeline from Alberta's oil sands to refineries in Ontario, Quebec, and New Brunswick. Undeterred, Irving, an early backer of this pipeline came up with a plan to circumvent provincial and environmental opposition. They continue to connect the oil sands to refineries by shipping oil from Alberta on foreign ships via the Panama Canal to New Brunswick.[18]

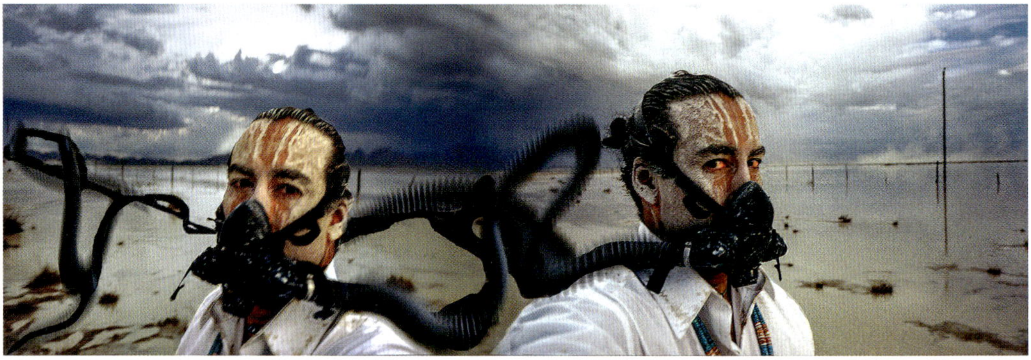

FIGURE 8.8 Will Wilson (Citizen of the Navajo Nation [Diné], born 1969), *Auto Immune Response No. 5*, 2004. Archival pigment print, 44 × 110 in. Hood Museum of Art, Dartmouth: Purchased through the William S. Rubin Fund; 2019.6. © Will Wilson.

The Irving Institute for Energy and Society's promise of realizing the futures of "Black, Brown, Indigenous, and other people of color and other marginalized groups" disguises the voracious, predatory greed of extraction and pollution that renders human beings, in the words of Achille Mbembe, "Discounted bodies . . . bodies at the limits of life, vulnerable and porous. Trapped in uninhabitable worlds and inhospitable places, they generate multiple kinds of tumors."[19] The consequences of the predatory greed of extraction and pollution are visible in *This Land*.

Dominating the central wall of the first gallery is Will Wilson's *Auto Immune Response No. 5*, from the series *Auto Immune Response (AIR)* (2004–2021), which so far consists of sixty-five artworks, a major artistic accounting of the creation of toxic environments (fig. 8.8). How to render visible what travels through the air, how to see what is invisible to the eye? "Toxic clouds colonize the air we breathe across different places and durations from . . . the incident to epochal latencies."[20] In Wilson's work clouds become evidence, environmental and political, they are lethal. Wilson places himself in the series as a Diné man we know only as "the protagonist": the artist performs a postapocalyptic Navajo man's journey through a vacant world, a survivor placed in landscapes of detritus and decay. Where has everyone gone? What cataclysm has transformed the familiar and strange landscape where he wanders? Why has the land become toxic to him? How will he respond, survive, reconnect to the earth?[21]

How to think and how to represent that which has vast spatial and temporal variance in scale? It was clear by 1970 that the uranium industry was producing a devastating and deadly epidemic of a variety of forms of cancers and "other radiation-related diseases not limited to the men and women working for the mines and mills" but having effects outside of the industry. Radioactive geographies have been difficult to map spatially and temporally at a variety of scales "from the scale of Diné Bikéyah . . . to the more local scales" where the risk of toxic contamination from individual tailings piles circulates "with the rain, wind, and animals." Toxic contamination is ubiquitous, found in the building materials of homes and at the most intimate scale of all, in the cells and organs of bodies.[22] How to measure the time scales of uranium exposure from the penetration of the cells of bodies, human and nonhuman, to the millennia of potential contamination when uranium toxicity has a half-life of 4.5 billion years? These are the temporalities that haunt Wilson's project. The title *Auto Immune Response* refers not only to the causal relations between the toxicity of the environment and human diseases where the immune system attacks the body but also to how environmental pollution is causing an autoimmune response in the planet itself.

In *Auto Immune Response No. 5*, the figure evokes the Hero Twins of the Navajo creation story. Wilson, doubled, is in the foreground, heads and shoulders at a 45-degree angle, heads turned outward from the photograph, bloodshot eyes looking accusingly(?) out of the frame, implicating the viewer. Who will accept responsibility? The tubes of their breathing apparatus curl and flap and appear to be attached to each other's masks. There are no oxygen tanks. Are they breathing each other's exhalations? Their hair, faces, shirts, and masks are covered in what we imagine to be radioactive dust, ash. Are we looking at humans who have been rendered disposable, waste? Are we looking at a death sentence, a planetary death in a palette of red, white, and blue? The landscape is liquid, leached out; it can only contaminate, as it is incapable of supporting life. The two figures are sharply defined, exposed in multiple ways; their eyes stare, demanding recognition, a witnessing, a reckoning.

The planetary crisis we face is not new, as Indigenous writers and activists keep telling us, and as Amitav Ghosh writes, "It represents the Earth's response to the globalization of the ecological transformations that were set in motion by the European colonization of much of the world."[23] In the words of la paperson, the avatar of Wayne Yang, "The exercises of supremacist sovereign power over life and death are most chillingly undisguised when we consider the ways the life worlds of land, air, water, plants and animals, and Indigenous peoples are reconfigured into natural resources, chattel, and waste: statuses whose capitalist 'value' does not depend on whether they are living or dead but only on their fungibility and disposability."[24]

Contemporary Indigenous artists, artists who expose the *longue durée* and contemporary consequences of extraction, dispossession, and destruction give voice to those who protest and oppose colonial corporate predation and refuse to die. In the face of planetary catastrophe, their art is an aid in thinking otherwise, demanding and fomenting a revolution in thought, in practice, and in politics.

For museums wishing to fulfill their role as public educators in spaces welcoming to a broad audience and who employ curators seeking to expand their collections of Indigenous and Black artists, for universities seeking to expand the diversity of their student body, unearthing, confronting, and acting to repair the violence and violations of settler colonialism and racial capitalism will require more than platitudes. The current white noise of diversity and inclusion, with its empty language and superficial gestures of belonging, is designed to subvert, if not obliterate, critical and creative thought. These institutions have to decide who they want to stand with and stand alongside. Perhaps this could begin with a public acknowledgment of whose ground they stand on, an acknowledgment comparable to the public artwork by Andrea Carlson, *Bodéwadmikik ėthë yéyék/You Are on Potawatomi Land* (2021) installed on the Chicago Riverwalk (fig. 8.9).[25]

Decolonizing museums, decolonizing minds, requires explicit recognition of the dispossession, displacement, and massacre of Indigenous peoples; the enslavement of Africans; the capitalist transformation of land into private property, land, its mountains, rivers, and forests and the oceans demolished, denuded, rapaciously stripped of all forms of life. Universities and museums

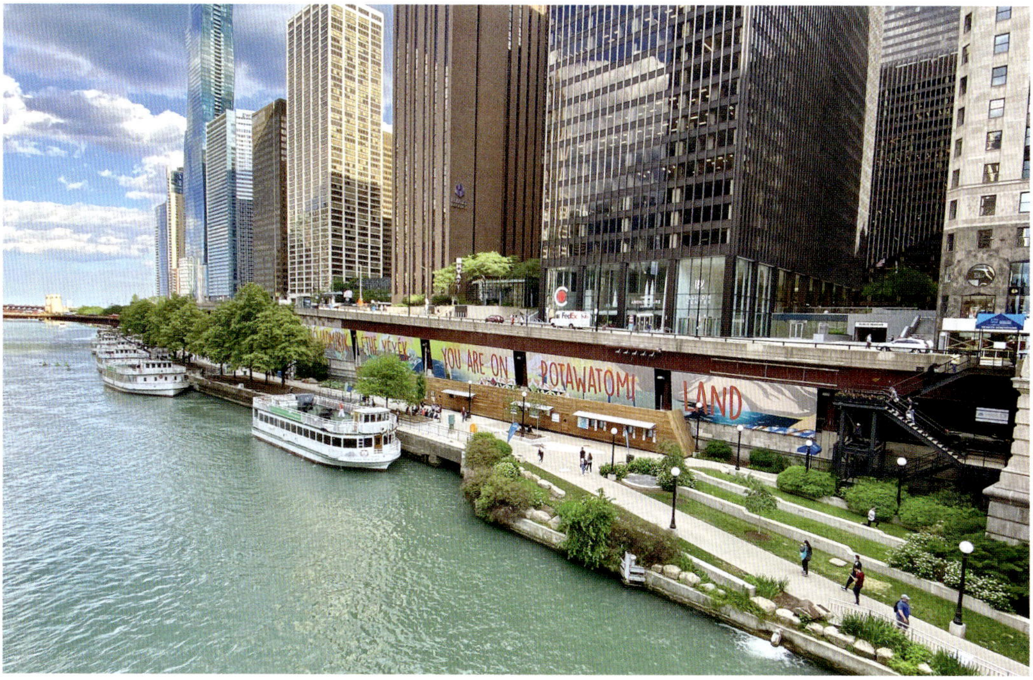

FIGURE 8.9 Andrea Carlson (Grand Portage Ojibwe descendant, born 1979), *Bodéwadmikik ėthë yéyék–You Are on Potawatomi Land,* 2021–23. Printed vinyl banners along the Chicago Riverwalk. Commissioned by the Department of Cultural Affairs and Public Events, Chicago, Illinois. Image courtesy of the artist. © Andrea Carlson.

must acknowledge their complicity in this exploitation and extraction and publicly expose the historic and contemporary sources of their wealth, from enslavement to fossil fuels. Decolonization also demands action to remediate and repair. Life devalued as resources, life as a source of energy, of fuel, enslaves the earth.[26]

NOTES

1. Katharine Swindells, "London Ranks as the World's Top City for the Wealthy," *Spear's Magazine*, March 1, 2022, https://spearswms.com/london-top-city-for-the-wealthy/; "Poverty Rates by London Borough," *Trust for London*, https://trustforlondon.org.uk/data/poverty-borough/.

2. Achille Mbembe, "Futures of Life and Futures of Reason," *Public Culture* 33, no. 1 (93) (2021): 11–33, https://doi.org/10.1215/08992363-8742136/.

3. Darby English, "Don't Be Intimidated by Museums. They Belong to Everyone," *The Guardian*, May 31, 2015, sec. Opinion, https://www.theguardian.com/commentisfree/2015/may/31/museums-not-white-spaces-belong-everyone/.

4. See, for example, Romare Bearden, *To Preserve Their Freedom*, from *The Life of Toussaint Louverture*, 1988, silkscreen on paper, 20½ x 30½ in. Colby College Museum of Art, accessed January 28, 2023, https://museum-exhibitions.colby.edu/explore-jacob-lawrence/.

5. For a recent example, see Hazel V. Carby, "The Limits of Caste," *London Review of Books* 43, no. 2 (2020), https://www.lrb.co.uk/the-paper/v43/n02/hazel-v.-carby/the-limits-of-caste/.

6. Such as "American Paintings," *National Gallery of Art*, accessed January 28, 2023, https://www.nga.gov/collection/paintings/american.html/; Eleanor Beardsley, "At the Louvre, a Rare Showcase for American Art," *NPR*, January 25, 2012, sec. Europe, https://www.npr.org/2012/01/25/145850981/at-the-louvre-a-rare-showcase-for-american-art/; "Just in from Paris: Crystal Bridges Opens Partnership Exhibition | Crystal Bridges Museum of American Art," May 14, 2012, https://crystalbridges.org/news-room/just-in-from-paris-crystal-bridges-opens-partnership-exhibition/; Charles Hosmer Morse Museum of American Art, "Nineteenth-Century American Landscapes," accessed January 28, 2023, http://morsemuseum.org/on-exhibit/landscape-in-nineteenth-century-america/.

7. One of the most powerful responses to this genealogy is Julie Mehertu's' *Howl, eon* (*I, II*), 2016–2017, ink and acrylic on canvas, each panel 324 x 384 in. SFMOMA, Gift of Helen and Charles Schwab, 2017, commissioned by the San Francisco Museum of Modern Art (SFMOMA). See "Julie Mehretu," accessed January 28, 2023, https://sfmoma.org/artwork/2017.237.A-B/.

8. Hood Museum, *This Land: American Engagement with the Natural World*, September 2, 2021, https://hoodmuseum.dartmouth.edu/explore/exhibitions/land/.

9. Another important leader transforming and expanding the range of artists, artworks, and exhibitions included in their institutions is Courtney J. Martin, the first Black director of the Yale Center for British Art. These two visionary women are demonstrating how to reimagine the practices of art museums and visually represent other worlds and other ways of seeing.

10. Alex Hull, "Museum Current: 'The Power of Place: Public Art and Indigenous Representations,'" *The Terrace: The McMullen Museum of Art's Student*

Publication, April 13, 2021, https://theterracebc.com/2021/04/13/museum-current-the-power-of-place-public-art-and-Indigenous-representations/.

11. Nick Estes and Jaskiran Dhillon, eds., *Standing with Standing Rock: Voices from the #NoDAPL Movement* (Minneapolis: University of Minnesota Press, 2019), 3.

12. Michel-Rolph Trouillot, *Silencing the Past: Power and the Production of History* (Boston: Beacon Press, 1995).

13. Trouillot, *Silencing the Past*.

14. "Dartmouth Receives $80 Million for Institute of Energy and Society," *Candid: Philanthropy News Digest,* September 20, 2016, https://philanthropynewsdigest.org/news/dartmouth-receives-80-million-for-institute-of-energy-and-society/.

15. John Woodside, "Canada's 100 Dirtiest Emitters," *Canada's National Observer,* October 21, 2021, https://www.nationalobserver.com/2021/10/21/news/canadas-100-dirtiest-emitters/.

16. "Inclusivity, Equity, and Justice: Background and Context," Arthur L. Irving Institute for Energy and Society, June 2020, https://irving.dartmouth.edu/about/about-institute/inclusivity-equity-and-justice/.

17. Natural Resources Defense Council and Environmental Defence Report, "One Trillion Litres of Toxic Waste and Growing: Alberta's Tailings Ponds," June 26, 2017, https://www.nrdc.org/sites/default/files/media-uploads/edc-and-nrdc-one-trillion-litres-of-toxic-waste-and-growing-albertas-tailings-ponds-june-2017.pdf/.

18. Geoffrey Morgan, "Irving Oil Finally Gets Approval to Source Alberta Oil—but through the Panama Canal," *Financial Post*, May 5, 2020, https://financialpost.com/commodities/energy/irving-oil-finally-gets-approval-to-source-alberta-oil-but-through-the-panama-canal/.

19. Achille Mbembe, "Futures of Life and Futures of Reason," *Public Culture* 33, no. 1 (2021). 23.

20. *Forensic Architecture: Cloud Studies*, 2020, https://forensic-architecture.org/investigation/cloudstudies/.

21. Portions of this discussion on *Auto Immune Response No. 5* were previously presented in a slightly different form in Hazel V. Carby, "Remembering the Future," *London Review of Books* 46, no. 7 (2024), https://www.lrb.co.uk/the-paper/v46/n07/hazel-v.-carby/remembering-the-future/.

22. Traci Brynne Voyles, *Wastelanding: Legacies of Uranium Mining in Navajo Country* (Minneapolis: University of Minnesota Press, 2015), 141.

23. Amitav Ghosh, *The Nutmeg's Curse: Parables for a Planet in Crisis* (Chicago: University of Chicago Press, 2021), 167.

24. la paperson, *A Third University Is Possible* (Minneapolis: University of Minnesota Press, 2017), 14–15.

25. Andrea Carlson, *You Are on Potawatomi Land*, 2021, total dimensions 15' x 266'. Installed on the Chicago Riverwalk (Photo by Andrea Carlson), https://monumentlab.com/bulletin/dont-look-to-my-work-for-reconciliation-a-conversation-with-andrea-carlson/.

26. N. K. Jemisin, *The Stone Sky,* 1st edition, The Broken Earth trilogy, book 3 (New York: Orbit, 2017), 335.

9

Alexandra M. Thomas

BRAIDING, STITCHING, SWEEPING

Black Feminist Domesticity and Art History

Dear Us. The plural pronoun here signifies the same "us" summoned by Toni Morrison when she wrote, "I think about us, black women, a lot" in her 1985 love letter "A Knowing So Deep" for *Essence* magazine.[1] The notion of an "us" evokes what postcolonial scholar Gayatri Spivak calls "strategic essentialism"[2]—while Black women are not a monolith, there is still a collective "we" when it comes to Black women's fraught navigations of certain institutions, especially the home. Further attention to transnational practices of Black women braiding, stitching, and sweeping encourages a closer look at the art, resistance, and homemaking of Black women that is often sidelined in art historical genealogies that ignore the everyday and the domestic. Whether it is hairstyles, quilts, baskets, or brooms, the visual culture of Black feminist domesticity teaches us about the relationship between African and African Diaspora art forms as well as Black women's tendency toward bricolage. If it is true, as Audre Lorde believed, that "the master's tools will never dismantle the master's house," then we must build and keep our own home using the critical methods we design.[3]

The concept of "Black feminist domesticity" includes a range of Black women's political and aesthetic concerns related to homemaking and kinship. As such, this essay is for Black women and the allied individuals who believe in the urgency of Black feminist world making in museums, academia, and beyond. The original form of "Braiding, Stitching, Sweeping: Black Feminist Domesticity and Art History" was a direct address to an audience of primarily art historians and museum professionals during the March 2022 convening "Re-Envisioning Histories of American Art" at the Hood Museum of Art at Dartmouth College. My panel, "Redefining American Art across Disciplinary Boundaries," included incredible scholars and interlocutors Dr. Kirsten Pai Buick and Dr. Teresa Montoya and was moderated by the monumental Black feminist critic Dr. Hazel V. Carby. Our dialogue extended beyond the realm of American art history and dove into the critical depths of women-of-color feminisms, political solidarity, and what it means to collaborate on a vision for a different world through our work and its intersections with creative practice. Since then I have adapted my offering to address the stakes of Black feminist domestic art history in a fuller sense, including commentary on the labor of love that is *Homecoming: Domesticity and Kinship in Global African Art*, the exhibition I curated at the Hood Museum (July 2023–May 2024).

In writing to the "us" that is Black women and our communities, two questions that undergird my project are *What are the gestures, feelings, and ethics that make up a Black feminist art history?* and *How do notions of "home" fit into that vision?* I am invested in exploring what it means to proliferate an abundance of Black feminist ideas and aesthetics into the institutional fabric of art history and museums. Might these institutions feel less *obsolete* if we accept the work of Black feminism as an urgent task: not just increased representation of Black women in museums but a fundamental shift of material circumstances?[4]

Black feminists in and outside the museum space and the field of art history have long attempted to dislodge the hierarchies and borders of the art world.[5] To begin, Black feminism offers political consciousness that reflects the needs of the most marginalized in our communities: drawing from the Combahee River Collective's 1977 Black lesbian feminist manifesto: "If black women were free, it would mean that everyone else would have to be free since our freedom would necessitate the destruction of all the systems of oppression."[6] Black feminism carries with it a tradition of transnationalism and solidarity across geographic borders; no one scholar could study and teach the entirety of Black and African art and culture throughout time and space, but one must still be wary of academic and curatorial discourse that advocates a strict separation between African art history and its global diaspora. A Black Atlantic and diasporic lens reckons with specificity while emphasizing the global condition of anti-Blackness that produces similar conditions and traditions in geographically distant places. This essay and my exhibition at the Hood Museum push the notion that Black women's art-making practices within and concerning the home, or what I call the visual culture of Black feminist domesticity, are important to the history of American art. In doing so, I propose three intimate gestures—braiding, stitching, and sweeping—as a lens through which to engage Black feminist art histories.

BRAIDING

Braiding is the first gesture this essay introduces as a mode through which to consider Black feminist art histories (fig. 9.1). Throughout the Black Atlantic world, braiding hair and wearing one's hair braided are markers of beauty and pride. Braiding hair can be meditative, and Black beauty salons around the globe are spaces of community building where Black women practice love and care for one another. Braiding is considered a protective style, meaning it protects the hair from breakage caused by over-styling, but it is also protective in the sense that Black women form a sisterhood around the art of braiding. Nigerian photographer J. D. Okhai Ojeikere (1930–2014) is one of the artists in *Homecoming* and has documented hundreds of Black women's highly stylized coiffures, serving as portraits of Black women's beauty culture. Braiding hair is absolutely an art form: braiders are subject to meticulous criticism based on length, style, and shape, and years of practice are required to perfect one's technique.

In Ojeikere's *Abebe* (1975), a Black woman's hair is plaited flat to her head (cornrows) at the bottom, with long box braids braided into one massive bun atop her head. Her earrings, concentric circles, mirror the rhythm and delicate repetition of her hairstyle. Captured in black-and-white against a blank background, the hairstyle is the central feature of the photograph. In

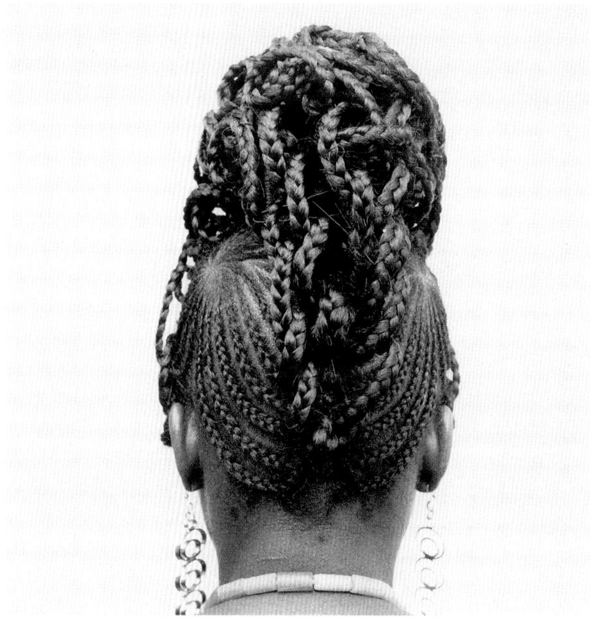

FIGURE 9.1 J. D. Okhai Ojeikere (Nigerian, 1930–2014), *Abebe,* 1975. Gelatin silver print, 23⅝ × 19¹¹⁄₁₆ in. Hood Museum of Art, Dartmouth: Gift of Robert J. Grey; 2017.55. Image by Jeffrey Nintzel © Estate of Okhai Ojeikere.

documenting these ethereal braided hairstyles designed, created, and worn by women of African descent, Ojeikere is highlighting the radical artistry of Black women's braiding culture. "In any black neighborhood you cannot escape noticing the presence of so many barbershops and hairdressing salons; so many haircare products and so much advertising to help sell them all; and, among young people especially, so much skill and sheer fastidiousness that goes into the styles you can see on the street," writes art historian Kobena Mercer in his 1987 essay "Black Hair/Style Politics."[7] These crafty and experimental hairstyles are innovative while being rooted in traditions of Black beauty culture in the face of racist ideology that equates beauty with Eurocentric beauty standards. As a Black feminist aesthetic practice, Black women and girls braid each other's hair into intricate designs, constantly experimenting with new styles. Whether inside the home or in a salon, braiding hair is often communal, an act that creates space for women to discuss and theorize their lives, or what bell hooks identifies as women making feminist transformation possible through a "theory that emerges from the concrete"—or Patricia Hill Collins's concept of "black women's standpoint" that then becomes black feminist thought.[8]

Braiding is an action defined by intentional entanglement—of hair and communities—for aesthetic and protective purposes. In fall of 2020, with Diné art historian Isabella Robbins, I co-organized a Zoom event called "Braiding Black and Indigenous Intimacies." We invited two collaborative artist pairs—First Nations artists Jeneen Frei Njootli and Tsēmā Igharas and Black British artists Tamar Clarke-Brown and Isaac Kariuki[9]—to share their work and have a dialogue about their shared interest in braiding. Njootli and Igharas lectured on their performance "Sinuosity," in which they weave fluorescent multicolored flagging tape into a long braid that stretches between them—tethering themselves to each other in an intimate gesture that fuses ancestral modes with contemporary aesthetics. Clarke-Brown and Kariuki shared their performance and digital startup "Coding: Braiding: Transmission," in which Black women braid one another's hair while GoPro cameras and movement detection software document coded messages to one another—grounding fugitive communication as an aesthetic practice, inspired by legends of enslaved women braiding escape routes into their hair.[10] One example of this practice is a sixteenth-century legend of a West Central African king, Benkos Biohó, who was formerly enslaved by the Portuguese and who successfully escaped to Colombia after enslaved women mapped escape routes and braided them into their hair to guide him. Braiding hair is an aesthetic and fugitive practice.

With time, it has become even clearer to me that our event was born from a serious commitment to braiding and weaving together Black and Indigenous feminisms as opposed to seeing these movements as distinct and unrelated. Since then, curator Anya Montiel's (Mexican and Tohono O'odham descent) *Ancestors Know Who We Are* exhibition of artwork by six Black-Indigenous women artists at the National Museum of the American Indian is a compelling illustration of curating Black and Indigenous intimacies through a feminist lens.[11] As a virtual exhibition featuring basket weaver Rodslen Brown (Black/Cherokee Nation of Oklahoma), graphic designer Joelle Joyner (African American and Kauwets'a: ka [Meherrin] descent), photographer Moira Pernambuco (African and Amerindian [Wapishana]), multidisciplinary artist Paige Pettibon (Black, Salish, and White descent), visual artist Monica Ricker T-Bolter (Prairie Band Potawatomi, Black, and German), and interdisciplinary artist/poet Storme Webber (Alaskan Sugpiaq [Alutiiq] and Black descent), the website itself has become an archive of multigenerational visual culture by Black-Indigenous women across various media and from different tribes, nations, and diasporic experiences.[12]

STITCHING

Stitching is a Black feminist gesture of care, repair, and creative expression, often taking the form of textiles and beadwork.[13] *Homecoming* includes a broad display of indigo textiles from West Africa and beyond, including Nigerian artist Nike Davies Okundaye's (born 1952) *Untitled (Adire Quilt)* (2002) and the Hood Museum's recent acquisition, Bhasha Chakrabarti's *It's a Blue World* (2021). *Adire* is indigo-dyed cloth that comes from Yoruba women in southwest Nigeria who use resist-dye techniques such as tying, stitching, and folding the fabric while applying color from the indigo or industrialized blue dye (fig. 9.2). By the early twentieth century, Yoruba women artists who used this technique were able to sell *adire* cloth to support their economic livelihood. Okundaye is likely the best-known Nigerian artist trained in the indigo adire cloth tradition. Born in 1951, she was raised in North Central Nigeria and learned classical dyeing and weaving processes from the women in and around her family.[14] Textile production is the art form most popularly associated with women's work and domestic arts, and West African indigo textiles are deep in hue and meaning. Generations of Yoruba women maintain the tradition of making and wearing indigo textiles.

In *Homecoming* the expanse of indigo textiles from West Africa is accompanied by a new acquisition, Bhasha Chakrabarti's *It's a Blue World* (figs. 9.3 and 9.4). The dual-sided quilt represents the globalized histories of indigo, the etymology of which identifies the blue dye as a "product of India." Major eighteenth-century indigo plantations were established in India and the American South; Chakrabarti maps these imperial cartographies in yellow thread—tracing ancient and colonial-era indigo trade routes. The work itself is crafted with indigo sourced from throughout the world. There are patches of adire textiles stitched together throughout the quilt that parallel the adire textiles made by Nigerian women, including Davies-Okundaye, also on view in this gallery. The alternative side of the quilt is inspired by the Gee's Bend quilters in Alabama. These quilters have been quilting for centuries, and their techniques have been passed down through generations. Some of the women still live directly on the land where their ancestors were enslaved. Some describe their creative process as God-given, while others describe it

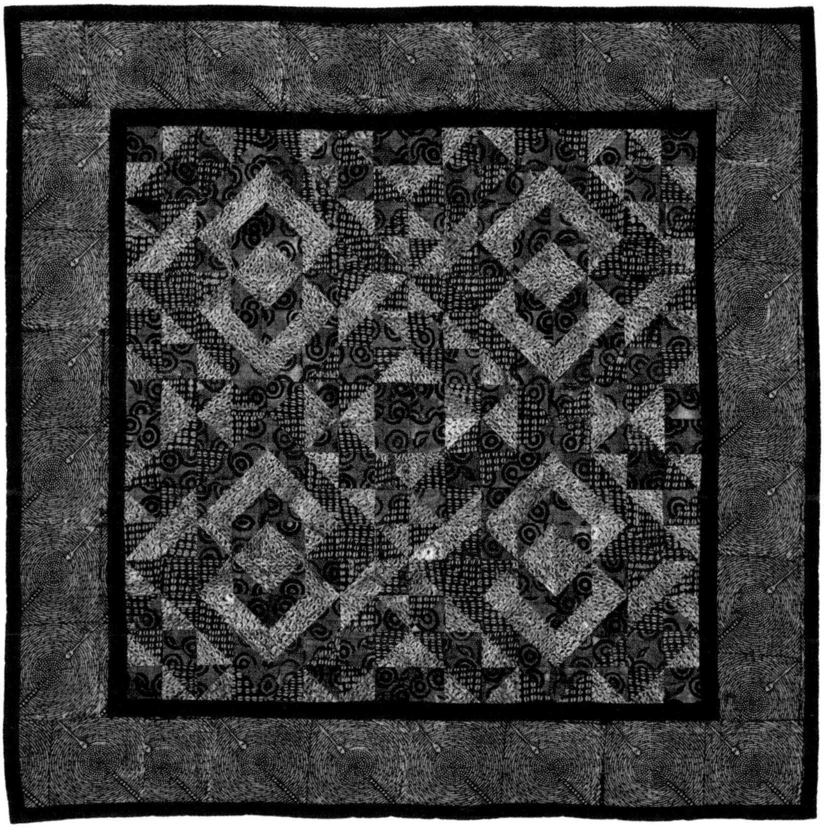

FIGURE 9.2 Nike Davies-Okundaye (Nigerian, born 1952), *Untitled (Adire Quilt)*, 2002. Indigo-dyed cotton and thread, 92 × 90 in. Hood Museum of Art, Dartmouth: Purchased through the William B. Jaffe and Evelyn A. Jaffe Hall Fund and through gifts from the Dickey Fund and the Leslie Humanities Center; T.2003.6. Image by Jeffrey Nintzel © Nike Davies-Okundaye.

as a meditative process in which women can commune and quilt together. Chakrabarti spent time in Gee's Bend in 2020 learning from China Pettway, Mary Ann Pettway, and numerous other esteemed quilters. As a South Asian woman, Chakrabarti was drawn to the Gee's Bend quilters, whose work reminded her of textiles she had seen in India. Gee's Bend quilters are masterful bricoleurs and often use scraps of different fabrics to make their vibrant creations. The denim used is Chakrabarti's collection of old jeans,

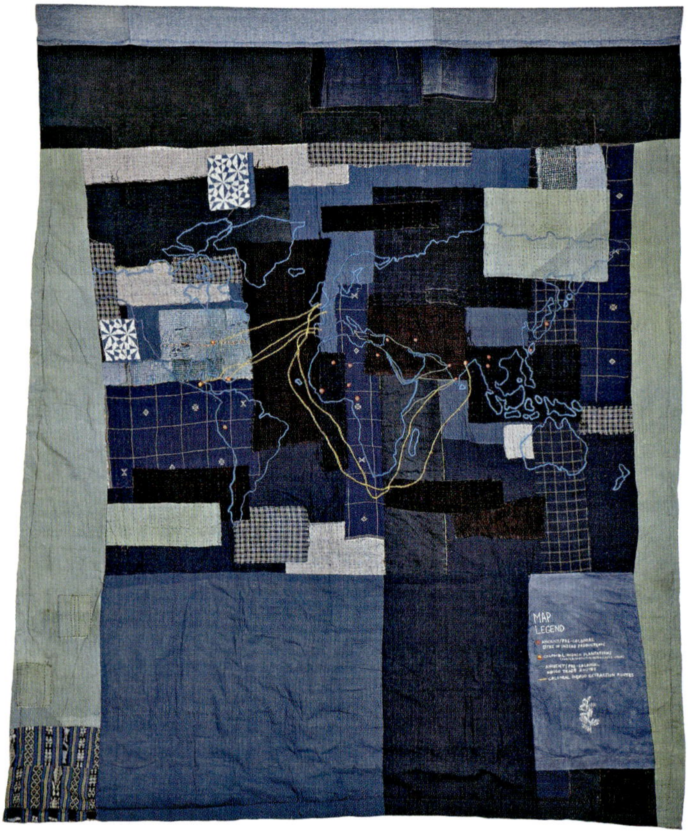

FIGURE 9.3 Side 1, Bhasha Chakrabarti (American, born 1991), *It's a Blue World*, 2021. Used jeans, indigo-dyed handloom fabric, and thread, 83 x 74 in. Hood Museum of Art, Dartmouth: Purchased through the William S. Rubin Fund and the Stephen and Constance Spahn '63 Acquisition Fund; 2022.61. Photo by Sara Jamback. © Bhasha Chakrabarti.

a nod to practices of bricolage that Gee's Bend quilters are known for, but also an homage to the revolutionary history of indigo, especially the 1739 Stono Rebellion in South Carolina and the 1859 Indigo Revolt (Nil Bidroha) in Bengal. Chakrabarti represents overlapping African, Asian, and American imperial cartographies in *It's a Blue World* by threading ancient and colonial-era indigo trade routes on a global map. Crafting these works with indigo sourced from around the globe on quilted fabric, Chakrabarti traces the transnational history of this blue pigment and dye.

The making and display of *It's a Blue World* mobilizes intergenerational and women of color feminist approaches to formal comparison. Chakrabarti refers to her practice of stitching as "mending" and a form of repair that "confronts fragility, precarity, and impermanence while embodying hope,

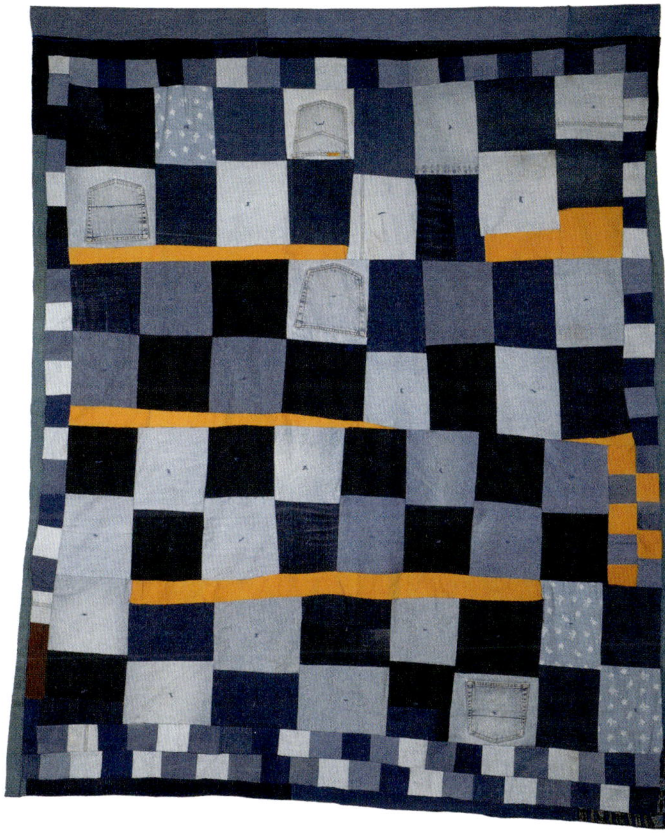

FIGURE 9.4 Side 2, Bhasha Chakrabarti (American, born 1991), *It's a Blue World*, 2021. Used jeans, indigo-dyed hand-loom fabric, and thread, 83 x 74 in. Hood Museum of Art, Dartmouth: Purchased through the William S. Rubin Fund and the Stephen and Constance Spahn '63 Acquisition Fund; 2022.61. Photo by Sara Jamback. © Bhasha Chakrabarti.

continuity and futurity."[15] Metaphorically and materially, stitching is a gesture of care rooted in textile traditions from the global South that, as Chakrabarti continues, "[resist] colonial and capitalist systems that deny the existence of black and brown bodies as sites of pleasure, knowledge, and value."[16] Stitching is utilitarian *and* political.[17]

SWEEPING

As the third and final gesture analyzed in this essay, *sweeping* is a nod to the often exploited and underpaid maintenance work done by Black women to sustain their homes and communities. Culturally and politically, the symbol of the broom is found extensively through global African cultures. African

Americans "jump the broom" at weddings, and brooms throughout the African continent and diaspora are used to sweep away evil spirits and past wrongdoings.[18] Brooms conjure notions of cleansing—be it spiritual or physical. Two brooms are on view in *Homecoming*, both made by unidentified Zulu artists in South Africa. These brooms are associated with the labor of Black South African women who craft and use them for domestic work while also evoking the pan-African religious practice of spiritual cleansing. Both brooms were likely collected (in the nineteenth and twentieth century) because they are crafted by hand and had a spiritual purpose as well.

A different broom, not in *Homecoming* but acquired by the Smithsonian's National Museum of African American History and Culture, is more important for how it is used than for how it was made (fig. 9.5). The Smithsonian collected a broom used by community members to clean up after Baltimore protests in 2015. It was gifted by the Newborn Community of Faith Church in Baltimore. One imagines Christian Black women, perhaps mothers or elders, using this typical broom to care for the streets left in shambles after local demonstrations honoring the life of Freddie Carlos Gray Jr., who was killed in police custody by a group of Baltimore officers. Sweeping the streets after protests is a quiet mode through which the labor of cleaning is politically oriented. Such a gesture is not an attack on Black Lives Matter organizing but rather a manifestation of care. Both protesting police brutality, in all forms, and cleaning up afterward are public demonstrations of love and care for community.

Whether it is in Apartheid South Africa or in the long history of US racism, Black women have historically worked as domestic laborers in White households. The broom thus becomes a symbol of the maintenance work that Black women do and that makes domestic labor a central organizing principle within Black feminist movements. In "White Women Listen! Black Feminism and the Boundaries of Sisterhood," Hazel V. Carby argues that "ideologies of black female domesticity and motherhood have been constructed, through their employment (or chattel position) as domestics and surrogate mothers to White families rather than in relation to their own families."[19] The labor performed by Black women in their own homes, neighborhoods, and workplaces (including in academia and museums) often

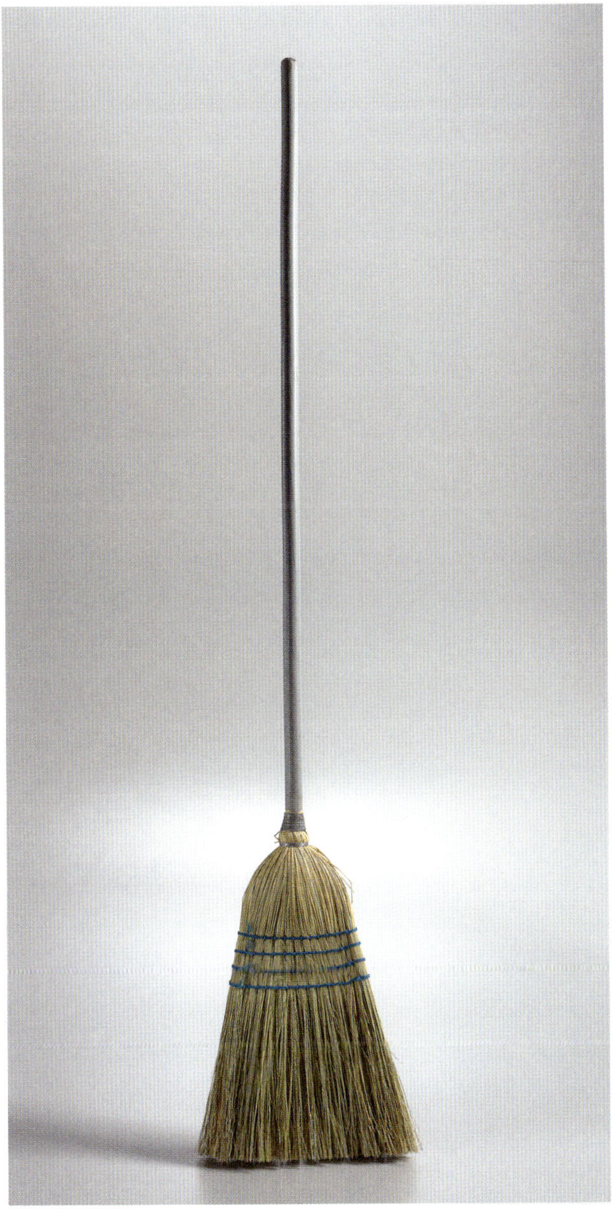

FIGURE 9.5 Broom used by the community members to clean up after Baltimore protests, ca. 2015. Wood, straw, wire, 54 × 10½ × 1⁹⁄₁₆ in. Collection of the Smithsonian National Museum of African American History and Culture: Gift of Newborn Community of Faith Church; 2015.210.2.

goes unacknowledged and unpaid even though it sustains communities and institutions. Domesticity is fraught for Black women; however, we know that the domestic sphere—and the care work performed there—can be a source of resistance.[20]

CONCLUSION

Braiding. Stitching. Sweeping. These gestures are metaphorically rich within, and beyond, the domestic sphere. Regarding braiding and stitching—both being actions of entangling different forms in an intentional design—if we are to take these seriously as modes of study and creative production, then they should encourage us to focus on the interconnectedness, solidarities, frictions, and entanglements in American art history. Whether it is a topic like cross-cultural quilting, Black and Native women's beadwork practices, or basketry using sweetgrass, there are infinite topics that can be pursued through this methodological approach. Away from the hyper-individualism of the neoliberal academy and the borders it constructs and maintains, we must push for braiding and stitching intimacies across different groups and the multiplicity of human experiences. Sweeping—associated with sweeping away evil spirits in Afro-Atlantic religions, the labor of Black women in political movements, *and* tending to homes and neighborhoods by cleaning—has a metaphorical purpose, too, that can become method. Much of this research requires "broad sweeps" across different time periods and geographies as opposed to distinct periodization, which is intellectually demanding but possible to do if one builds a "home" in more than one discipline.

To conclude, consider an image of an elegantly poised Black woman who appears self-assured and in charge of the space in which she resides (fig. 9.6). Toyin Ojih Odutola's drawing *Pregnant* is a highlight in *Homecoming*. A domestic image of a Black woman exuding power and grace: her manicured nails, chic domestic interior, matching blue gems, and gold jewelry are marks of luxury and prestige. Although she is not visibly pregnant, the title alludes to the sense of a growing family and distinct lineage. Her uniquely sheer woven skirt and floral long-sleeved blouse convey the power of fashion to show a sense of glory and experimentation with textiles. In this series of

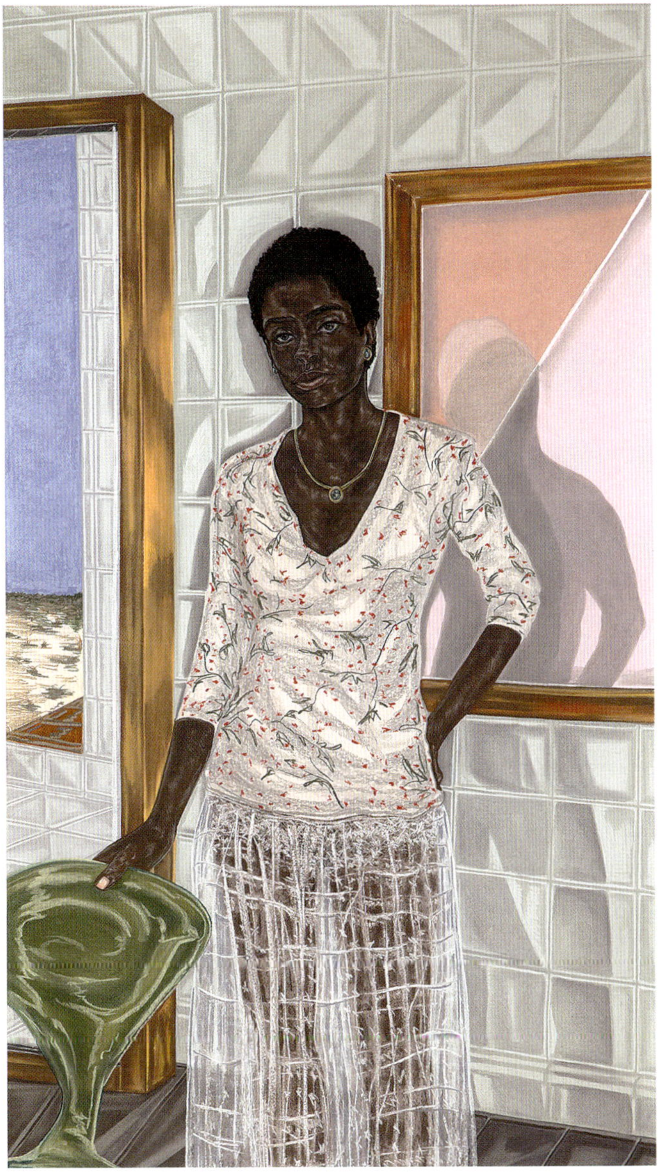

FIGURE 9.6 Toyin Ojih Odutola (Nigerian, works in New York City, born 1985), *Pregnant*, 2017. Charcoal, pastel, and graphite on paper, 74½ × 42 in. Hood Museum of Art, Dartmouth: Purchased through the Florence and Lansing Porter Moore 1937 Fund; 2018.8. Image courtesy of Jack Shainman Gallery, New York. © Toyin Ojih Odutola.

drawings, Odutola imagines a Nigerian family in a parallel universe where racism and colonialism never existed. In this fictional world, opulence and abundance are the norm. This is precisely the type of domesticity I am advocating for—a world in which Black women's creative labor, innovative designs, and speculative worlds are celebrated for their abundant offerings. Black feminist domesticity has tremendous significance to the fields of art history, museum studies, and curatorial practice.

NOTES

1. Toni Morrison, "A Knowing So Deep," in *What Moves at the Margin: Selected Nonfiction* (Jackson: University Press of Mississippi, 2008), 31.

2. In "Everybody's Afraid of Gayatri Chakravorty Spivak: Reading Interviews with the Public Intellectual and Postcolonial Critic," Mridula Nath Chakraborty notes that Gayatri Spivak coined the term "strategic essentialism" in a 1984 interview with Australian feminist philosopher Elizabeth Grosz.

3. Audre Lorde, *The Master's Tools Will Never Dismantle the Master's House* (London: Penguin UK, 2018).

4. Angela Davis's 2003 book *Are Prisons Obsolete?* (New York: Seven Stories Press, 2003) radically theorizes the failed promises and necessary obsolescence of prisons through an abolitionist lens. Leftist art historians and cultural workers, myself included, have extended an abolitionist perspective to museums—emphasizing the carceral ethics of Western museums and unpacking what it might mean to abolish and start anew.

5. The genealogy of Black feminist art historical criticism includes people like Freida Tesfagiorgis, Tribotia Hayes Benjamin, Sharon Patton, Judith Wilson-Pates, Jontyle Theresa Robinson, Sylvia Ardyn Boone, Lowery Stokes Sims, Leslie King-Hammond, Michele Wallace, Samella Lewis, Regenia Perry, Lorraine O'Grady, Adrian Piper, and many others.

6. This statement has been met with criticism from endless points of view. Some of it is valid, but much of it denies the reality that most marginalized identities already overlap with Black feminist concerns. Black women can also be Asian, Latine/x, Indigenous, disabled, undocumented, queer, trans, poor, etc. Focusing on Black feminism does not necessarily exclude any key voices in the leftist community.

7. Kobena Mercer, "Black Hair/Style Politics," *New Formations* 3 (1987): 34.

8. bell hooks, "Theory as Liberatory Practice," *Yale Journal of Law & Feminism*

4 (1991): 8; Patricia Hill Collins, "The Social Construction of Black Feminist Thought," *Signs* 14, no. 4 (1989): 745–73.

9. Alexandra M. Thomas, "Coding, Braiding, Transmission: On the Aesthetic Life of Dark Sousveillance," *Women & Performance: A Journal of Feminist Theory* 30, no. 3 (2020): 391–97.

10. Some of this description is pulled directly from the article Isabella Robbins and I coauthored after the "Braiding Black and Indigenous Intimacies" event we co-hosted for the *Yale Daily News*. Alexandra Thomas and Isabella Robbins, "Braiding Black and Indigenous Intimacies," *Yale Daily News,* November 29, 2020, https://yaledailynews.com/blog/2020/11/29/braiding-black-and-indigenous-intimacies/.

11. Art historian and curator Anya Montiel was one of the participants at the March 2022 convening "Re-Envisioning Histories of American Art" at the Hood Museum of Art at Dartmouth College.

12. The exhibition *Ancestors Know Who We Are* is archived on the Smithsonian website https://americanindian.si.edu/ancestors-know/, accessed July 10, 2023.

13. While this essay focuses on textiles as opposed to beading, it is worth noting that Joyce Scott's *Mammy under Undue Influence* (2007) is a beadwork sculpture in *Homecoming.* A blend of stitched glass beads and blown and cast glass, Scott's *Mammy under Undue Influence* combines the artist's training in traditional African and Native American beading practices with cultural criticism. Resulting in an uncanny sculptural portrait of a Black domestic worker ("the mammy"), Scott reinvents the historically racist archetype with an experimental aesthetic.

14. Much more can be learned about Nike Davies's life and her influence on global African arts in Kim Marie Vaz's 1995 book, *The Woman with the Artistic Brush: A Life History of Yoruba Batik Artist Nike Davis* (Armonk, NY: M. E. Sharpe, 1995), as well as several other articles, recent dissertations, and exhibition catalogs.

15. Bhasha Chakrabarti discusses her practice in a feature on The Here & There Co website, https://thehereandthere.co/artists/bhasha-chakrabarti/, accessed July 10, 2023.

16. The Here & There Co website, https://thehereandthere.co/artists/bhasha-chakrabarti/.

17. The book *Stitching Love and Loss: A Gee's Bend Quilt* (Seattle: University of Washington Press, 2023) by Dartmouth alumna Lisa Gail Collins is another example of stitching as a social and political practice used for personal and communal healing. Collins meditates on mourning, creativity, and resilience in an in-depth study of a 1942 work-clothes quilt made by Missouri Pettway with her husband's old clothing while mourning his death.

18. Contemporary African artists Adejoke Tugbiyele and Usha Seejarim have used brooms throughout their sculptural work with a feminist and experimental vision. African American abstract artist Ed Clark used a janitorial broom to sweep paint across his canvases.

19. Hazel V. Carby, "White Woman Listen! Black Feminism and the Boundaries of Sisterhood," in *The Empire Strikes Back: Race and Racism in 70s Britain* (Oxfordshire, UK: Routledge, 1982), 113.

20. Angela Davis taught us this in the classic Black feminist essay "Reflections on the Role of the Black Woman in the Community of Slaves" (1971), which she wrote while incarcerated. On the nineteenth-century plantation, in the living quarters, away from the master and overseer, enslaved African women forged kinship structures to protect themselves and their communities under the brutal regime of racial slavery. Caring for one's kin becomes a radical act within a system that devalues Black life and familial structures.

10

Yinshi Lerman-Tan

TYRUS WONG'S ASIAN AMERICANA

In December 2021 I found myself waiting for the Blue and Gold Fleet ferry that would take me from Pier 41 in San Francisco to Angel Island. On this foggy Sunday, I stood alone on the pier, among the boarded-up shops. After a cold ride across the Bay, I stepped onto an island that was wild with trees battered by the Pacific Ocean wind. A park ranger in a pickup truck said I was one of the only people on the island that day. He directed me to a path through the forest, where at the end of the mile-long road I would find the Angel Island Immigration Station.

Listening to the birdsong, I walked past the forest expanse, looking out at a view of the sea through wire fences. I arrived at the historic barracks where hundreds of thousands of immigrants had been detained and interrogated between 1910 and 1940. As Erika Lee and Judy Yung described in *Angel Island: Immigrant Gateway to America*, Angel Island is not simply the Ellis Island of the West. Rather, it has come to represent the exclusionary and racist policies that heavily restricted Asian immigrants from coming to the United States during the era of Chinese and Asian exclusion as well as the resilience of the individuals, families, and communities who persisted in their journeys.[1] Angel Island holds all of that and a poetics of migration in its walls, where, beginning in 1910, immigrants carved hundreds of poems and inscriptions about their experiences of wind, clouds, hope, despair, deportation, family, and moonlight.

This volume asks how we might rethink American art, and this section asks how we might reconsider American art history across disciplinary boundaries. I went to Angel Island as not only a historian and curator of American art but also a mixed-race Chinese American scholar working in the field of Asian American art, a subfield of art history that is crucially informed by Asian American studies.[2] I was there because of my research about American artist Tyrus Wong, who passed through Angel Island in 1920 at the age of ten, immigrating with his father and leaving behind his mother and sister in Guangdong, China. On the island, Wong was separated from his father, detained for about a month, and subjected to interrogation. Like so many who were barred from entry into the United States under the Chinese Exclusion Act of 1882 and subsequent legislation, Wong was a "paper son." In order to challenge exclusion, paper sons and daughters purported to be the children of someone with immigration status (or another class exempt from exclusion). Wong's father had previously lived in the United States under an assumed identity, as a merchant named Look Get, and Wong adopted the name Look Tai Yow in order to enter the country with his father.[3]

From that moment of precarious entry through the landscape that I explored nearly a century later, Wong would go on to have an eighty-year career as an artist, most famously as the visionary who shaped Disney's iconic 1942 film, *Bambi*. In the past few decades, Wong has been the subject of increasing interest: he features in best-selling author Lisa See's 1995 memoir *On Gold Mountain*, and he has been the longtime subject of Los Angeles writer and curator Sonia Mak. In 2013 he was the subject of a retrospective at the Walt Disney Family Museum curated by Michael Labrie.[4] Documentarian Pamela Tom released the definitive film about him, *Tyrus*, in 2015,[5] and English scholar Karen Fang has published about Wong, including research on his greeting card designs.[6]

I learned about Wong while serving as a teaching assistant for Marci Kwon's 2016 survey of Asian American art at Stanford University. I watched Tom's documentary and *Bambi* with my Chinese American grandmother, Hsiao Chin Tan, who, in her nineties, was inspired by Wong's art and life. After losing my grandmother, I began work on a major project about Wong as a kind of tribute to her. I am very grateful to Kim Wong, who has shared materials, memories, and information with me as I embarked on this research about her father. I presented a version of this essay at the Midwest Art Historical Society annual conference in 2021, and as a curator at The Huntington Library, Art Museum, and Botanical Gardens, I acquired major artworks by Wong for the museum, including his *Dragon's Den Mural* (ca. 1935) (discussed in this essay) and his monumental masterpiece, *Jesus* (ca. 1936).

Taking Angel Island as a beginning point, this essay explores how the work and career of Tyrus Wong helps us productively rethink American art history in two crucial ways. First, to consider Wong—rightfully—as part of the history of American art, we must recognize how his early career was shaped by his experiences as a Chinese American immigrant in California in the era of Asian exclusion. To understand his historical situatedness, a historian of American art must not only rely on the disciplinary tenets of American art but also expand to draw upon the concepts of Asian American and ethnic studies, including major historical forces that affected American artists of Asian descent—such as lack of citizenship status, Chinese and Asian exclusion and anti-Asian sentiment, and the incarceration of Japanese Americans. Marci Kwon's invaluable historiography of the field of Asian American art explains, "In the decades since the Asian American movement, a small but active cohort of scholars has worked tirelessly to trace new lines of inquiry in the study of Asian American art."[7] Kwon describes how foundational scholars (including Margo Machida, Mark Dean Johnson, Gordon Chang, and ShiPu Wang) built a disciplinary context for Asian American art—a context in which Wong's art and experience, inextricably bound, become more legible. My own interpretation of Wong in the first section of this essay, and my argument that his approach to images self-fashioned an Asian American citizenship and identity in the era of Chinese exclusion, are examples of how expanding the disciplinary boundaries of American art informs our interpretation and understanding of historic artists of color.

In the second part of this essay, I argue that Wong's work constitutes what I call "Asian Americana," and his career helps us understand how artists of color have always been central in shaping major parts of American art and culture. His life and career transcend the conventional racial and media boundaries of the study of American art, historically focused on pre-1945 painting and sculpture by White artists trained in New York and New England.[8] Wong's formative training as a modernist painter in 1920s and 1930s Los Angeles, steeped in the early twentieth-century California modernism of the Otis Art Institute as well as his circle of 1930s Asian American modernist artists, gave way to his work at the Disney studios and the production of an icon of American pop culture: *Bambi*. I argue that Wong's work for *Bambi*, as well as his work across media, from his early art school paintings, to his work in film and animation, illustrations for cookbooks and book jackets, murals, Christmas cards, and ceramics, constitute a body of "Asian Americana." I borrow the word "Americana" from Wong himself in a 1965 interview, describing an illustration for *Coronet* magazine as a "typical Americana scene."[9] In 1933, for an exhibition that featured a group of young artists called "the independents," the curator Hammond Sadler referred to Wong as having "a background that reads like an Oriental Tom Sawyer"—a racialized characterization of Wong by a White curator in the 1930s—but one that does seem to get at Wong's quintessentially American story and style.[10] While his artistic production might be dismissed as kitsch or popular culture, this essay suggests that Wong's work in these seemingly humble media achieves a radical layering of American icons typically coded as White with an Asian American sensibility and politics, including one of Disney's most iconic films.

Further, his career defies the disciplinary divisions of medium specificity that have typically siloed our field and encourages us to think about how the investments of Asian American and ethnic studies can inform our understanding of artists of color who have been historically marginalized by American art scholarship and museums.[11] This also has implications for collecting institutions. As a curator of American art, I conclude this essay with a discussion of an acquisition I made at my previous institution—The Huntington—of one of Wong's murals, originally painted for a Los Angeles Chinatown restaurant around 1935, an example of how expanding our boundaries of American art necessarily means expanding institutional collecting interests and practice to more robustly include and display the varied media produced by artists like Wong.

SELF-FASHIONING ASIAN AMERICAN IDENTITY AND CITIZENSHIP

A watercolor self-portrait by Wong is preserved in the collection of the Chinese American Museum in Los Angeles (fig. 10.1). He holds an ink brush in one hand and a stem with leaves in the other, connecting the artist's act of creation with organic growth. Although the paper before him is blank, the image takes shape around the figure, as if in process. Wong fashions himself simultaneously in the style of a pensive Chinese scholar, or *luohan*, lounging on a tree; a dapper 1920s art student in a white shirt, slacks, and suspenders; and a reclining Michelangelesque body, as a curator of his work noted in 1933.[12] Wong likely made this picture while a student at the Otis Art Institute in Los Angeles. A detail of a class photo of faculty and students on the first day of class in November 1928 from the Otis College archives shows Wong dressed in a crisp white shirt with slicked-back hair, as in the self-portrait. In the full class photograph, students and faculty bear painted name tags

FIGURE 10.1 Tyrus Wong (American, born in China, 1910–2016), *Self Portrait*, late 1920s, watercolor on paper, 14½ x 21⅜ in. Chinese American Museum, gift of Sanora Babb Howe. Image courtesy of Kim Wong. © Tyrus Wong Family Estate.

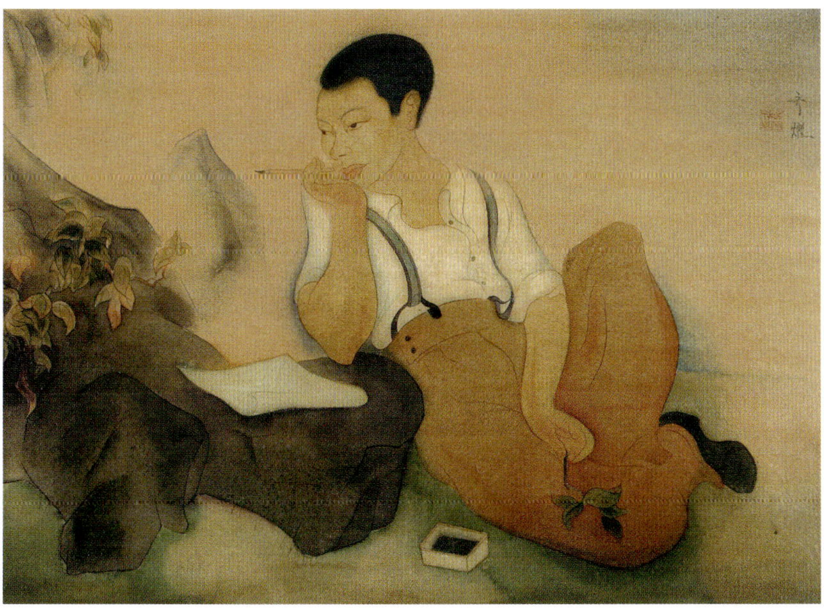

with their surnames—Anderson, Baker, Tanaka—however, Wong bears his first name, not his Chinese name, Gen Yeo, or paper name, Tai Yow, but his English name, a singular moniker: "Tyrus."

In both self-portrait and class picture, Wong is engaged in a kind of savvy self-fashioning. As historian Anna Pegler-Gordon has argued, portraiture, and in particular photography, was a visual method of policing and establishing citizenship for Chinese Americans in the era of exclusion. Pegler-Gordon explains, "By 1909, almost all people of Chinese descent in the United States, including U.S. citizens, were required to possess photographic documentation," which could be demanded at any time by immigration officials.[13] Wong was subject to this kind of imagistic surveillance from childhood. A 1919 immigration photo of nine-year-old Wong shows him before he immigrated through Angel Island; it is pasted on a card that reads "A. Fong, Hong Kong, Emigrants' Photographer."[14] Pegler-Gordon also notes that the act of having a portrait made could also be a mode of resistance that Chinese Americans used to establish their own American identities in visual terms. Chinese American photographic portrait studios were visited by immigrants not only for the purposes of identification documents but also for individual and family studio portraits, and even the visual reunification of families who had been separated by migration.[15] Formal studio portraits show Tyrus and his father together in 1925, thus reclaiming the photographic portrait medium for family and community purposes rather than purposes of complying with (or duping) immigration enforcement.

Wong's preserved albums and scrapbooks of photographs from his childhood and art school days reveal some of how he understood his own image. On pages of his albums, he is pictured among other students on the steps of Benjamin Franklin Junior High School in Pasadena or playing leapfrog with his art school buddies.[16] He embellishes the photos by drawing in the margins, cheekily adding bodies around head shots. One page enshrines three studio portraits of Tyrus as a child—including the immigration photograph—and the studio portrait of his father. Tellingly, around these, Tyrus has drawn four exaggerated caricatures of the heads of grimacing White men: two with mouths open and teeth and tongues exaggerated, and two with eyes narrowed nefariously. To me, these read as the immigration officials Wong would have confronted.

Wong's work self-consciously crafts an Asian American identity with more agency than he legally experienced. Around the time Wong made this self-portrait, he was detained by American immigration authorities for a second time. On October 31, 1931, while a student at Otis, Wong departed on a weekend drawing trip to Tijuana, Mexico. According to his interrogation files (which remain in the archives of the Chinese American immigration lawyer Y. C. Hong, preserved by The Huntington Library, where I viewed them with Wong's daughter Kim), Wong presented his papers issued at the port of San Francisco in 1921, including his immigration photo: "Cert. of identity bears photograph which is a good likeness of the present applicant."[17] The thirteen-page document contains transcripts of Wong's interrogation by immigration authorities and the transcript of a hearing with Wong's father—both with an endless stream of questions typical of the interrogations used in the Chinese exclusion era, in which inconsistencies in respondents' answers would be used as a method of deportation or denial of entry.[18] The file also contains the transcriptions of a striking letter written by artist and Otis Art Institute dean, E. Roscoe Shrader on behalf of the school, in which he implores the Immigration Service at San Ysidro to "expedite the entrance of Tyrus Wong into the United States." Shrader goes on to use Wong's excellent track record as an art student as grounds for his return: "Tyrus Wong has been a student at Otis Art Institute continuously from July 6, 1928, to October 31, 1931, when he left for the week-end to Mexicali. During this period he has done outstanding work in art and each year he has been awarded a scholarship in the school because of his superior ability."[19] Reading this contemporaneous account of Wong's brush with exile—literally in the context of a sketching trip across the border—the stakes of his self-portrait and his art school education are starkly revealed. Making a self-portrait, Wong controls his own image completely. As someone who experienced being racialized through images and official processes as a child and adult, Wong's self-portrait is a kind of visual act of resistance through his ability to quote from art historical and contemporary sources across geographies and time periods in a way that his own literal body could not traverse borders without physical, visual, and verbal policing.

ASIAN AMERICANA: MOVIES, MURALS, AND MENUS

Wong was interested in visually establishing an Asian American identity, something he would continue to do in the "Asian Americana" he would go on to produce throughout his career in Hollywood, at Disney, and as an illustrator and muralist working across nontraditional media. Not long after finishing his training at Otis, Wong—a painter trying to make it during the Depression—got a day job. In 1938 he joined the Disney studios as an "in-betweener" on the animation assembly line.[20] Wong's 1938 Disney contract, written on *Snow White and the Seven Dwarves* stationery, reads, "Our reaction to your work is that you possess talent and that your work is worthy of consideration." The letter (typed below smiling Snow White surrounded by squirrels and above the Evil Witch holding a red apple) invites Wong to participate in a four-week unpaid training period and, if he is subsequently hired, a salary of eighteen to twenty-five dollars per week.[21]

In the late 1930s, the Disney studios were beginning work on a film based on Felix Salten's 1923 best-selling novel, *Bambi: A Life in the Woods*.[22] Salten, a Jewish writer from the artistic hotbed of Vienna, wrote the book not as a children's story but as an allegory of the Jewish experience in Europe, using animals to convey the perils of assimilation and risks of violence looming in the metaphorical forest of an increasingly anti-Semitic Europe.[23] In the 1930s, Hitler banned Salten's book and the author was forced to flee Vienna.[24] While Salten took refuge in Switzerland, Hollywood (and eventually Disney) acquired the rights to his book. Until this point, much of Disney's production had been slapstick and gag-based, and *Bambi* was something different: an emotionally laden coming-of-age tale, an animal world of discovery and trauma.[25] Wong, despite his unremarkable position at Disney, was the perfect artist to receive Salten's pathos-laden story, as they were both modernist artists and immigrants who left their homes either because they were forced to or in pursuit of opportunity.

After starting his new job at the studios, Wong went to the library and picked up a copy of Salten's book and began making little watercolor and pastel landscape sketches.[26] Wong's sensibility would go on to shape the film's groundbreaking minimalist aesthetic, a stark departure from the maximalist animation style the Disney studios used prior to this point in films like their 1937 production, *Snow White*.[27] The forest in Wong's sketches was poetically simplified—taking a visual cue from both the reduced forms of modernism Wong was steeped in as an artist in 1930s America and the negative space of Asian art that Wong studied and to which he had cultivated a visual relationship. It was upon seeing the sketches that Walt Disney decided that Wong's work would guide the film's look.[28]

Many of Wong's miniature landscape sketches for *Bambi* are about five inches by four inches, small enough to fold and fit in a pocket—a contrast to his large-scale WPA-inflected canvases and murals. In one, a lone deer stands on the edge of a forest (fig. 10.2). The little deer's ears are pushed back as if he has heard a sound, the grass also swept backward as if echoing his alarm. He looks into a clearing in the woods, a negative space in the composition suggested by the organic bleeding edge of the watercolor and a few spindly trees that indicate recession in space. In the film, Bambi's mother warns him not to enter the meadow, unprotected from hunters, foreshadowing the terrible moment where she is shot in one such open space. In that pivotal scene, Bambi is bewildered and horrified, realizing he has escaped and his mother has not. Seeing Wong's miniature landscape, which still somehow manages to dwarf the tiny, fearful deer, I am reminded of the windswept forest landscape of Angel Island and the photograph of nine-year-old Wong, who would soon be separated from his own parent. There is a rhyme between Wong's experience with the film he helped to shape, about a child confronting the violence and loss as well as the magic of his forest universe—in Wong's case, the violence of the American immigration system in the era of Chinese Exclusion and the possibility of opportunity and a better life in America.[29]

Wong's work on *Bambi* necessarily rethinks American art by revealing how the Asian American experience surprisingly resides within one of the most important American films of all time.[30] Wong's major role in the film also speaks to the underlying origins of *Bambi* as the product of the lives of not only one—but two—immigrant artists, revealing the dovetailed experiences

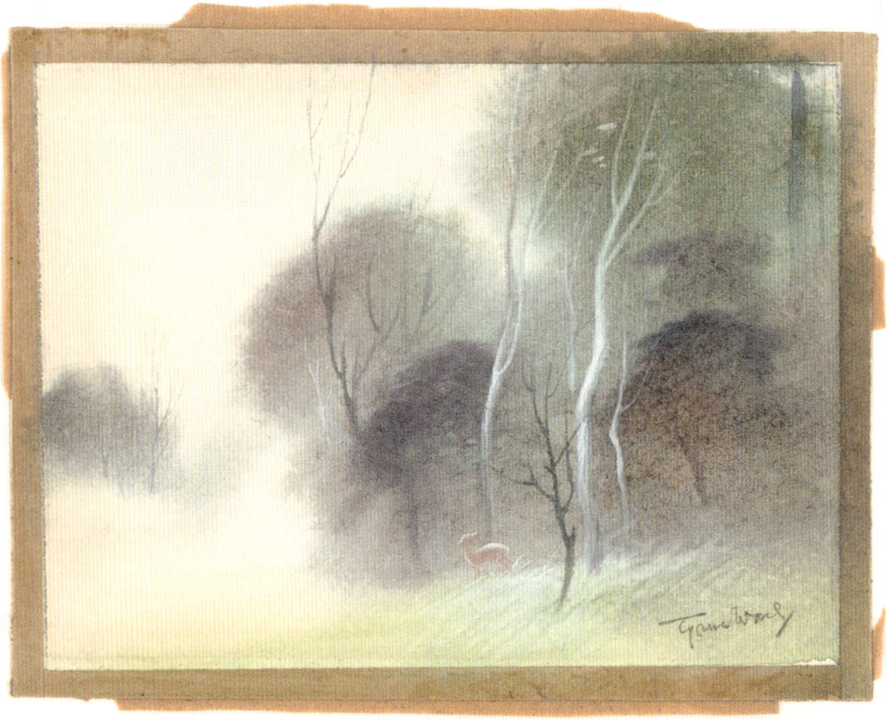

FIGURE 10.2 Tyrus Wong (American, born in China, 1910–2016), visual development for *Bambi*, 1942. Watercolor and pastel on paper, 5 x 4 in. Image courtesy of Kim Wong. © Tyrus Wong Family Estate.

of a Jewish Austrian writer during Hitler's rise to power and an Asian American artist in the era of exclusion. Acknowledging Wong is not a recuperative project but one that recognizes how iconic pieces of Americana represent the immigrant American experience. Wong was let go before the film was released in the kerfuffle of a heated animator's strike in 1941 a year before the film's release in 1942. Wong went uncredited for his major impact on the film's art until 2001, when Disney named him a Disney Legend.[31]

Bambi is the most famous example of Wong's art as "Asian Americana," but his career both before and after that point were spent traversing media that traditionally lie outside the fine art context: illustrations on the covers and interiors of books, the covers of restaurant menus, the interior walls of restaurants and exterior walls of buildings, holiday cards, ceramic plates, and finally, in his later years, three-dimensional kinetic kites.[32] In her deep dive about Wong's greeting cards, Karen Fang has argued that his card designs are undervalued, despite the importance that commercial art held for minority and other marginalized artists. Researching Wong, I have seen towers of works on paper with images of birds, mice, fruit, snowscapes, and summerscapes in rooms where his kites (owls, goldfish, butterflies, caterpillars) hang from the ceiling and his murals decorate the walls. Among them are genres unto himself, like cowboy pictures—cowboys carrying Christmas trees on horseback or watching the sun set in a Western landscape.[33] Wong's *Bambi* preparatory sketches even take on an afterlife in his illustrations for books and Christmas cards. In a 1970 illustration for *Reader's Digest* titled *Starbright,* the lone deer continues to stand alert on the precipice of the glade twenty-eight years later.[34] This motif is similar to one nicknamed "the pink tree" from 1955—it sold over a million copies.[35] In Wong's successful line of holiday card designs, which he produced annually for more than twenty years, two icons—Bambi and a Christian shepherd—are almost interchangeable.

The legacy of Wong's artistic production across film, consumer goods, and middle-brow media are evidence of how he made his living and supported his family as an Asian American artist in a predominantly White American art world. After gaining his citizenship in 1949, Wong turned to commercial media and goods to capitalize upon the fine art and painterly production in which he was trained in his early career.[36] There is a distinctly Chinese American, or even more broadly immigrant, aesthetic in Wong's undiscriminating use of materials—in particular, in his penchant for using recycled items to make works of art.[37] This scrappiness in Wong's work and various modes of artistic production were products of the exclusion he experienced as an artist of color. In seeking to recognize the contributions of artists of color, I want to suggest in the context of this volume that by expanding our definitions of the media worthy of consideration, we make American art more equitable.

How does this idea of collecting outside traditional media occur in practice for collecting institutions? At The Huntington Library, Art Museum, and Botanical Gardens, I pursued this philosophy through acquisitions of

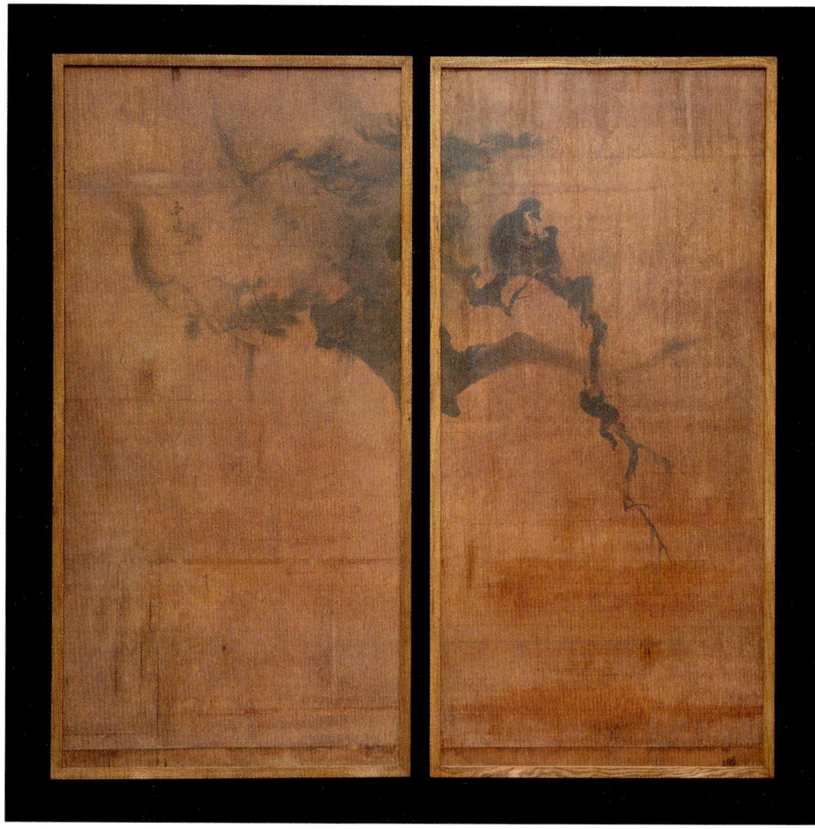

FIGURE 10.3 Tyrus Wong (American, born in China, 1910–2016), *Dragon's Den Mural*, ca. 1935. Oil and charcoal pencil on plywood (two panels), 96 × 48¹⁄₁₆ in. each. Huntington Library, Art Museum, and Botanical Gardens. © Tyrus Wong Family Estate.

works by Tyrus Wong. As a curator, I acquired a circa 1935 mural by Wong originally created for the Los Angeles Chinatown restaurant the Dragon's Den (fig. 10.3).[38] A monumental eight feet by eight feet, it shows a descending composition of pine tree branches and boughs, delicately rendered in oil and pencil on two varnished plywood panels that come together like a folding screen. The grain of the plywood almost reads like the texture of silk, a Depression-era alternative for a would-be silk painting. A family of five monkeys sits in the forest: a mother clutches a baby, and a link of three mischievous adolescents climbs the branches, passing a fruit down the line. Wong's composition traverses diagonally across the negative space of the panels, evoking both the visual traditions and iconography of historical Chinese and Japanese animal painting along with the distinctive language of muralism and modernism drawn from Wong's context in WPA-era California. The mural was preserved by the major Asian American writer Lisa See, whose own family history is intertwined with Wong's in the early twentieth-century history of the Chinese American community in Los Angeles.[39] The acquisition of the mural was preceded by acquisitions of archival material at The Huntington led by the curator of Pacific Rim Collections, Li Wei Yang, and supported by Strategic Initiatives director, Sian Leong Adams, including a major collection of papers given by Leslee See Leong containing the business records of the Dragon's Den and Wong's hand-painted menus for the restaurant.[40]

The visual presence of the mural cannot be separated from the context for which it was originally created. The Dragon's Den, which opened in 1935, was the Depression-era business idea of Wong's friend Eddy See (novelist Lisa See's grandfather), who operated an art gallery in the mezzanine of the See family's successful store, F. Suie One.[41] Serving up Chinese American family-style dishes, the Dragon's Den was an artistic celebrity and queer hangout during Hollywood's Golden Age. The signatures of figures like Anna May Wong and Groucho, Harpo, and Chico Marx are inscribed in its guestbook.[42] Eddy See commissioned his artist friends, including Wong (whom See showed in his gallery) and the Japanese American modernist painter Benji Okubo, to paint murals on the walls. In the dark basement restaurant, Wong's diaphanous charcoal monkeys and tree branches would have appeared to intertwine with the swirls of cigarette smoke—the upward swoop of the tree's leaves like smoke puffs rising to the ceiling.

The Dragon's Den mural helps us productively rethink the history of American art as a locus for Asian American modernism in the early twentieth century. In art historical terms, the restaurant itself was an unconventional exhibition space for two major members (Wong and Okubo) of the Los Angeles Oriental Artists' Group, a pan–Asian American group comprised of both Japanese American and Chinese American artists who exhibited together—long before the establishment of the term "Asian American" in 1968.[43] Also known as the California Oriental Artists and the Modern Oriental Artists of

California, the group represented a pan–Asian American artistic renaissance that took place in Los Angeles, and more broadly in California, during the interwar period. The artists (including Wong, Okubo, Hideo Date, and Gilbert Leong, as well as Keye Luke, Tokio Ueyama, and Bay Area artists such as Miki Hayakawa, and others) developed a homegrown style of American modernism.[44] Wong's mural would have been displayed alongside Okubo's mythological paintings of the Eight Immortals on the brick walls (visible in period photos of the Dragon's Den preserved in The Huntington's archives); and the exterior mural signage designed by Wong and painted by Okubo with the name of the restaurant in both English and Chinese.

Surrounded by paintings made by then-contemporary Asian American artists, diners would look at menus with covers painted with Wong's signature sparse compositions, each a vignette featuring one object: a pear, fish, lobster, spring onion, and handful of mushrooms, an egret—or in one that gestures toward the walls, a little seated monkey. Wong's hand-painted menu covers are also preserved in the See Leong papers at The Huntington, and in collaboration with my colleague Li Wei Yang, we displayed a menu alongside Wong's Dragon's Den mural in the Virginia Steele Scott Galleries of American Art at The Huntington in 2024. Opening the menu, diners would have been able to choose from Chinese American fare, like Tomato Chow Mein, Egg Foo Young, Fish Chop Suey, and Chinese Fortune Cakes,[45] which they would eat off of candy-colored floral china and blue-and-white willow-patterned plates, using chopsticks emblazoned with the restaurant's name. As Jennifer 8. Lee explains in *Fortune Cookie Chronicles*, the ubiquitous dishes of American Chinese food like chow mein, chop suey, General Tso's chicken, and fortune cookies are all American inventions without precedent in actual Chinese cooking.[46] In the same way, it is tempting to think of Wong's monkey mural as representative of Chinese painting, but like the food served at the Dragon's Den, it is less representative of China and rather an American phenomenon and a distinctly American Chinese experience specific to Los Angeles in the 1930s.

Wong's mural still retains physical records of its original use. A conservation exam by The Huntington's Mary Ann and John Sturgeon Senior Paintings Conservator, Christina O'Connell, revealed condition impacts seemingly made by use in the restaurant and a long afterlife in the home of the See family (including as a headboard for a bed and sliding screen)—not issues you usually encounter with works on canvas. This case study reveals that by collecting an artwork that might normally be dismissed for being outside the scope of a collecting institution or rejected for its unique conservation issues, we gain the opportunity to preserve the underrepresented material culture of an Asian American history of Los Angeles and Hollywood, as well as the important Asian American art history of a physical site where a diverse group of artists and creatives gathered and collaborated in the early twentieth century.

Wong's monkey mural brings into the museum a work that ties into the artist's wider presence in still extant and disappeared Asian American spaces of Los Angeles—reimagining, too, not just American art but American urban space via Wong's art. The Dragon's Den stood at 206 Marchessault Street—an address that no longer exists but is still emblazoned on the matchbooks and business cards that remain in The Huntington's archives. However, if you drive down the Arroyo Seco Parkway from The Huntington about ten miles to Chinatown, some of Wong's public art still survives. On Broadway you will pass Wong's cartoon logo of a potbellied little boy carrying a gift box behind his back, made for the beloved Phoenix Bakery. Farther down, you can see the mural *Celestial Dragon* that Wong was commissioned to paint in 1941 at Broadway Plaza for the "new" Los Angeles Chinatown, established in 1938 after the city demolished "old" Chinatown to build Union Station. Like an evolution of his self-portrait, a photograph taken in 1941 shows Wong painting the mural, the dragon like a projection of him, emerging from the tip of his brush (fig. 10.4). Made the year he was let go from Disney, Wong's *Celestial Dragon* seems to have some of the fantasia of the studio built into it, concretizing the flickering magic of animation into the physical architecture of the center of Chinese American experience in Los Angeles. It bears noting that Wong's dragon mural was adjacent to the offices of Chinese American immigration lawyer Y. C. Hong, who assisted Wong when he was detained at the Mexican border as an art student.[47] Sketches Wong made for the mural show the dragon's head from four different angles. Another features a close-up sketch of the bony fingers and claws of the dragon's extended arm. And yet another small gouache watercolor sketch recalls a single cel of

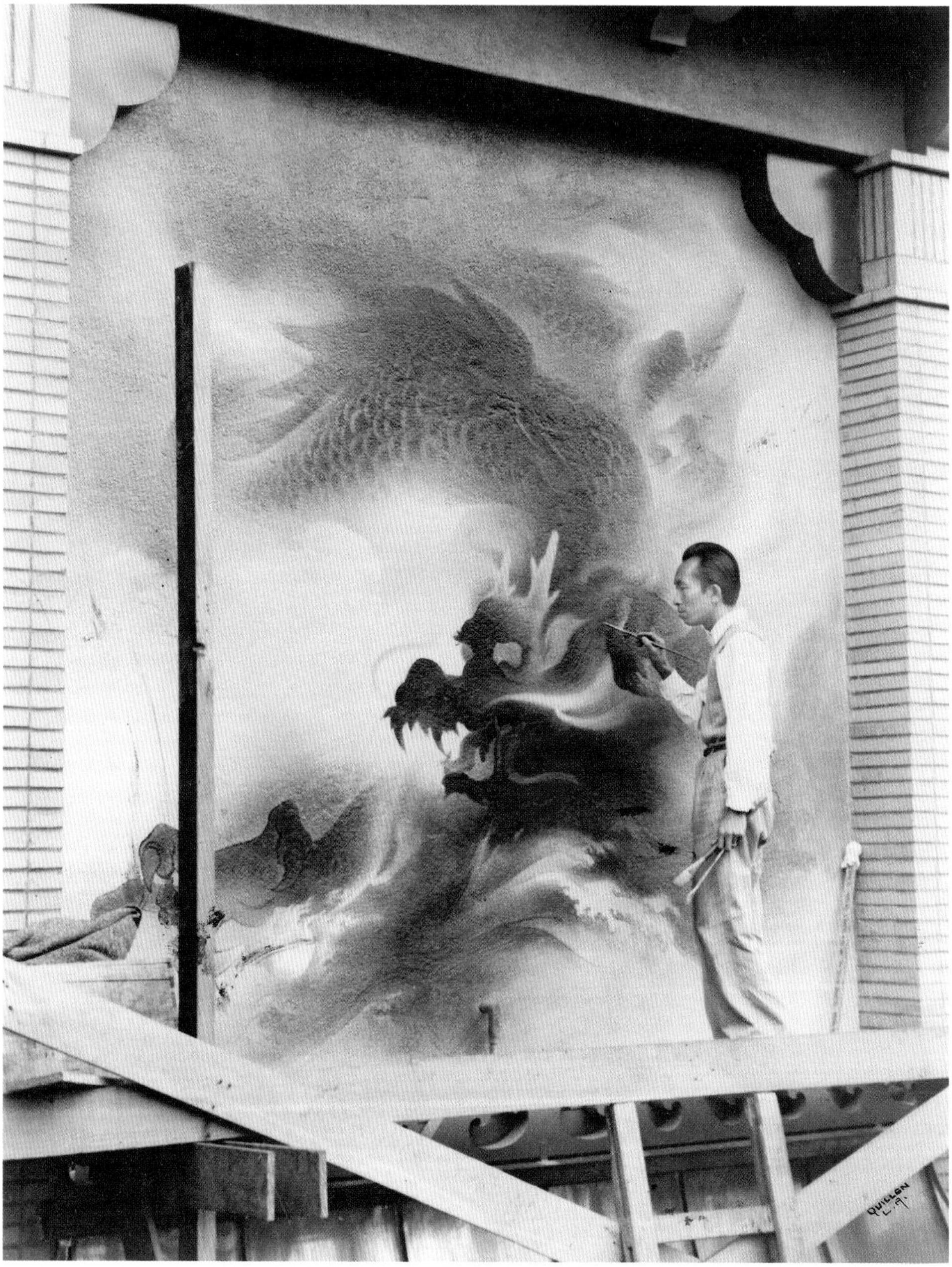

FIGURE 10.4 Tyrus Wong painting *Celestial Dragon*, ca. 1941. Archival photograph. Image courtesy of Kim Wong. © Tyrus Wong Family Estate.

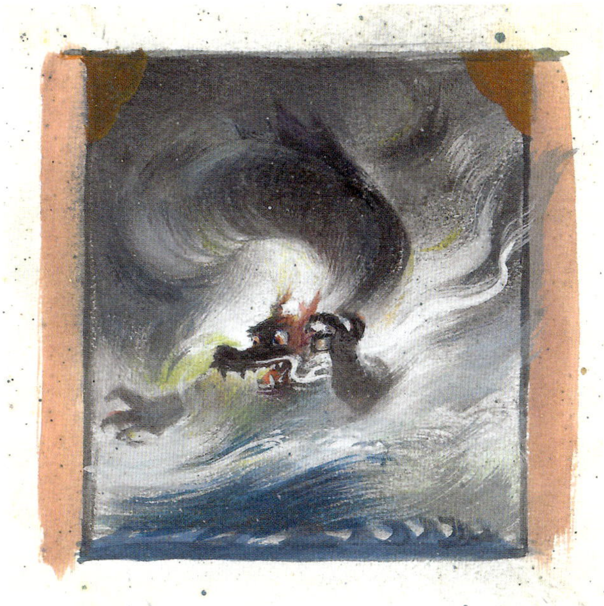

FIGURE 10.5 Tyrus Wong (American, born in China, 1910–2016), sketch for *Celestial Dragon*, ca. 1941. Gouache. Image courtesy of Kim Wong. © Tyrus Wong Family Estate.

animation that would be blown up not on a theater's big screen but to the scale of the wall (fig. 10.5).[48]

The protruding claw, teeth, and swirling clouds of Wong's still-extant dragon resonate with the iconography of Orientalism in twentieth-century Los Angeles—a tactic of self-Orientalizing that both historic and contemporary Asian American artists and performers used to succeed in predominantly White artistic structures.[49] For instance, in 1934, a few years before Wong painted his mural, Chinese American movie star Anna May Wong posed in publicity shots for her new movie, *Limehouse Blues*, wearing her iconic black silk "dragon dress," with a twisting, sequined ornamental dragon body echoing the curves of her own.[50] Anna May Wong and Tyrus Wong occupied similar artistic circles—the movie star even threw a dinner party for guests at the Dragon's Den and was well-acquainted with the See family[51]—and Anna May wrote to Tyrus and his wife, Ruth, congenially in 1960:

> I think it's high time we replace the "orientally yours" picture with a new one of a recent vintage taken by Richard. It was so good to see you both at dinner the other evening and we were happy to find you looking hale and hearty in spite of the wear and tear of modern life.[52]

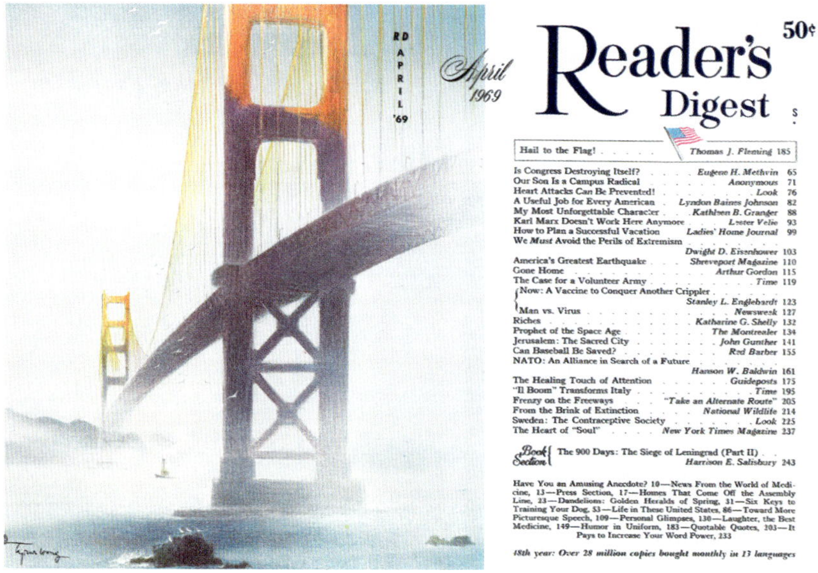

FIGURE 10.6 Tyrus Wong (American, born in China, 1910-2016), *Golden Gate Bridge, San Francisco*, illustration for cover of *Reader's Digest*, April 1969. Image courtesy of Kim Wong and *Reader's Digest*. © Tyrus Wong Family Estate.

In her correspondence, Anna May references her habit of signing her publicity photos "Orientally Yours" (a phrase that scholar Yunte Huang has characterized as having "a touch of defiance"[53]). She communicates with a kind of wink of insider knowledge of their shared experience as Asian American artists contending with stereotypes and racialized expectations—both self-consciously trafficked in the very Orientalist tropes that were foisted upon them and fetishized by the White spaces in which they moved, turning those tropes back on themselves and reclaiming them.

Seeing Tyrus Wong's career across these media, we see the ever-present historical threads that connect Angel Island, Los Angeles Chinatown, and American Chinese food to Hollywood Disney, Hallmark, and popular media. While Wong's large-scale murals shaped the visual identity of spaces in Los Angeles Chinatown, Wong's small works on paper and illustrations—like his sketches for *Bambi*—carry a somewhat quieter pathos. In an illustration from 1969 for the cover of *Reader's Digest*, Wong depicts the Golden Gate Bridge in a seemingly benign picture of an American landmark, but it is also a picture of a borderlands: the threshold of California and the Pacific Rim.[54] The Golden Gate Bridge did not exist in 1920 when Wong arrived from Guangdong, but he passed through the waters of the Golden Gate on his way to Angel Island as a child, sailing on the water underneath where the bridge would be finished in 1937. In this illustration and across Wong's oeuvre, we see Americana anew.

NOTES

1. Erika Lee and Judy Yung, *Angel Island: Immigrant Gateway to America* (Oxford: Oxford University Press, 2010).

2. See Marci Kwon, Introduction to "Asian American Art, Pasts and Futures," *Panorama: Journal of the Association of Historians of American Art* 7, no. 1 (2021), https://doi.org/10.24926/24716839.11446/.

3. "Tyrus Wong, 'Bambi' Artist Thwarted by Racial Bias, Dies at 106," *New York Times*, December 30, 2016, https://www.nytimes.com/2016/12/30/movies/tyrus-wong-dies-bambi-disney.html/; Tyrus Wong, Michael Labrie, and Walt Disney Family Museum, *Water to Paper, Paint to Sky: The Art of Tyrus Wong* (San Rafael, CA: Weldon Owen, 2013), 14–17.

4. Lisa See, *On Gold Mountain: The One-Hundred-Year Odyssey of My Chinese-American Family* (New York: Vintage Books, 2012); Sonia Mak, *'Round the Clock: Chinese American Artists Working in Los Angeles* (Monterey Park, CA: Vincent Price Art Museum, East Los Angeles College, 2012); Wong, Labrie, and Walt Disney Family Museum, *Water to Paper, Paint to Sky*.

5. *Tyrus,* dir. Pamela Tom, Apricot Films, 2015.

6. Karen Fang, "Commercial Design and Midcentury Asian American Art: The Greeting Cards of Tyrus Wong," *Panorama* 7, no. 1 (2021), https://doi.org/10.24926/24716839.11548/.

7. Kwon, Introduction to "Asian American Art, Pasts and Futures."

8. See Wanda M. Corn, ed., *The Great American Thing: Modern Art and National Identity, 1915–1935,* Ahmanson Murphy Fine Arts Imprint (Berkeley: University of California Press, 1999).

9. Betty Hoag, Oral history interview with Tyrus Wong, Archives of American Art, Smithsonian Institution, January 30, 1965, https://www.aaa.si.edu/collections/interviews/oral-history-interview-tyrus-wong-13010/.

10. Hammond Sadler, *Exhibition of Paintings: "Independents"* (Palos Verdes

Estates, California, 1933, Tyrus Wong papers, 1932–1963, Archives of American Art, Smithsonian Institution.

11. This issue is explored in Aleesa Pitchamarn Alexander's important article about the responsibility of museums to address the historic lack of representation of Asian American artists in museums. Aleesa Pitchamarn Alexander, "Asian American Art and the Obligation of Museums," *Panorama: Journal of the Association of Historians of American Art* 7, no. 1 (2021), https://doi.org/10.24926/24716839.11446/.

12. Sadler, *Exhibition of Paintings*; Sonia Mak meditates on the power of Wong's self-portrait in "The Curator's Corner," *Southern California Quarterly* 88, no. 3 (2006): 384–85.

13. Anna Pegler-Gordon, "Chinese Exclusion, Photography, and the Development of U.S. Immigration Policy," *American Quarterly* 58, no. 1 (2006): 55.

14. "Tyrus Wong photograph attributed to A. Fong" (1919), Tyrus Wong Family Estate.

15. The Huntington also holds a rare collection of glass-plate negatives donated by Lisa See that depict street and studio scenes taken in Los Angeles Chinatown from the late nineteenth and early twentieth centuries. For discussion of photography in San Francisco Chinatown, see Anthony W. Lee, *Picturing Chinatown: Art and Orientalism in San Francisco* (Berkeley: University of California Press, 2001). The visual reunification of families in photo collages made by San Francisco Chinatown–based May's photo studio is discussed in Marci Kwon, "The Evasive Bodies of May's Photo Studio," lecture, Stanford University, December 11, 2017, https://www.youtube.com/watch?v=nPw8kofyHDc/.

16. "Wong Photo Album and Scrapbook" (ca. 1920s–1940s), Tyrus Wong Family Estate.

17. I viewed Wong's immigration files in the You Chung Hong papers in The Huntington Library with Li Wei Yang, curator of Pacific Rim Collections at The Huntington, and the artist's daughter, Kim Wong, in 2022.

18. Li Wei Yang, "The Lawyer Who Beat Back a Racist Law, One Loophole at a Time," *What It Means to Be American* (blog), April 5, 2016, https://www.whatitmeanstobeamerican.org/identities/the-lawyer-who-beat-back-a-racist-law-one-loophole-at-a-time/.

19. "Tyrus Wong Immigration File, Interrogation Transcript," The Huntington Library, San Marino, California, 1931, You Chung Hong legal papers.

20. Wong, Labrie, and Walt Disney Family Museum, *Water to Paper, Paint to Sky*, 45.

21. "Letter to Tyrus Wong from Walt Disney Productions," March 15, 1938, Tyrus Wong Family Estate.

22. "Books to Be Read or Read About: '*Bambi,*' The Life Story of a Deer. Translated from the German," *Evening Sun*, July 7, 1928; "Books and Authors: Latecomers Make Season Noteworthy," *Scranton Republican*, July 5, 1928; Ollie Johnston and Frank Thomas, *Walt Disney's* Bambi*: The Story and the Film* (New York: Stewart, Tabori, and Chang, 1990), 106.

23. The Jewish aspect of *Bambi*, and its origins as work by prominent Jewish intellectuals and writers, has been discussed occasionally in articles in Jewish magazines like *Tablet* and *Haaretz* and in a few academic works, including Paul Reitter, Bambi's *Jewish Roots and Other Essays on German-Jewish Culture* (New York: Bloomsbury Academic, 2015). Also see Maya Balakirsky Katz, "Bambi Abroad, 1924–1954," *AJS Review* 44, no. 2 (2020): 286–316, https://doi.org/10.1017/S0364009420000070/.

24. For a biographical treatment of Salten, see Beverley D. Eddy, *Felix Salten: Man of Many Faces*, Studies in Austrian Literature, Culture and Thought (Riverside, CA: Ariadne Press, 2010). For discussion of his artistic circle, see Alex Ross, "The Schorske Century," *The New Yorker*, September 28, 2015, https://www.newyorker.com/culture/cultural-comment/the-schorske-century/.

25. Johnston and Thomas, *Walt Disney's* Bambi, 106.

26. Yinshi Lerman-Tan phone conversation with Kim Wong, June 30, 2019.

27. Wong, Labrie, and Walt Disney Family Museum, *Water to Paper, Paint to Sky*, 45; *Tyrus* (film), 2015; Johnston and Thomas, *Walt Disney's* Bambi, 136, 152.

28. *Tyrus* (film) 2018; Pierre Lambert, *Bambi* (Paris: Huginn and Muninn, 2017).

29. This parallel is also noted in "Tyrus Wong, '*Bambi*' Artist Thwarted by Racial Bias, Dies at 106," *New York Times*, December 30, 2016, https://www.nytimes.com/2016/12/30/movies/tyrus-wong-dies-bambi-disney.html.

30. *Bambi* is quintessential classic Disney, from the original suite of Disney animated films that laid the blueprint for seemingly everything that came after it, from Disney's *The Lion King* to Smokey Bear (not a film but a US Forest Service character), both of which it spawned. It ranks number three on the American Film Institute's top ten most important animated movies of all time, topped only by two earlier Disney films, *Pinocchio* and *Snow White.* Chicago film critic Roger Ebert called *Bambi* "a perennial classic, seen by every generation, remembered long after other movies have been forgotten."

31. "Tyrus Wong," n.d., Disney Legends, Walt Disney Archives, https://d23.com/walt-disney-legend/tyrus-wong/.

32. For more on greeting cards, see Karen Fang, "How Tyrus Wong's Christmas Cards Captivated the American Public," *Smithsonian Magazine,* December 2020, https://www.smithsonianmag.com/arts-culture/tyrus-wong-christmas-card-captivated-american-public-180976239/. For more on Wong's ceramics, see Tyrus Wong, Bill Stern, and Craft and Folk Art Museum (1973–1997), *Mid-Century Mandarin: The Clay Canvases of Tyrus Wong* (Los Angeles: Museum of California Design, 2004). Sonia Mak has spoken and written about Wong's murals.

33. I have discussed how Wong's cowboys read through the proliferation of cowboy iconography among Asian American contemporary artists like Kenneth Tam and Stephanie Mei Huang. Yinshi Lerman-Tan, "Asian American Cowboys," conference paper (College Art Association Annual Conference, online, 2022).

34. "*Starbright* cover for *Reader's Digest*" (1970), Tyrus Wong Family Estate.

35. Fang, "How Tyrus Wong's Christmas Cards Captivated the American Public."

36. Karen Fang also notes that "Wong's cards and their extraordinary reach illustrate the opportunities that minority and marginalized artists might have found in commercial art." Fang, "Commercial Design and Midcentury Asian American Art."

37. Perhaps there is an academic article I can cite, but those children of immigrants and Asian American families do not need scholarship to confirm the widespread immigrant parent and grandparent impulse to reuse and recycle household items from yogurt containers to Popsicle sticks.

38. The mural was purchased with funds from the Art Collectors' Council, with additional support from the Steve Martin Fund for American Art. And many thanks go to my museum colleagues Christina Nielsen, Dennis Carr, and Lauren Cross.

39. See, *On Gold Mountain*.

40. "News Release—The Huntington Acquires the Papers of the Chinese American Family Featured in the Book 'On Gold Mountain' by Lisa See," May 13, 2020, https://huntington.org/news/news-release-huntington-acquires-papers-chinese-american-family-featured-book-gold-mountain/.

41. See, *On Gold Mountain*.

42. "Dragon's Den Guestbook" (ca. 1935), Private Collection.

43. Marian Yoshiki-Kovinick, "A Bit of Paris in Heart Mountain," in *A Seed of Modernism: The Art Students League of Los Angeles, 1906–1953* (Pasadena: Pasadena Museum of California Art, 2008).

44. The group showed at the Los Angeles Museum in 1936 and the Foundation of Western Art in 1934, 1935, and 1937.

45. "Tyrus Wong Hand-Painted Menus for the Dragon's Den" (ca. 1935),

Gilbert, Florence, and Leslee See Leong Collection, The Huntington Library, San Marino, California.

46. Jennifer 8. Lee, *The Fortune Cookie Chronicles: Adventures in the World of Chinese Food* (New York: Twelve, 2009).

47. Sonia Mak has discussed the relationship between Tyrus Wong and You Chung Hong, and Wong's portrait of Confucius for Hong's office in Los Angeles Chinatown.

48. Tyrus Wong, "Sketches for Celestial Dragon Mural" (ca. 1941), Tyrus Wong Family Estate.

49. Lerman-Tan, "Sadakichi Hartmann's American Art."

50. Designed by Travis Banton, this dress is preserved in the Costume Institute at the Met.

51. "Dragon's Den Publicity News Clippings" (ca. 1935), Gilbert, Florence, and Leslee See Leong Collection, The Huntington Library, San Marino, California.

52. Anna May Wong, "Anna May Wong to Tyrus and Ruth Wong," September 4, 1960, Tyrus Wong Family Estate.

53. Yunte Huang, *Daughter of the Dragon: Anna May Wong's Rendezvous with American History*, 1st edition (New York: Liveright Publishing, 2023).

54. "Cover for *Reader's Digest*" (1969), Tyrus Wong Family Estate.

Michael W. Hartman / Jami C. Powell

CONCLUSION

An Invitation

As Anya Montiel explained in her essay in this volume, the Renwick Gallery's "half-century anniversary provided an opportunity for the Renwick to embark on a vigorous acquisition campaign, thereby adding more works by Native artists and other underrepresented groups into the permanent collection." Institutional anniversaries and national milestones provide not only occasions for celebratory reflection but also calls to action that ultimately serve as a springboard for change. Many museums commemorated the 1976 US bicentennial with self-congratulatory, nationalistic exhibitions, such as the Smithsonian's *Freedom Is the Only King*, which centered on Emanuel Leutze's iconic history painting *Washington Crossing the Delaware*.[1] Largely uncritical of the nation's history of settler colonialism, slavery, and dispossession, this exhibition and others ignited responses from artists of color, most notably with Robert Colescott's painting *George Washington Carver Crossing the Delaware: Page from an American History Textbook* (1975).[2]

By the Columbus Quincentenary in 1992, many commemorative exhibitions across the United States began to challenge some of the prevailing narratives celebrated in 1976, offering revisionist accounts surrounding Columbus and his legacy.[3] For many Native American artists, this was also the first time many mainstream art museums showed an interest in displaying their work, a point that was not lost on artists working at the time.[4] In a

1991 interview, James Luna famously quipped, "Now everyone is saying, let's have an Indian show or let's have a colonialism show. So, when people call me, I have to ask why didn't you call me before? You're calling me now, but are you going to call me in '93?"[5] Here, in classic Luna style, he uses humor and what some might wrongly assume as an irreverent question to open a critical space and ask whether or not the interest in Native American art was sustainable or simply a trend, followed by a return to the status quo and the exclusion of Indigenous artists and narratives from mainstream museums and collections.

As many institutions prepare for 2026, the 250th anniversary of the signing of the Declaration of Independence, arts workers and museums find ourselves at another critical inflection point. While these conversations are taking place across the field of American art, the authors and projects featured in this volume can serve as starting points, guides, or frameworks for temporary and permanent collections reinstallations. The collaborative and co-curated approach, emphasized by several authors in this volume, who themselves shared their knowledge by coauthoring essays, is a model that is certainly not new within the museum field, but it is one that could be used more broadly in American art. Their examples can guide institutional dialogues for these projects and others, inviting us to keep our audiences in mind and hold our collections accountable. What does care look like when we exhibit historical and contemporary artworks that reckon with histories of violence rooted in setter colonialism, slavery, and dispossession? How do we undertake the impossible task of knowing that we cannot tell every story due to the limitations of space and our own collections?

The essays in this volume suggest multiple paths forward as more and more institutions commit to a sustained engagement with all of their constituents that extends beyond 2026. As each author has demonstrated, there is no "one size fits all" approach to telling more inclusive, complicated, entangled, and truthful histories of American art. Every collection, every community, merits specialized attention to interpretation and care. It is our intention that this book serves as a springboard to help ourselves and our colleagues, present and future, reconsider lasting commitments and collaborations with the diversity of artists working within the field of American art.

NOTES

1. Barbara S. Groseclose, *Emanuel Leutze, 1816–1868: Freedom Is the Only King* (Washington, DC: Smithsonian Institution Press, 1975), published in conjunction with an exhibition of the same title on view January 16–March 14, 1976.

2. Other responses to the bicentennial by artists of color included Fritz Scholder's (Luiseño) 1975 *Bicentennial Indian*, as well as Chicanx artist Rudolfo O. Cuellar's *Humor in Xicano Arte 200 Years of Oppression*, 1976 and Chicanx artist Ricardo Favela's *Centennial Means 500 Years of Genocide!* (1976). These latter two works were recently included in the Smithsonian American Art Museum's traveling exhibition *¡Printing the Revolution! The Rise and Impact of Chicano Graphics, 1965 to Now*, curated by E. Carmen Ramos.

3. This included the exhibition *The West as America*, which was perceived as too "revisionist" by Republican members of Congress who threatened to defund the Smithsonian Institution. See William H. Truettner, ed., *The West as America: Reinterpreting Images of the Frontier, 1820–1920* (Washington, DC: Smithsonian Institution Press, 1991), and Michael Kimmelman, "Old West, New Twist at the Smithsonian," *New York Times*, May 26, 1991, section 2, p. 1. More recent exhibitions have continued to update, revise, and rethink these narratives, including *Knowing the West* at Crystal Bridges Museum of American Art, the subject of Mindy Besaw's essay in this volume. See also *Circa 1492* at the National Gallery of Art (October 12, 1991–January 12, 1992) and *Seeds of Change* at the National Museum of Natural History (October 27, 1991–April 1, 1992).

4. The 1993 Whitney Biennial was curated by Thelma Golden, John G. Hanhardt, Lisa Phillips, and Elisabeth Sussman and included works by James Luna (Luiseño) and Jimmie Durham, who claimed, and at that time was thought, to be Cherokee. See also Jaune Quick-to-See Smith and ATLATL, *The Submuloc Show/Columbus Wohs: A Visual Commentary on the Columbus Quincentennial from the Perspective of America's First People. Curated by Jaune Quick-to-See Smith* (Phoenix: ATLATL, 1992), as well as Anya Montiel, "After Columbus," in *Art in America* 105, no. 9 (2017): 86–91.

5. Steven Durland, "Call me in '93: An Interview with James Luna," *High Performance*, no. 56 (Winter 1991): 34–39.

CONTRIBUTORS

AUSTEN BARRON BAILLY, PhD, is chief curator of Crystal Bridges Museum of American Art. Since joining the museum in 2019, Bailly has co-curated *We the People: The Radical Notion of Democracy*; *Bethany Collins—America: A Hymnal*; and *In American Waters: The Sea in American Painting*. Bailly previously served as the George Putnam Curator of American Art at the Peabody Essex Museum, where she received two Association of Art Museum Curators awards for excellence: Outstanding Exhibition of 2015 for *American Epics: Thomas Hart Benton and Hollywood* and Outstanding Exhibition Catalogue of 2020 for *Jacob Lawrence: The American Struggle*.

LAYLA BERMEO is the Kristin and Roger Servison Curator of Paintings, Art of the Americas, at the Museum of Fine Arts, Boston. She previously held curatorial positions at the Philadelphia Museum of Art, Williams College Museum of Art, and the African American Museum in Philadelphia. She holds an MA from Williams College and received her PhD from Harvard University in 2024. At the MFA, Bermeo co-organized *Collecting Stories: Native American Art,* curated *Frida Kahlo and Arte Popular* and authored the accompanying bilingual catalog, and developed the Curatorial Study Hall program for local teens. In 2019, WBUR, a National Public Radio news station, named Bermeo as one of the twenty-five millennials of color impacting Boston arts.

MINDY N. BESAW, PhD, is director of research, fellowships, and university partnerships and curator of American art at Crystal Bridges Museum of American Art. Besaw's projects and exhibitions include the 2018 renovation and reinstallation of the Early American art galleries; co-curator of *Art for a New Understanding: Native Voices 1950s to Now* (2018); co-curator of *Cross-Pollination: Martin Johnson Heade, Thomas Cole, Frederic Edwin Church and Our Contemporary Moment* (2020), and co-curator of *Knowing the West* (2024). Besaw was previously curator at the Buffalo Bill Center of the West in Cody, Wyoming. She holds a PhD in American art history from the University of Kansas.

KIRSTEN PAI BUICK, PhD, is a professor of art history at the University of New Mexico and the inaugural chair of the Department of Africana Studies. She specializes in the visual and material culture of the first British Empire; art of the United States; landscape representation; and African American art. Her book *Child of the Fire: Mary Edmonia Lewis and the Problem of Art History's Black and Indian Subject* was published by Duke University Press. Her second book, *In Authenticity: "Kara Walker" and the Eidetics of Racism* is in progress.

HAZEL V. CARBY, PhD, HonFLSW, is the Charles C. and Dorathea S. Dilley Professor Emeritus of African American studies and professor emeritus of American studies at Yale University. A fellow of the Royal Society for the Arts and member of the American Academy of Arts and Sciences, she is currently Centennial Professor, International Inequalities Institute, London School of Economics. She is the author of *Imperial Intimacies, A Tale of Two Islands*, which was awarded the British Academy's Nayef Al-Rodhan Prize for Global Cultural Understanding. Dr. Carby is also the author of *Cultures in Babylon: Black Britain and African America*; *Race Men*; and *Reconstructing Womanhood: The Emergence of the Afro-American Woman Novelist*; as well as the coauthor of *The Empire Strikes Back: Race and Racism in 70s Britain*.

JANET DEES is assistant director of arts at the Smithsonian National Museum of African American History and Culture (NMAAHC) in Washington, DC. She was previously the Steven and Lisa Munster Tananbaum Curator of Modern and Contemporary Art at the Block Museum of Art, Northwestern University, and held affiliations with the Department of Art History and the Center for Native American and Indigenous Research. Prior to her appointment at the Block in 2015, Dees was curator at SITE Santa Fe. She was a 2023 fellow of the Center for Curatorial Leadership and is the recipient of a 2018 curatorial fellowship from the Andy Warhol Foundation for the Visual Arts. Dees is editor of and contributor to several publications, including *A Site of Struggle: American Art against Anti-Black Violence* (Block Museum of Art, Northwestern University, and Princeton University Press, 2022) and *If You Remember, I'll Remember* (Block Museum of Art, Northwestern University 2022).

MORGAN E. FREEMAN is a PhD candidate in American studies at Yale University. Her areas of concentration include the contemporary art and visual cultures of Black and Native practitioners. She is interested in this work as it relates to belonging, defining indigeneity, and place specificity. Freeman was previously the Native American Art Fellow (2018–20) at the Hood Museum of Art, Dartmouth, serving as co-curator for the exhibitions *Form and Relation: Contemporary Native Ceramics*; *The Embodiment of Language*; and *This Land: American Engagement with the Natural World*. She graduated from Tufts University with a BA in American studies.

MICHAEL W. HARTMAN is the Jonathan Little Cohen Associate Curator of American Art at the Hood Museum of Art at Dartmouth College. He holds a BA in art history and in German from the University of Arkansas; an MA from Williams College; and a PhD in art history from the University of Delaware. His recent exhibitions include *Historical Imaginary*; *Liquidity: Art, Commodities, and Water*; *Gather, Move, Resonate: Nick Cave & Jeffrey Gibson*; and *This Land: American Engagement with the Natural World*. He is coeditor of book reviews for *Panorama* and has previously held positions at the Biggs Museum of American Art; the Clark Art Institute; Crystal Bridges

Museum of American Art; the Dallas Museum of Art; and the Winterthur Library, Museums, and Gardens.

KAREN KRAMER is the Elizabeth and Stuart Pratt Curator of Native American and Oceanic Art and Culture at the Peabody Essex Museum (PEM). Her long-standing commitment to presenting and interpreting Indigenous art and culture and her broad experiences working with Native artists and scholars has led to groundbreaking exhibitions and catalogs, including *T. C. Cannon: At the Edge of America*; *Native Fashion Now*; and *Shapeshifting: Transformations in Native American Art*. Kramer also directs PEM's innovative Native American fellowship program. She is currently a PhD candidate in American studies at Harvard University, where she is writing a dissertation on Native American public art (1969–2024).

YINSHI LERMAN-TAN, PhD, is a curator and scholar of American art. She received her PhD in art history from Stanford University and her BA in American studies from Yale University. Previously, she has served as a curator of American art at The Huntington and San Antonio Museum of Art. At The Huntington, she co-curated *Betye Saar: Drifting Toward Twilight* and coedited the accompanying catalog, and she strategically expanded the museum's collecting and installation of American and Asian American art. She has also held positions at the Cantor Arts Center at Stanford, the Yale Center for British Art, and the Smithsonian American Art Museum. Her work has been supported by the Douglass, the Andrew W. Mellon, and the Coates Foundations.

ANYA MONTIEL, PhD, is a curator at the Smithsonian's National Museum of the American Indian in Washington, DC. Previously she was curator of American and Native American Women's Art and Craft, a joint position between the Renwick Gallery and the National Museum of the American Indian and funded by the Smithsonian American Women's History Initiative. She received her doctorate and master's degrees in American studies from Yale University and holds bachelor's degrees in Native American studies and anthropology from the University of California, Davis.

ROGER PAUL was born on the Motahkomikuk Indian reservation near Princeton, Maine, to a Passamaquoddy mother and a Maliseet father. Paul grew up speaking both languages and began learning English around the age of five. After touring the world with the US Marine Corps, he earned his BA in sociology at the University of Maine at Presque Isle. Paul has worked as a cultural director, teacher, counselor, storyteller, and consultant and is presently working as a teacher with the Penobscot Nation and the University of Maine at Orono. A *mihtaqs* (father) of three and a *muhssumss* (grandfather) of five, he works diligently to share and ensure the continuing growth and prosperity of the Wabanaki language and culture.

JAMI C. POWELL, PhD, is associate director for curatorial affairs and curator of Indigenous art at the Hood Museum of Art, Dartmouth, where she also serves as a senior lecturer in Native American and Indigenous studies. She is an enrolled citizen of the Osage Nation. Her curatorial projects include *Form and Relation: Contemporary Native American Ceramics*; *CIPX Dartmouth with Kali Spitzer and Will Wilson*; *Madayin: Eight Decades of Aboriginal Bark Painting from Yirrkala*; and *Gather, Move, Resonate: Nick Cave and Jeffrey Gibson*. Powell is on the board of directors for the Native American Art Studies Association (NAASA) and the advisory board for *Panorama*. She is a recipient of the 2020 New Leadership Award from ArtTable.

THOMAS H. PRICE is a PhD candidate in the art history department at the University of Delaware, specializing in nineteenth- and early twentieth-century American art, landscape representation, and queer art. His dissertation, "Body Work: Masculinity and Extraction in Late Nineteenth-Century American Art," explores the visual culture of natural resource extraction in the United States and its display and reframing of masculine identity. He was formerly the curatorial assistant for American art at the Hood Museum (2018–20), where he was part of the *This Land* curatorial team.

JOHN R. STOMBERG is the Virginia Rice Kelsey 1961s Director of the Hood Museum of Art at Dartmouth College. Before joining Dartmouth in January 2016, he served as the Florence Finch Abbott Director of the Mount

Holyoke College Art Museum and the Joseph Allen Skinner Museum, and he held leadership positions at the Williams College Museum of Art and the Boston University Art Gallery. He holds a BA from Georgetown University and both an MA and PhD from Boston University—all in art history. The primary focus of his curatorial work is American art and culture since 1900. Moving between photography, prints, paintings, sculpture, media art, and installation work, his exhibitions have been conceived to broaden our understanding of how art operates in, and often shapes, society. He publishes on modern and contemporary art and issues directly related to museums, education, and academia.

ALISA SWINDELL is associate curator of photography at the Hood Museum of Art. Her exhibitions include *And I'm Feeling Good: Relaxation and Resistance* and *Femme Is Fierce: Femme Queer Performance in Photography*. She has worked at the Block Museum of Art, the Art Institute of Chicago, Gallery 400, and the Saint Louis Art Museum. Swindell has been published in *Newcity*, *Gastronomica*, and the catalogs for *Who Says, Who Shows, What Counts*; *Let Me Be an Object That Screams*; and *Selfish*. She is a PhD candidate in art history at the University of Illinois–Chicago, holds MAs from the School of the Art Institute of Chicago and the University of New Orleans, and has an AB from Bryn Mawr College.

ALEXANDRA M. THOMAS, PhD, is an assistant professor of art history at Fordham University. Formerly she was the 2021–23 curatorial research associate in African art at the Hood Museum, where she curated the exhibition *Homecoming: Domesticity and Kinship in Global African Art*. She holds a PhD in African American studies and history of art with a certificate in women's, gender, and sexuality studies from Yale.

INDEX

Italicized numbers refer to figures.

CRITICAL ETHNIC STUDIES AND VISUAL CULTURE

Reenvisioning Histories of American Art: Transforming Museum Practice
Edited by Michael W. Hartman and Jami C. Powell

Queer World Making: Contemporary Middle Eastern Diasporic Art
Andrew Gayed

Resisting the Nuclear: Art and Activism across the Pacific
Edited by Elyssa Faison and Alison Fields